Dumbing Down

Dumbing Down

culture, politics
and the
mass media

edited by
Ivo Mosley

IMPRINT ACADEMIC

Contents

Dumbocracy in the Visual Arts

Dumbocracy in Education

Dumbocracy and Science

Dumbocracy and Religion

Dumbocracy and 'The Environment'

Authors

Adam Boulton was educated at Oxford and Johns Hopkins and has been a lobby correspondent since 1983. He has been political editor and presenter on *Sky News*, a political columnist on *Sunday Business*, and has worked for TV-AM, BBC External and IPS Third World Wire.

Robert Brustein is founder and artistic director of the American Repertory Theatre at Harvard and theatre critic for *The New Republic*. Twice winner of the George Jean Nathan Award for dramatic criticism, his books include *The Theatre of Revolt* and *Dumbocracy in America*.

Tam Dalyell is Labour MP for Linlithgow and Westminster correspondent for *New Scientist*.

C.D. Darlington FRS was Sherardian Professor of Botany in the University of Oxford, Keeper of the Botanic Gardens and Fellow of Magdalen College. He wrote on botany, genetics and the study of man and his magnum opus was *The Evolution of Man and Society*.

Roger Deakin, writer and filmmaker, studied English at Peterhouse, Cambridge. A founder-director of the charity Common Ground, until recently he was a director of the Eastern Arts Board. He is the author of *Waterlog: A Swimmer's Journey Through Britain* (1999).

Claire Fox is publisher of *LM* magazine. She writes on education, culture and the media. In 1999 she was co-Director of the conference 'Culture Wars: Dumbing Down, Wising Up?' and she is organizing an Institute of Ideas to be held from 16 June to 16 July 2000.

Laura Gascoigne is a freelance writer and journalist. She studied Classics at Oxford, and combines two of her passions by writing about art. For several years editor of *Artists and Illustrators* magazine, she is completing a book on the business of being an artist.

Anne Glyn-Jones read PPE at Oxford then worked for the National Film Board of Canada. On her return she spent five years in the theatre, then was research archivist to Harold Macmillan. For 12 years Devon Research Fellow at the University of Exeter, her most recent publication is *Holding up a Mirror: How Civilizations Decline* (1996).

Bill Hare studied art history at Edinburgh University and the Courtauld Institute. Formerly Assistant Curator, Talbot Rice Gallery, he now teaches at the Open University and the University of Edinburgh. Among his books are *Contemporary Painting in Scotland*, 1992.

Dominic Hobson, educated at Magdalene College, Cambridge, publishes financial magazines. His most recent book, *The National Wealth: Who Gets What in Britain* (1999), is a popular and comprehensive look at the distribution of wealth in Britain today.

Michael Johnson joined the Board of Trade in 1960 and worked in the senior civil service for 35 years. He took early retirement in 1995 and is now an independent consultant specializing in international trade policy.

Jaron Lanier is Visiting Professor of Computer Science at Columbia University. He is one of the original pioneers of virtual reality technology and an accomplished artist and classical musician.

Joan Leach is lecturer in Humanities and Science Communication at Imperial College London. She is editor of the journal *Social Epistemology* and has published on science popularization and the rhetoric of science as well as discourse ethics in science.

David Lee trained as an art historian at Nottingham University and University College London. A well-known writer and broadcaster on contemporary art and photography, he is editor of *Art Review*.

Shaun Mosley read Agriculture and Economics at Oxford. He has a PhD in Applied Mathematics from Nottingham University. He has published on causality and quantum physics in *The American Journal of Physics* and *Physics Letters* and has directed two feature films.

Ivo Mosley read Japanese at Oxford. A ceramicist for twenty years, he developed new techniques in high-temperature glazing. Now a full-time writer, he edited *The Green Book of Poetry* and *Earth Poems*. His musical *Danny's Dream* was produced in York in 1999.

Nicholas Mosley is the author of fourteen novels, including *Accident* and *Impossible Object* (both filmed), two biographies, a travel book, an autobiography and a book about religion. His novel *Hopeful Monsters* was Whitbread Book of the Year in 1990. He lives in London.

Redmond Mullin has degrees in philosophy and ancient literature. He has been a Jesuit, an advertising executive, and is non-executive director of many charitable foundations. A founder of the Institute of Charity Fundraising Managers, he is chairman of a fundraising company and has published on fundraising and philosophy.

Michael Oakeshott (1901–90) was one of the most important British political philosophers of the twentieth century. His Selected Works are being published by Yale University Press and *Rationalism in Politics* was republished by The Liberty Fund Press in 1991.

Oliver O'Donovan is Regius Professor of Moral and Pastoral Theology at Christ Church, Oxford. His many publications on Christian ethics and theology include *The Desire of the Nations: Rediscovering the Roots of Political Theology* (CUP, 1996).

Helen Oppenheimer is internationally known as a writer on Christian ethics and theology. She was awarded a Lambeth DD in 1993. Her publications include *The Marriage Bond* (1976), *The Hope of Happiness* (1983), and *Finding and Following* (1994).

Michael Polanyi (1891–1976), scientist turned philosopher, published over 200 scientific papers and several books on the nature of knowledge, meaning and freedom; among them *Personal Knowledge* (1958). His concern was to define and defend high ideals of freedom.

Peter Randall-Page is a sculptor with an international reputation whose work is held in collections including the Tate Gallery and the British Museum. His public work includes commissions for cities such as Edinburgh and London. He lives and works in Devon.

Philip Rieff is well known as an interpreter of Freud and a critic of contemporary culture. His books include *Freud: The Mind of the Moralist, The Feeling Intellect, The Triumph of the Therapeutic* and *Fellow Teachers of Culture and its Second Death*. He was Benjamin Franklin Professor of Sociology at Pennsylvania University.

Mark Ryan is a writer and broadcaster on questions of art and culture, and arts editor of *LM* magazine. He co-directed with Claire Fox the conference 'Culture Wars: Dumbing Down, Wising Up?' and is the author of *War and Peace in Ireland*, 1994.

Ravi Shankar is a celebrated Indian classical musician who has performed with many Western musicians, including the Beatles and Yehudi Menuhin. He has made many recordings. His autobiography *Raga Mala* appeared last year.

Demelza Spargo is an art historian who has specialized in the links between art and agriculture. She has written for publications including the *Burlington Magazine* and *Art Monthly* and she organised the exhibition 'This Land Is Our Land' at the Mall Galleries in 1988.

Andrew Williams read Modern History at Oxford. He has been a secondary school teacher for twenty-five years, and Head of Corfe Hills School (1600 pupils) in Broadstone, Dorset for the last ten years.

John Ziman FRS is Emeritus Professor of Physics at the University of Bristol. He has published many books upon the epistemology of science, including *Reliable Knowledge*. His book *Real Science: What it is and What it Means* will be published this year by CUP.

Ivo Mosley

Introduction

The intellectual leaders of the peoples have produced and propagated the fallacies which are destroying liberty and Western civilization. The intellectuals alone are responsible for the mass slaughters which are the characteristic mark of our century. They alone can reverse the trend and pave the way for a resurrection of freedom.

Ludwig von Mises, 1947

Never before in human history has so much cleverness been used to such stupid ends. The cleverness is in the creation and manipulation of markets, media and power; the stupid ends are in the destruction of community, responsibility, morality, art, religion and the natural world.

As a result, a kind of numbness has taken over. In the face of an uncertain and alarming future, which holds little inspiration for present living, people fight off gloom and stupefaction by withdrawing into trivia, sensation-seeking or addictions to money, drugs, or power.

Both the process and its results are to be seen in Dumbing Down, a phenomenon observable in almost all walks of life; politics, culture, civil administration, the media, science, education, even the law. It is so widespread that a new term has been coined: dumbocracy.

Dumbocracy is the rule of cleverness without wisdom. It looks always for the short-term gain, forgetting that we could be around on this planet for a long time – provided dumbocracy does not get out of hand.

Some insist that dumbing-down does not exist; it is an illusion created by an elite to shore up its own waning power. My own opinion is that elites are a necessity in the human affairs of any great civilization. We should try to get the best elites we can, for when one elite is got rid of, another — often worse — takes its place; those who promise to rid us of one elite are bent on replacing it with themselves. As Franz Kafka wrote, 'Every revolution evaporates, leaving nothing behind it but the slime of a new bureaucracy.'

Dumbocracy in Government

The subject of dumbocracy in government is in the air, as argument rages over whether the 'Third Way' constitutes a new vision of democracy or an encroaching totalitarianism. The attempt by one party to be the voice of the people, regulating all our activities in the name of the people, disempowering traditional institutions and other pockets of self-government including the family, is not a new kind of manoeuvre, but something that has been tried many times. The outcome is never fruitful. There is an expression, 'Those who ignore history are condemned to repeat it'; but sometimes a good deal worse than repetition lies in wait.

At the heart of the democratic debate is whether the sentence 'Give us your vote and we'll take care of everything' is an adequate expression of democracy. The idea that casting a single vote every five years can ensure that everything is taken care of — from the buses, to art funding, to defence spending, the health service and the safeguarding of basic freedoms — is far-fetched.

Those who have thought profoundly about democracy realize it is best achieved through a diversity of democratic institutions, as well as by voting politicians in and out of office. Civil associations, of which there are thousands in any civilized country, are places where people may participate in democracy directly. Their actions and participation actually make a difference and the choice of who rises in the hierarchy is decided by merit, by choice among those who know, rather than by whoever offers the most effective spin to a remote electorate.

A more long-standing conflict over democracy concerns, to quote from **Demelza Spargo**'s essay, 'whether we elect representatives for their wisdom, honesty, devoutness and foresightedness; or whether we elect them because they promise to give us what we want.' As the parties increase their hold on who is made available to 'represent' the people, so true democracy recedes into a dim and hazy distance; our representatives are only human in default; in action, they are loyal party units.

Dumbing-down democracy is perhaps the most shameful of the many dumbings-down that are taking place, for it opens the way to totalitarian government. Few would argue with the proposition that democracy represents the most ambitious and hopeful programme for managing human affairs. Indeed, in a complex modern society it is the only conceivable way.

In the essays in this section, **Tam Dalyell** views with despair the decline of intelligent government in Westminster, as the art of conversation is replaced by spin. **Ivo Mosley** looks at how perversions in democratic thought and practice are pushing us into a new kind of pseudo-liberal totalitarianism. **Michael Oakeshott**'s classic essay looks at history since the Middle Ages as a struggle between individualism and those who have found individualistic society a burden. **Michael Johnson** describes the long process of change and modernization in the British Civil Service since the War, and how this process now links with the new political culture to undermine the service's capacity for independent thought and policy advice. **Redmond Mullin** emphasizes the importance of other areas of democratic activity outside the executive machine, and how we must resist the efforts of government to extend control. **Dominic Hobson** looks at the state's efforts to run or regulate business — and now to even transform itself into a business — with a jaundiced eye.

Dumbocracy and Culture

As democracy widened its constituency in the nineteenth and twentieth centuries, the race was on in the West to absorb the newly-enfranchised classes into high culture, with its sense of responsibilities and its high calling for the human race.

However, over the following century high culture changed more than the newly-enfranchised classes. It became, **Philip Rieff** argues, more concerned with flouting than with maintaining its traditions, and therefore an anti-culture - not much high about it but the smell.

Meanwhile, a new form of high culture emerged (in music) from one of the Earth's most disadvantaged nations: Black America.

As we enter a new millennium, the effort to interest the majority in traditional high culture has run out of steam. Populists discredit the word 'high' by calling it elitist, and re-define the word 'culture' as 'what you choose to get up to'.

Ravi Shankar regrets that commercial interests have overtaken the interests of civilization in bringing up our young people. He also presents a very positive picture of cultural diversity, of tradition, and of cross-cultural fertilization; how rich the world can be when we all get on. **Robert Brustein** presents a quite different picture, of cultures at war with each other, with all the suppressions of truth, the ugly struggles for power and the loss to the world of what might be, which war entails.

Anne Glyn-Jones sees parallels in earlier declines of civilization. Finding practical lessons from the past is difficult, but she argues that the bad effects of minimalizing censorship outweigh the bad effects of unbridled commercialism.

With the advent in Britain of the lottery, huge amounts of money are extracted from the populace by means of a state-licensed monopoly on gambling. They are disbursed by state *apparatchiks* to various so-called 'cultural' activities, with results ranging from dubious to outright banditry. **Roger Deakin** examines the process and asks if living culture, in contrast to the preservation of dead culture, is properly an object of charitable subsidy. **Mark Ryan** writes on efforts to make high culture accessible by turning it into a branch of the entertainment industry.

Dumbocracy and the Media

It is convenient to blame the media for almost everything. In reality, of course, we can switch off, we can not-buy, we can avert our eyes; or we could all vote for censorship. The one thing it's entirely unreasonable to do is expect businessmen not to chase a lucrative market.

When every programme, article or book has to seek the widest possible audience, the 'lowest common denominator' effect kicks in. No media provider who wants to maximize profits will take on difficult and demanding material. A background of jolly-seeming nonsense takes over, interrupted by sensationalism or extreme forms of 'entertainment' that test the boundaries of what's acceptable, in order to excite ever more jaded taste buds.

The power of the mass media is one of the phenomena that are really new to the human race, and it is clear that the tenor of society is overwhelmingly affected by the constant stream of pandering which pours into our brains from TV screens, newspapers and magazines. Abstinence may be recommended, but people are hardly going to leave the comforts of being pandered to unless they sense a greater gain somewhere else. What greater gain is on offer?

Oliver O'Donovan examines one of the narcissistic corruptions that have invested the media and through them our lives, drawing general observations upon how the media have affected the way we experience the world and calling for a recovery of authority in religion.

Adam Boulton puts up a heroic defence of the soundbite, often associated with dumbing-down. The soundbite, he says, symbolizes the pledges of politicians in a form they can actually be held to.

Dumbocracy and the Visual Arts

The visual arts present a very special case. When sliced-up cows and unmade beds are celebrated as the epitome of contemporary visual art in Britain, almost everyone senses something is — well, at the very least missing. **David Lee** argues that this is structural; the state, corporations and individuals with financial rather than cultural interests have combined in using public money to corrupt the arts.

There is, however, one way in which the state constructively and indiscriminately supports the arts: the dole.

Laura Gascoigne is intrigued by the infatuation of the *haute bourgouisie* with the peculiar brand of nihilism that calls itself 'cutting edge'. **Peter Randall-Page**, after giving a more positive view of what art can be about, reflects on some of the reasons why the current state of affairs has come about.

Bill Hare presents a hopeful picture of the potential for art to reflect the interests of people at large, and of the importance that art can have in giving a community a sense of identity.

Dumbocracy in Education

As early as 1794, Prussian law recognized the principle of state supremacy in education. Almost a century later, when the state in Britain decided education should be state-funded, a decision was made not to fund the numerous schools that existed already to serve the poor, but to start up brand new schools under state control.

Meanwhile, as other states decided compulsory education was needed to compete in the modern world, they mostly came to similar conclusions; the rich and powerful could be left to educate their children in any manner they saw fit, but the education of the rest must be managed from the state.

The result has been the disempowering of parents and a permanent revolution in education, as political parties change their minds about the kind of results they want to achieve and how best to achieve them — whether those results are nationalism, equalization, civilization, technical excellence, development of the individual, or just keeping young people off the streets.

In Britain, it was James Callaghan who declared that the curriculum was a 'secret garden' which should be opened up to government inspection and supervision. Since then, political power over what teachers teach has spread by direct and indirect means. In primary and secondary education the means are direct; in higher education it is indirect, as funding is conditional to approval by the state. Pupils can now pass through the whole education system without even encountering one of the central principles of Western civilization; that every increase of state power pushes a free citizenry towards passive serfdom.

Michael Polanyi, in a classic essay written before political correctness spread its influence, examines how a materialist conception of man, denying higher spiritual ideals, led to totalitarianism in thought and then in politics.

Claire Fox observes higher education being used as a tool for social inclusion, and laments the loss of respect for higher knowledge that this entails. **Andrew Williams** laments the disappointing results of a century of compulsory education in introducing young people to a higher culture.

Dumbocracy and Science

For scientists, dumbing down has a single and particular meaning; that is, pressure upon them to make their work comprehensible to badly-educated or unintelligent audiences. For the rest of us, other worries are more pressing. One is the way multitudes of 'experts' overrule tradition and common sense and spread about all kinds of baloney. Another is the stupid uses to which genuine science is put.

'Popular science' can consist of perfectly respectable attempts to explain scientific concepts and development in lay terms. Just as often, it seems to consist of what the poet Auden called 'resonant lies'; that is, hocus-pocus masquerading as serious thought, designed to justify some cherished but shameful social behaviour. Thus, soon after Darwin explained his theory of natural selection, Spencer coined the phrase 'the survival of the fittest' and the Social Darwinists were using this soundbite to argue that charity was a bad idea; 'The law of the survival of the fittest was not made by man. We can only, by interfering with it, produce the survival of the unfittest.'[1]

Soon, popular corruptions of scientific theory were in overdrive. In the 1920s, psychomorphic interpretations of relativity theory became all the rage among intellectuals and barber-shop philosophers, in support of anything from atheism to adultery to self-pitying despair. In the thirties, bogus racial theories were used to justify anti-Semitism. In the 1960s, the sexual revolution was 'scientifically' justified by mistaken observations of sexual life in Samoa. In the '80s, a culture of selfish individualism was justified by Richard Dawkins' 'The Selfish Gene'.

The phenomenal public and commercial success of simplified and corrupted scientific ideas feeds back into serious science. Difficult, subtle and complex ideas are left unex-

---

[1]   W.G. Sumner, 1885, quoted in Galbraith, *The Affluent Society*.

plored, while simple and 'successful'[2] ideas gain ground.

A greater worry is the stupid uses to which genuine science is put. The dangers of scientific weapons creation is obvious enough. It is rapidly becoming obvious, also, that the vast industries surrounding industrial food production and scientific medicine create new problems as they solve old ones. In this context, it is worth noting that the science industries profit twice from every destruction of the natural world; once during the destruction itself, and again when they are called in to clear things up.

As the problems (environmental changes, iatrogenic disease, weaponry) pile up, it seems science has become another model dumbocracy; very clever people doing very stupid things that jeopardise our well-being. The problem is, how can science be properly regulated? This subject is explored by **Joan Leach, Shaun Mosley** and **Ivo Mosley.**

Do we expect too much from science? **John Ziman** explains the stupidity of looking to science to provide for all our needs. His essay is that of a scientist speaking to the public, arguing that we should not listen to science as if it were one voice promising us the answer to all our ills. **Walter Freeman** laments the stupidity of seeking happiness out of bottles and looks for a more sociable and human understanding of how to achieve that lofty goal. **Jaron Lanier** argues that certain developments in information technology 'make people redefine themselves into lesser beings'. A pioneer in the field, he speaks with authority on a brand-new problem that can only grow in importance.

Dumbocracy and Religion

When we lose religion, it is not just our sense of guilt that goes astray. We also lose a sense of meaning and significance in what we do. We lose the confidence of a shared moral framework; we lose the teaching embedded in religious stories. Gone from our lives are rites of celebration and passage, the rituals that make a community out of individuals. We also lose our sense that, living in an enterprise not of our making, we

---

[2] 'It is not truth but opinion that can travel the world without a passport' —
Sir Walter Raleigh, *History of the World,* (preface) 1612.

may live in some fulfilling relationship with the higher power that made it. People forget that atheism is the most illogical of all creeds—a belief in something out of nothing.

For many centuries, religion pitted itself against science; now science is being blamed for the demise of religion, because its emphasis on literal truth has undermined belief. If religious devotees must view their stories as metaphors, does not scientific truth, literal and powerful though it be, seem paradoxically trivial? Is there no higher truth than the laws governing the behaviour of particles? God forbid such boredom!

Many essays in this book lament the departure of religion as an active force in our lives. What else can provide the kind of absolute horror that we need, to restrain us from certain kinds of behaviour? Some power of the taboo, which in certain societies can kill stone dead with the mere uttering of a curse, is sorely needed among us so-called 'civilized' people; otherwise, the host of dreary evils that fall outside the law cannot be fought. When people can betray their families, sell arms or drugs, devote their ingenuities to peddling entertainments that are nothing but mental poison, all without a seeming twinge of conscience or a flicker of social rebuke, then it's clear that religion is defunct—and sorely needed.

Meanwhile, complaints about life's dissatisfactions, which used to be part of the dialogue between man and God, are laid at society's door, and society has its work cut out to deal with them. The state has taken on many of the functions that religion used to provide. Charity, community, patronage of the arts, rites of passage; it is now proposing to take on moral teaching ('citizenship'). Without the transcendent teachings of religion, our concept of freedom is belittled and our concern for the future cannot find expression.

Helen Oppenheimer deals in her essay with the importance of truth. With the relativization of everything, even historians have taken on the fashionable notion that there is no such thing as truth. **Nicholas Mosley** deals with the erosion of mystery in religion, as banality is introduced into the one human sphere that can best do without it.

A mention should be made here of **Oliver O'Donovan**'s essay, for though it is included in the section on media, and its insights into the nature of publicity are general, it is written by a theologian from a specifically religious point of view.

Dumbocracy and the Environment

The word 'environment' implies that all of nature just exists for us to live and cavort about in. Even if we accept this desiccated philosophy, we presumably want the 'environment' to stay nice and healthy. Human stupidity vis-à-vis the natural world has had a lot written about it, much of it hysterically biassed, from both sides of the debate.[3] Whatever the case, two facts at least are undeniable. The first is that people in the past have frequently rendered their environment uninhabitable to themselves and have had to move on. The second is that our ability to degrade our environment grows with our command of, and our skill at using, technology. Countering these is the hopeful possibility that, with wisdom and forethought, the same technology and the scientific understanding behind it will enable us to restrain ourselves before it's too late. The outcome of this struggle may be the primary factor in determining how long our civilization lasts.

The essays in this section are firstly a historical overview of the problem from **C.D. Darlington**, an outspoken botanist, geneticist and historian; then an impassioned and very contemporary plea for changes in agricultural practice from **Demelza Spargo**.

---

[3] My own contributions to this debate (their bias declared in their titles) are the anthologies *The Green Book of Poetry* (Frontier Publishing) and *Earth Poems* (HarperSanFrancisco).

Tam Dalyell

On the Decline of
Intelligent Government

*The veteran Labour MP Tam Dalyell converses with **Ivo Mosley** about the changing role of the Westminster Parliament. He started by discussing the marginalization of the House of Commons and the increasing power of the executive lodged in Downing Street.*

When I was first elected to the House of Commons in May 1962, as a result of the West Lothian by-election, it simply did not occur to its Members that there was any other centre of power in Britain. Harold Macmillan, in his retirement at Birch Grove, testified that he had often felt physically sick at lunch time on Tuesdays and Thursdays preparing for the ordeal of twice-weekly Prime Minister's Questions. Prime Minister's Questions were a serious matter. How he answered was a genuine measure of the Government's stock, and when, once every three weeks or so, Hugh Gaitskell, as leader of the Opposition, asked a question, it was an event.

The serious nature of Prime Minister's Questions persisted throughout the premiership of Sir Alec Douglas-Home (1963–4), throughout the term of the incoming Labour Government, and the Heath Government of 1970–4. Then the rot set in and, as so often in public life, it was a matter of chance — a development which nobody could have foreseen, or at least a development which nobody actually foresaw. It came about like this.

On 29 April 1975, a day on which the Prime Minister was scheduled to answer parliamentary questions at the Despatch Box, Harold Wilson was due to be away at a conference of

Commonwealth Leaders of Government. The Labour MP John Golding, Member for Newcastle-under-Lyme and a prominent and controversial member of the National Executive Committee of the Labour Party, hit on the wheeze of asking a question: 'To ask the Prime Minister if he would state his official engagements for April 29th.' The Deputy Prime Minister, Edward Short, replied 'As the House knows, my Right Honourable Friend is attending the Commonwealth Heads of Government meeting in Kingston, Jamaica, until May 7th.' By asking a purely formal question, acceptable to the Table Office and the stringent rules of Parliamentary order, John Golding had outflanked the vetting system on questions to the Prime Minister and gained the opportunity to put a supplementary question on almost any aspect of policy which might be on his mind.

The genie was out of the bottle. Pandora's Box was opened. From now on MPs could ask the Prime Minister about virtually anything under the political sun. The Prime Minister was put in the position of having to be seen as a Universal Expert — he or she who must not be caught out — who must appear to be conversant with everything that his or her Government was doing. This meant delving into the relative minutiae of departments of state — Mrs Thatcher and Mr Blair becoming inquisitive about the work of Cabinet colleagues to an extent which would not have occurred to Mr Macmillan or Mr Attlee. But in order for a Prime Minister to be briefed on such an unprecedented diversity of topics it was necessary to have a considerable apparatus in Downing Street.

In November 1965 Richard Crossman had a bout of sickness; the Prime Minister asked me, as Crossman's PPS, to go to Downing Street from time to time to tell him how his Secretary of State was progressing. Apart from the 'Garden Girl' typists, the Prime Minister's staff appeared to be his personal secretary Lady Falkender, his press secretary Sir Trevor Lloyd-Hughes, and the cat. Twenty years later I witnessed Tony Blair's Downing Street, bustling with special advisers — a veritable parallel government to the great departments of state. Cabinet Ministers and their junior ministerial colleagues are meaningfully answerable to MPs in the Commons and indeed to the House of Lords. Not so the parallel government. The Commons is sidelined.

IM: Do you think that there has been a change in the character of the average MP? There seems to be a public perception of MPs as being ingratiating and on an increasingly lucrative gravy train, as Europe and the devolved United Kingdom assemblies are added to the list of possibilities of public office.

Have MPs changed in character? Yes. When I was first elected to the House of Commons in May 1962 there were questions to a Secretary of State for the Colonies and a Secretary of State for Commonwealth Affairs, apart from questions to the Foreign Secretary. Great issues were the aftermath of what happened at the Hola Camp and the treatment of the Nigerian Chief Enahoro. The affairs of the Central African Federation and of Rhodesia occupied many hours on the floor of the House, besides much Prime Ministerial time. Some 40 years later it is significant how few — very few — parliamentary contributions there have been from the back benches on the US/UK aggression against Iraq and on the Balkan war. It may be partly that after the 'End of Empire' we British have turned in on ourselves. But it is also that MPs are either expected to, or like to, second guess local councillors. One can understand Duncan Sandys saying to some constituent who chided him for not taking up a housing case — he had been a noteworthy Minister of Housing — 'I represent Streatham at Westminster, not Westminster in Streatham!'

But are MPs gravy-train seekers? No. Men and women who submit themselves to the arduous sweat of becoming an MP would be able to command a substantially higher income outside politics, in many fields of business and the professions. If MPs give the impression, to the public, of being ingratiating, two other sets of reasons suggest themselves. Too often parliamentary questions to the Prime Minister are seen as opportunities for job applications to the PM for junior ministerial office. But there is a second set of considerations which bother me rather more. It is perceived that the party central machine has more to say than ever before over whether a parliamentary candidate is re-selected. Members of the parliamentary awkward squad could find that a National Executive Committee, unprecedentedly under the thumb of No. 10 Downing Street, by some alchemy does not endorse their re-selection the next time around. Therein lies the real pressure to ingratiate.

IM: It seems to me that the public have a decreasing attention span and interest in politics. Do you think that this follows from, or leads to, the demoralization of politics?

There is a real problem of decreasing public attention span and interest in politics — or, to be more precise, in other than instant political solutions. This is largely a result of the electronic media. Winston Churchill was never grilled on air by journalists; and Clement Attlee, when asked, 'Have you anything to say about the Berlin Airlift?', than which nothing was more important in 1948, famously replied to the reporter, 'No thank you, no comment today' — and the heavyweight reporter, unsurprised, accepted the Prime Minister's response without demur.[1] Half a century later, in an age of irreverence, it is inconceivable that any politician would get away with that. It would be interpreted as 'hauteur'. Comment is expected on the heels of a headline. I doubt if most politicians are noticeably demoralized by such a situation; what is true is that politicians' comment, often necessarily ill-considered, is devalued in the public perception.

IM: Is the much-paraded anti-elitist passion of recent Governments responsible for the destruction of responsibility in government?

This is a very delicate question. I cannot conceal my contempt for focus-groups, spin-doctors and all the paraphernalia that emphasizes presentation and pleasing the whims of the electorate. Certainly there has been much anti-elitist rhetoric, but are we sure that, since 1945, there has been an elite against whom to rage and fume? Personally, I think not. I was elected to a Parliament, in 1962, which was the fag-end of a military structure and hierarchy — incidentally alive and well in the Labour Party, no less than in the Tory Party. Most MPs had been in the Services in World War II. DSOs, MCs, MMs (not to mention a couple of VCs) abounded. But Cabinet and Shadow Cabinet (the Parliamentary Committee of the Parliamentary Labour Party) were not an elite. The PLP's Thursday-evening meetings were a restraining factor.

One of my abiding memories of the House of Commons is that of a huge frame padding through the door to the right of

[1] More to the point, so did his editor, the legendary Arthur Christiansen, for a quarter of a century the unquestioned boss of Beaverbrook's *Daily Express*.

the Speaker's chair and beseating himself in a corner. Should any colleague have happened to occupy the space when the frame loomed in the doorway he or she moved up or, if there were not spare seats, evaporated. The frame belonged to Major John Morrison, Wiltshire and Islay landowner, who quite simply spoke not a word in the Chamber. He was the Chairman of the 1922 Committee. His function was to go along to the Prime Minister, having gauged opinion and Commons performance and say to Harold Macmillan or Sir Alec Douglas-Home, 'The boys won't wear it', or 'Such and such a minister does not bat very well at the dispatch box'. The Parliament of 1959–1964, an era in which the first Prime Minister was an aspiring aristocrat, married to the Duke of Devonshire's daughter, and the second an impeccably genuine aristocrat, was the Indian Summer of Bagehot's concept of 'government by conversation'.

IM: Is Bagehot's idea of 'government by conversation' now dead, as Members are increasingly puppets on their master's strings?
Alas yes, and I regret it in many ways, 'government by conversation' entered its declining years in 1964. But the causes of the decline were, in my view, largely threefold. It would be misleading to attribute them simply to the advent of a new-broom Labour Government.

First there was the situation, though not the character, of Harold Wilson as incoming Prime Minister. By temperament he was friendly and gossipy and I never had difficulty in talking to him about anything. But Wilson was determined to be different from his predecessor Hugh Gaitskell, who had been much damaged by being seen to encourage the Frognal Gardens Coterie. Wilson did not want to be seen to have favourite courtiers and that meant being more distant from everybody.

Second the selection of the then fourteenth Earl of Home as Conservative Prime Minister and the pithy description of the process of Iain MacLeod as 'Choice by the Magic Circle', led to a counter-reaction. Informality of decision by grandees was thought to be no longer acceptable. Years later, during the days following the rejection of Ted Heath and before Margaret Thatcher was elected, I teased Edward DuCann, then Chairman of the 1922 Committee, 'Come back the Magic Circle!'

'Tam, m'boy', said DuCann in total solemnity, 'the Magic Circle had a great deal to be said for it!'

The third factor is mundane/physical/environmental. MPs now have offices, many of them rather lavish, but minutes away from the hub of the Commons around the chamber, whereas in the past we had to make do with lockers. I am not persuaded that this change necessarily represents progress. Instead of talking to one another, MPs are increasingly cooped up in their cabins, dealing with constituency business in the company of 'research' assistants. My suspicion is that these 'research' assistants do precious little research and a lot of constituency propaganda/casework, too often usurping business which is more properly that of the local council. I was deeply shocked at the sparse attendance in the Commons Chamber for the important debates on Kosovo and the Balkan War. The excuse that many Members were in their offices, eyeing proceedings on their in-house TV monitors fails to convince. What is certain beyond peradventure is that the Commons Smoking Room, which would be full to capacity every evening in the 1960s from 8pm onwards, is now virtually empty. If Parliament is about 'parleying with one another', in a way that served Britain well for centuries, that has ceased to happen. Parleying helped keep Britain out of the Vietnam War, by pressurizing Wilson not to accede to Lyndon Johnson's request to send a 'Battalion of Bag-Pipers' as a token British force. I believe that under the old system Blair might have been made to desist from the folly of the Balkan bombing.

There is another inhibition on government by conversation which is much vaguer, but nonetheless pervasive. An ambitious MP feels that he or she has to be more circumspect as to what they say, as words, thanks to modern technology, are not only likely to be more recorded than in previous decades, but are certainly more easily traceable. Thirty years ago, if any Member went to the excellent Commons Library and said, 'What did Dalyell say about chemical weapons on Monday 6 May 1968?' — with considerable trouble they might have traced such nuggets of wisdom, or they might not. Three decades later, to get such information takes seconds — by pressing the right knobs on a computer. That scourge of modern politics, the Instant Rebuttal Unit, certainly renders no service to serious political argument and therefore to wise decision making. The Instant Rebuttal Unit is just one of the creations — now creatures — of the 'party machine'.

IM: Does the increasing control exercized by party machines, and the role of 'spin doctors', make modern democratic politics seem increasingly totalitarian?
Well, my use of 'party machine' begs a number of questions. In the case of the present Government, is it the party machine or the 10 Downing Street machine? I think the latter is the more accurate description. If people talk to those of my generation about the party machine or party policy, we tend to think in terms of the policy of the National Executive Committee of the party, hammered out on the anvil of resolutions at party meetings, particularly the former House Policy Committee of the National Executive Committee of the NEC, and endorsed by the Party Conference. Right or wrong, recent decisions on single mothers, incapacity benefit and a number of other matters were not, by any stretch of the imagination, *party* policy — they were *Government* policy. Equally, it is the Leader and his office in the Conservative Party who have been instrumental in the expulsion of Julian Critchley and other pro-Europeans from the Tory tribe. It would not have occurred to previous leaders to do anything of the kind. (The case of Viscount Hinchingbrooke in Dorset being rather different.)

'Rocking the boat' has escalated up the rungs of the ladder of political sin. Much fun has been made of MPs having 'pagers'. Actually, although I do not have a pager, ribaldry on this particular point is misplaced. With offices as far away as the Outer Mongolia of Number Seven Millbank, Members who are not Sebastian Coe do require warning of impending divisions. What is not a joke is the requirement to be 'on message' on matters of policy. Not only when a General Election looms, but even when there is a whiff of a by-election, there falls the veil of a taboo on tricky, albeit urgent, issues.

The trouble is that a ridiculous and ill-conceived yearning for day-to-day public approval prevents Government from tackling difficult social issues. If the attitude is not quite, 'one of these days is none of these days', it is at least, 'we'd better be careful not to offend too many voters until after the next election!' This does not synchronize with prompt good government!

*IM: So what do you feel is the role of the media in all these develop-
ments? Given the ubiquity and intrusiveness of television and the
tabloids, are these developments inevitable?*

Crucial to all these developments is the changing role of the
media. When I first was elected to the House of Commons and
became Parliamentary Private Secretary to the diarist and
Housing Minister, Dick Crossman, the most important media
occasion of the week for him was a small glass of sherry in his
room with James Margach, the veteran *Sunday Times* guru, on
a Thursday evening. Margach's visit to Room 18 on the ministerial corridor on a Thursday evening when Parliament was
sitting was a matter of the Law of the Medes and Persians.
Margach padded round other Cabinet Ministers. Wilson had
his 'white Commonwealth of Lobby Correspondents' —
David Wood of the *Times*, H.B. Boyne of the *Daily Telegraph*,
Francis Boyd of the *Guardian*, John Bourne of the *Financial
Times*, Walter Terry of the *Daily Mail* and others. The quiet,
serious chat has been superseded by raucous spin-doctors,
who in a different technical era are expected to answer
instantly. Ubiquitous and intrusive TV makes for instant and,
therefore, necessarily ill-considered responses. The response,
however ill-judged, has then to be defended. We live under
the Tyranny of Deadlines.

Ivo Mosley

Dumbing Down Democracy

The wise ruler takes no action;
  the people transform themselves.
The wise ruler is not meddlesome;
  the people prosper by themselves[1]

Lao Tzu

We are used to thinking of democracy and totalitarianism as opposites, so it comes as a surprise when, with grim regularity, totalitarian regimes emerge from democracies. But this surprise is misplaced, for in the liberal tradition of thought there are many warnings that a tendency towards loss of freedom is inherent in democracy itself.

Changes in the democratic cultures of Western countries have led to worries over whether some new kind of totalitarianism is creeping up on us. The cult of charisma, in the form of pop and film idols; the continual celebration of violence in the media; the cult of the body beautiful; the abolition of God; the division of society into middle-class and underclass— *ubermenschen* and *untermenschen*; more and more invasive state control over our lives, all remind us of well-documented totalitarian tendencies of the past.

Certain acts of government exacerbate these anxieties; the abolition of traditions and therefore the past; the creation of a new and ersatz national identity; the state's hijacking and corruption of art; ever-more pervasive state control in education;

---

[1] Lau Tzu, *Tao Te Ching*, LVII.

the sidelining of parliament and civil institutions; an increasing use of propaganda to supersede the processes of debate.

Other developments send out warning signals. There has been a huge increase in the amount of control that political parties exercise over their members. The powers of the executive arm of government extend increasingly into the judiciary and over parliament, as the Government takes it upon itself to release convicted torturers and murderers for political reasons, as it involved us in a war in Kosovo that it never had any intention of declaring, and as it inflicts by *diktat* a myriad of petty regulations, many of which are never ratified by parliament.

Most recently, we have seen attempts at introducing the cult of the leader as representing all the people (except for the 'dark forces of conservatism'). This is what the Nazis called *Gleichshaltung*: 'coordination, streamlining, bringing into line'. By this means 'the fuehrer, representing the will of the people, directed the flow of policy through the institutions of state and party down to the people'.[2] This semi-mystical process justified bypassing all the normal checks on state activities; vested interests, institutions, traditional groupings, the conservative forces of law and religion. All such groups— if they resist—were cast as 'backward-looking', 'anti-progressive'; 'enemies of the people'.

The Nature of Modern Western Democracies

What we have come to call democracy in the West is not what the ancients meant by democracy. When Plato and Aristotle talked about democracy they were talking about a system in which those in authority were chosen by lot. This kind of extreme democracy is not even contemplated in today's world and is one reason why the ancient philosophers were less admiring of democracy than we might expect.

Aristotle described three forms of government. Each form—monarchy, aristocracy and democracy—had a good and a bad manifestation, depending on whether the rulers ruled for the benefit of all or in their own interest.

---

[2] Klaus P. Fischer, *Nazi Germany—A New History*, p. 278 (New York: Continuum, 1996).

'The true forms of government', he wrote, 'are those in which the one, or the few, or the many, govern with a view to the common interest; but governments which rule with a view to the private interest—whether of the one, the few, or the many—are perversions.'[3]

Cicero, writing a few hundred years later, had this to say about government:

> Of the three basic types of government, I regard monarchy as the best; but a moderate, mixed type of government, combining all three elements, is much better. There should be a monarchical element in the state. The leading citizens also ought to have some power. And the people themselves should have some say in running the affairs of the nation.[4]

More than a thousand years later Aquinas said much the same thing. 'The best form of polity', he wrote, 'is partly kingdom, with one at the head of all; partly rule by the best, insofar as a number of persons are set in authority; partly democracy, that is, government by the people, insofar as the rulers can be chosen from the people, and the people have the right to chose their rulers.'[5]

It is evident that modern democracies are all of this mixed and complex type, whether the monarch is a President with great power or a hereditary monarch with little power. The elected representatives of the people hold the main power, but this is checked by the influence of autonomous institutions—composed of individuals who are held in respect and exert influence in society for reasons other than success in the struggle for power that is politics.

The complex structure of modern democracies is strong against some perversions, weak against others. I would argue that the push for more state power is the chief perversion to which democracy is vulnerable. Financial corruption and cronyism will always crop up, no doubt, but in open democracies they may be—and usually are—detected and dealt with. The desire of politicians for more power, however, is a force

---

[3] Aristotle, *Politics*, 1279a.
[4] Cicero, *Republic*, 1, 44.
[5] St Thomas Aquinas, *Summa Theologiæ*, 1–2, 105,1.

that has been pushing democracy towards a new kind of pseudo-benevolent totalitarianism. The simplification, the dumbing-down of democracy to a simple formula of 'Cast your vote and we'll take care of you', is a process dangerous to civilization itself.

Democracy and 'The State'

'The State' takes on a kind of abstract reality in our minds, though in fact it just consists of those people and their power whom we agree to let rule over us. It is only natural that the bureaucrats and politicians who make up the state should seek to increase their power, against all wise advice from the tradition of democratic thought. Edmund Burke wrote:

> 'It ought to be the constant aim of every wise public counsel to find out with how little, not how much, restraining the community can subsist; for liberty is a good to be improved, not an evil to be lessened. It is not only a private blessing of the first order, but the vital spring and energy of the state itself, which has just so much vigor and life as there is liberty in it.'[6]

The danger of governments granting ever-increasing power to themselves was addressed by John Stuart Mill in his essay *On Liberty*, published in 1859:

> The most cogent reason for restricting the interference of government is the great evil of adding unnecessarily to its power. Every function added to those already exercised by the government, causes its influence over hopes and fears to be more widely diffused, and converts, more and more, the active and ambitious part of the public into hangers-on of the government, or of some party which aims at becoming the government. If the roads, the railways, the banks, the insurance offices, the great joint-stock companies, the universities, and the public charities, were all of them branches of the government; if, in addition, the municipal corporations and

---

[6] Edmund Burke, *Letter to the Sheriffs of Bristol*, 3 April 1777.

local boards, with all that now devolves on them, became departments of the central administration; if the employees of all these different enterprises were appointed and paid by the government, and looked to the government for every rise in life; not all the freedom of the press and popular constitution of the legislature would make this, or any other country, free otherwise than in name. And the evil would be greater, the more efficiently and scientifically the administrative machinery was constructed.[7]

The scenario described by Mill is to some extent with us. The state has, by many methods, augmented its power since he wrote. One method it has used is to institute emergency provisions in war, then fail to revoke them when peace is restored. A recent instance of this in Britain was when the post-war Government of Clement Attlee declined to reverse the centralization of power that Churchill had instituted during the Second World War.

Another method the state has used is to promise to achieve, or impose, equality. State action to impose complete equality — in the sense of equal wealth for all — has to be so all-pervasive, so sapping of initiative, and so demanding of man-power, that the attempt can only succeed in reducing everyone to a condition of equal misery. This condition was often achieved in Communist countries, although — as Orwell pointed out in *Animal Farm* — some were always more equal than others. State officials were not immune from misery, however, for though they escaped economic misery, the spectre of a fall from grace, imprisonment or even death, dogged their waking and sleeping moments. The moral impulse towards equalization of wealth has been tempered by this experience, and now it generally aims at a moderate equalization by taxation.

Another way the state has increased its power is by convincing us that some things are too important to be left to private provision. Voters are keen that healthcare should be in the public domain; governments less so nowadays because, as

---

[7] J.S. Mill, *On Liberty*, V.

healthcare gets more and more expensive, decisions as to who gets what are bound to be unpopular. Governments are keener on state control in education; by that means they may influence our notions of what it is to be a citizen.

But the most powerful way that states in the modern age have been able to increase their power is by offering to look after citizens from cradle to grave. This offer is attractive to anyone who dislikes the idea of human distress, and it is especially attractive to two sections of the population; those who want to be looked after and those who want to look after them.

Thus a yearning for Utopia on earth gives birth to a third form of totalitarianism, a liberal totalitarianism, popularly known as the Nanny State. As Nanny increases her power, she turns from a benevolent and magical Mary Poppins into an image of stifling manipulation.

There is an expression 'the worst is the corruption of the best'. The three forms of totalitarianism were all born in answer to fine wishes: communism (the wish for equality); fascism (the wish for order); the Nanny State (the wish that there should be as little suffering in the world as possible). History tells us how the first two wishes went wrong; what about the third?

Liberal Totalitarianism

The word 'liberal' has undergone a slow change in meaning over the last 150 years. It used to mean a belief that the state should not interfere in the fundamental liberties of individuals, except to prevent the activities of one individual injuring another. In the definition of John Stuart Mill: 'The liberty of the individual must be thus far limited; he must not make himself a nuisance to other people.'[8]

This is not what liberalism has come to mean. It now has two meanings quite at odds with the traditional one.

One meaning signifies a sense of identification or sympathy with malefactors, who are no longer to be thought of as evil or abominable but as underdogs. Once we understand the harsh lives of those who do evil deeds we must forgive them, because the evil they do comes out of the evil done to them.

---

[8] Mill, *On Liberty*, III.

Kindness will interrupt the vicious circle and produce goodness. The other new meaning refers to the bossy interference that follows when liberals identify an evil and intrude with kindness to put it right.

The two meanings of the word share an economic as well as a political interest, as a great deal of employment arises from trying to put the world to rights.

This state of affairs was envisioned by Burkhardt towards the end of the nineteenth century:

> The social impulse would assign to the state never-heard-of and outrageous tasks, which can be accomplished only by a mass of power which is also never-heard-of and outrageous. Careerists will want to take this omnipotent state in hand and guide it.[9]

The establishment of liberal totalitarianism depends on an illusion, that the state can achieve what civil society cannot — that it can forge a steady Utopia out of our base human natures. The failures of liberal totalitarianism are obvious. The streets are full of the homeless as they've never been before — and in an age of unparalleled wealth, at that. Drug abuse threatens children everywhere. The family is in dire straits. Moral and social order are in decay. The state whisks away forty-odd percent of people's hard-earned cash, much of which it spends on an enormous bureaucracy and putting right its own mistakes. Unemployment sits at high levels, and crime with it. Those in work work longer and longer hours, the wealth gap is growing once again, and corporate powers fill our world with pollution.

One of the reasons for all this is that people with little experience or competence are put in charge of making rules and overseeing their implementation. The state's appointees are chosen primarily for their obedience as political creatures, not for their acumen in business or administration. Incompetence, waste and inappropriate expenditure are the results.

Regulators, administrators and overseers spread a new culture in society; that of conformity to the political will. People

---

[9] From Jacob Burkhardt, 'The State in the Newer Sense', in *Judgments on History and Historians*.

are always looking over their shoulders. Politicization gathers momentum as more and more people need the approval of the state just to stay in work.

To further this process a game is played, stirring up mistrust among people; it has been much played by both Mrs Thatcher and Mr Blair.

The game goes like this: We are told that teachers are incompetent; they need government supervision. A cheer goes up from the rest of us; we can all remember at least one incompetent teacher. Builders are getting away with murder, we are told, and need government supervision; everyone who's been let down by a builder gives a cheer. The health service is corrupt and incompetent; they need bureaucrats to supervise them; anyone who's waited in a hospital queue gives a cheer. Lawyers, broadcasters, farmers, doctors…as each new group is invaded by government the rest all cheer, ignoring for the moment that they may be next in line (if they haven't been processed already).

The media love to play the same game. 'It's an outrage!' they shout. 'The Government should do something about it!' The fantasy of one power that can cure all ills sells to the outraged child in each of us.

But as the state's regulators take over, fundamental problems in society are created. Politics spreads into every area of life and creates the scenario described earlier by John Stuart Mill. Voluntary organizations and associations disappear, to be replaced by state apparatus. Suddenly we are all politicians, or in fear of politicians, and life has become a mild form of hell. Everything is done in the name of 'the people', but is in fact done to benefit the political machine.

Attitudes to 'The People'

Democracy is described as 'government of the people, by the people, for the people'.[10] In reality, it means something less romantic; it means that every few years the people get to choose their rulers from a limited offer. And in practice, 'the people' have often been much abused by governments acting in their name.

---

[10] Abraham Lincoln, Gettysburg address.

For Nazis and Communists—and, more recently, New Labour—'the people' is a magic invocation. If those who invoke the magic name really believed in 'the people' they would trust the people to get on with their lives and organize themselves. What such politicians are really interested in is power.

Political extremists are divided into two camps by their attitudes to 'the people'. One camp, almost extinct in the modern world, makes no bones about its contempt; they believe that the people, alias the mob, are:

> an unwieldy rabble, with no natural sense of what is right and fit. It rushes wildly into state affairs with all the fury of a swollen stream in the winter, and confuses everything![11]

The other camp—the revolutionaries—pretends in public to believe that the people are the source of all wisdom; but among themselves they say the people do not know what is best for themselves and need to have their interests interpreted for them.

Either way, the attitude of extremists towards the people is contemptuous. If we turn to the writings of democrats we find a more enlightening picture. For instance, Edmund Burke:

> When popular discontents have been very prevalent, it may well be affirmed and supported, that there has generally been something found amiss in the constitution, or in the conduct of the government. The people have no interest in disorder. When they do wrong, it is their error, and not their crime. But with the governing part of the state, it is far otherwise. They may certainly act ill by design, as well as by mistake.[12]

Here we have a picture of the people as not malicious; but neither are they a fount of mystical wisdom. Gullibility is the worst the people stand accused of, but the price of gullibility can be high indeed. It was 'the people' who believed in the

[11] Otanes the Persian, as reported by Herodotus in the fifth century BC.
[12] Edmund Burke, *Thoughts on the Causes of the Present Discontents* (1770).

promise of the Third Reich, 'the people' who went with
Lenin's promises.

Gullibility is prey to flattery as well as to false promises. The
danger of flattery was well known and well recognized in the
courts of monarchs. In democracies it proceeds along similar
lines, except 'the people' have to be flattered *en masse.* 'Equality' is the rallying cry of those who flatter the people. There is
no need for elitism, they say; any of us could run the country.
No need for a culture of thought and learning and self-
restraint; all this can be replaced by self-belief. They point to
the injustice of inherited elites and thereby hope to discredit
all kinds of elitism.

When voters swallow this flattery they get charlatans, crafty
charmers, unscrupulous manipulators to rule over them. A
residue of instinctive deference prevents many from seeing
the true nature of such politicians until much damage has
been done. If the process goes too far a kind of hypnotized
worship of the leader occurs, such as we have seen in countries headed by Hitler, Stalin and Saddam.

Yet people are reluctant to return to dependence on civil
society, that mix of voluntary self-governing associations and
interdependencies by which we took care of each other in the
past. This is partly because we remember it as cruel, oppressive and arbitrary—so perhaps it must to some extent always
be, since all human systems are fallible. But in looking back we
sometimes forget one huge change that has occurred since the
retreat of civil society; that is, the enormous increase in affluence that has been made available to us by advances in technology and science, and by mechanization.

This affluence, because of the high degree of cooperation
required in extracting it from the natural world, is largely in
the hands of corporations. Since the state needs large amounts
of cash to finance its programmes, it must turn to them for the
wealth it needs.

Democracy and the Corporations

Burckhardt wrote, in the late 1860s:

> With all business swelling into big business, the
> views of the businessmen have taken the following
> line...the state should be no more than the protec-

tive guarantor of the businessman's interests, and of his type of intelligence, henceforth assumed to be the main purpose of the world.

There are now many corporations with internal economies larger than those of many small countries. Corporations, unlike small countries, do not have internal systems of justice or democracy; they are purely executive operations. In this respect they are like fascist states; and yet they are unlike fascist states in that they have to operate subject to control from outside sources. They are subject to control by international law, by the laws of the countries in which they operate, and by what consumers will put up with.

Because we all need the prosperity that corporations generate, all of us — governments, consumers and workforces alike — are prepared to give them a fairly free hand. To stay competitive, corporations must seek out the best locations and conditions to do business, and that may include — for instance — manufacturing in countries with lax environmental and employment laws, taking and giving bribes, and subsidising oppressive regimes.

Ultimately, directly through purchase or indirectly through political legislation, and sometimes even through the moral demands of shareholders, restraint over the activities of corporations belongs to the consumers and voters of the wealthy countries, which are also the democracies. The moral sentiments of consumers and voters determine how ruthlessly a corporation may behave. These moral sentiments, it turns out, are somewhat jaded or inert; they can cope with all kinds of slow outrages, such as the displacements of tribal peoples, the exploitation of workers abroad, the slow death of the natural world, the corruption of foreign governments, the trade in arms. Only on occasions of gross and sudden outrage, such as Shell were sponsoring a few years ago in Nigeria, does the consumer base make a show of resistance.

But when government makes too close an alliance with the interests of business, we should beware. We may be doubly stitched up, for both have tendencies to misbehave. In the words of Adam Smith:

> The violence and injustice of the rulers of mankind
> is an ancient evil, for which, I am afraid, the nature

of human affairs can scarce admit of a remedy. But the mean rapacity, the monopolizing spirit of merchants and manufacturers, who neither are, nor ought to be, the rulers of mankind, though it cannot perhaps be corrected may very easily be prevented from disturbing the tranquillity of anybody but themselves.[13]

We should beware the false promises of government and corporate power to deliver happiness via affluence alone. At the moment, unfortunately, this promise seems to be the one promise that politicians are expected to keep. When it comes to elections there is one main requirement, easily identified; 'It's the economy, stupid!', as President Clinton said during his re-election campaign. In the run-up to the last election in Britain, prospective Members of Parliament were told not to express opinions on any of the most pertinent and acute forms of distress in society; drugs, unemployment, crime, the welfare trap, the destruction of the natural world. This was in response to a perception that the public did not want to hear any such debate. The moral weariness on the part of voters who can only vote on the amount of money in their pockets signifies almost complete defeat in the face of a numbing and misunderstood power.

The growth of state power is like boiling a lobster; the victim doesn't notice until it is dead. The victim in this case is the free society, in the higher sense of freedom by which we mean freedom to espouse ideals higher than mere expediency and comfort. This freedom may seem abstract, but it is the freedom upon which Western civilization is built.

A hundred and fifty years ago, Alexis de Tocqueville described the process by which this loss of freedom could occur. After writing Part One of his book *Democracy in America*, which he wrote in order to recommend democracy to his fellow Frenchmen, he found himself haunted by the spectre of what could go wrong in democracies; of how they were vulnerable to an entirely new kind of despotism. In Part Two of the book he included some chapters to describe this vision. Here are some excerpts:

---

[13] Adam Smith, *Wealth of Nations*, Modern Library Edition, p. 461.

Above (the people) stands an immense and tutelary power, which takes upon itself alone to secure their gratifications and watch over their fate.

It would be like the authority of a parent if, like that authority, its object was to prepare men for manhood; but it seeks, on the contrary, to keep them in perpetual childhood.

It covers the surface of society with a network of small complicated rules, minute and uniform, through which the most original and the most energetic characters cannot penetrate.

It must not be forgotten that it is especially dangerous to enslave men in the minor details of life.

Such a power does not destroy, but it prevents existence; it does not tyrannize, but it compresses, enervates, extinguishes, and stupefies a people.

It is in vain to summon a people who have been rendered so dependent on the central power to choose from time to time the representatives of that power; this rare and brief exercise of their free choice, no matter how important it may be, will not prevent them from gradually losing the faculties of thinking, feeling and acting for themselves.

Let us then look forward to the future with that salutary fear which makes men keep watch and ward for freedom, not with that faint and idle terror which depresses and enervates the heart.[14]

---

[14] Alexis de Tocqueville, *Democracy in America*, from Part Two, Book IV, Chapters 6 & 7.

Michael Oakeshott

The Masses in Representative Democracy

I

The course of modern European history has thrown up a character whom we are accustomed to call the 'mass man'. His appearance is spoken of as the most significant and far-reaching of all the revolutions of modern times. He is credited with having transformed our way of living, our standards of conduct and our manners of political activity. He is, sometimes regretfully, acknowledged to have become the arbiter of taste, the dictator of policy, the uncrowned king of the modern world. He excites fear in some, admiration in others, wonder in all. His numbers have made him a giant; he proliferates everywhere; he is recognized either as a locust who is making a desert of what was once a fertile garden, or as the bearer of a new and more glorious civilization.

All this I believe to be a gross exaggeration. And I think we should recognize what our true situation is in this respect, what precisely we owe to this character, and the extent of his impact, if we understood more clearly who this 'mass man' is and where he has come from. And with a view to answering these questions I propose to engage in a piece of historical description.

It is a long story, which has too often been made unintelligible by being abridged. It does not begin (as some would have us understand) with the French Revolution or with the industrial changes of the late eighteenth century; it begins in those perplexing centuries which, because of their illegibility, no historian can decide whether they should properly be regarded as a conclusion or a preface, namely the fourteenth and fifteenth centuries. And it begins, not with the emergence of the 'mass man', but with an emergence of a very different kind, namely that of the human individual in his modern idiom. You must bear with me while I set the scene for the entry of the character we are to study, because we shall mistake him unless we prepare ourselves for his appearance.

II

There have been occasions, some of them in the distant past, when, usually as a consequence of the collapse of a closely integrated manner of living, human individuality has emerged and has been enjoyed for a time. An emergence of this sort is always of supreme importance; it is the modification not only of all current activities but also of all human relationships, from those of husband, wife and children to those of ruler and subject. The fourteenth and fifteenth centuries in western Europe were an occasion of this kind. What began to emerge, then, was conditions so pre-eminently favourable to a very high degree of human individuality, and human beings enjoying (to such a degree and in such numbers) the experience of 'self-determination' in conduct and belief, that it overshadows all earlier occasions of the sort. Nowhere else has the emergence of individuals (that is persons accustomed to making choices for themselves) either modified human relationships so profoundly, or proved so durable an experience, or provoked so strong a reaction, or explained itself so elaborately in the idiom of philosophical theory.

Like everything else in modern Europe, achievement in respect of human individuality was a modification of medieval conditions of life or thought. It was not generated in claims and assertions on behalf of individuality, but in sporadic divergencies from a condition of human circumstance in which the opportunity for choice was narrowly circumscribed. To know oneself as the member of a family, a group, a corporation, a church, a village community, as the suitor at a court or as the occupier of a tenancy, had been, for the vast majority, the circumstantially possible sum of self-knowledge. Not only were ordinary activities, those concerned with getting a living, communal in character, but so also were decisions, rights and responsibilities. Relationships and allegiances normally sprang from status and rarely extricated themselves from the analogy of kinship. For the most part anonymity prevailed; individual human character was rarely observed because it was not there to be observed. What differentiated one man from another was insignificant when compared with what was enjoyed in common as members of a group of some sort.

This situation reached something of a climax in the twelfth century. It was modified slowly, sporadically and intermittently over a period of about seven centuries, from the thirteenth to the twentieth century. The change began earlier and went more rapidly in some parts of Europe than in others; it penetrated some activities more readily and more profoundly than others; it affected men before it touched women; and during these seven centuries there have been many local climaxes and corresponding recessions. But the enjoyment of the new opportunities of escape from communal ties gradually generated a new idiom of human character.

It emerged first in Italy: Italy was the first home of the modern individual who sprang from the break-up of medieval communal life. 'At the close of the thirteenth century', writes Burckhardt, 'Italy began to swarm with individuality; the ban laid upon human personality was dissolved; a thousand figures meet us, each in his own special shape and dress.' The *uomo singolare*, whose conduct was marked by a high degree of self-determination and a large number of whose activities expressed personal preferences, gradually detached himself from his fellows. And together with him appeared not only the *libertine* and the *dilettante*, but also the *uomo unico*, the man who, in the mastery of his circumstances, stood alone and was a law to himself. Men examined themselves and were not dismayed by their own want of perfection. This was the character which Petrarch dramatized for his generation with unmatched skill and unrivalled energy. A new image of human nature appeared — not Adam, not Prometheus, but Proteus, a character distinguished from all others on account of his multiplicity and of his endless power of self-transformation.

North of the Alps events took a similar course, though they moved more slowly and had to contend with larger hindrances. In England, in France, in the Netherlands, in Spain. In

Switzerland, in Poland, Hungary and Bohemia, and particularly in all centres of municipal life, conditions favourable to individuality, and individuals to exploit them, appeared. There were few fields of activity untouched. By the middle of the sixteenth century they had been so firmly established that they were beyond the range of mere suppression: not all the severity of the Calvinist regime in Geneva was sufficient to quell the impulse to think and behave as an independent individual. The disposition to regard a high degree of individuality in conduct and in belief as the condition proper to mankind, and as the main ingredient of human 'happiness', had become one of the significant dispositions of modern European character. What Petrarch did for one century, Montaigne did for another.

The story of the vicissitudes of this disposition during the last four centuries is exceedingly complex. It is a story, not of steady growth, but of climaxes and anti-climaxes, of diffusion to parts of Europe at first relatively ignorant of it, of extension to activities from which it was at first excluded, of attack and defence, of confidence and of apprehension. But if we cannot pursue it in all its detail we may at least observe how profoundly this disposition imposed itself upon European conduct and belief. In the course of a few hundred years it was magnified into an ethical and even into a metaphysical theory, it gathered to itself an appropriate understanding of the office of government, it modified political manners and institutions, it settled itself upon art, upon religion, upon industry and trade and upon every kind of human relationship.

In the field of intellectual speculation the clearest reflection of this profound experience of individuality is to be seen in ethical theory. Almost all modern writing about moral conduct begins with the hypothesis of an individual human being choosing and pursuing his own directions of activity. What appeared to require explanation was not the existence of such individuals but how they would come to have duties to others of their kind and what was the nature of those duties; just as the existence of other minds became a problem to those who understood knowledge as the residue of sense experience. This is unmistakable in Hobbes, the first moralist of the modern world to take candid account of the current experience of individuality. He understood a man as an organism governed by an impulse to avoid destruction and to maintain itself in its own characteristic and chosen pursuits. Each individual has a natural right to independent existence: the only problem is how he is to pursue his own chosen course with the greatest measure of success, the problem of his relation to 'others' of his kind. And a similar view of things appeared, of course, in the writings of Spinoza. But even where an individualistic conclusion was rejected, this autonomous individual remained as the starting point of ethical reflection. Every moralist in the seventeenth and eighteenth centuries is concerned with the psychological structure of this assumed 'individual': the relation of 'self' and 'others' is the common form of all moral theory of the time. And nowhere is this seen more clearly to be the case than in the writings of Kant. Every human being, in virtue of not being subject to natural necessity, is recognized by Kant to be a person, an end in himself, absolute and autonomous. To seek his own happiness is the natural pursuit of such a person; self-love is the motive of the choices which compose his conduct. But as a rational human being he will recognize in his conduct the universal conditions of autonomous personality; and the chief of these conditions is to use humanity, as well in himself as in others, as an end and never as a means. Morality consists in the recognition of individual personality whenever it appears. Moreover, personality is so far sacrosanct that no man has either a right or a duty to promote the moral perfection of another: we may promote the 'happiness' of others, but we cannot promote their 'good' without destroying their 'freedom' which is the condition of moral goodness.

In short, whatever we may think of the moral theories of modern Europe they provide the clearest evidence of the overwhelming impact of this experience of individuality.

But this pursuit of individuality, and of the conditions most favourable to its enjoyment, was reflected also in an understanding of the proper office of government and in appropriate manners of governing and being governed, both modifications of an inheritance from the Middle Ages. We have time only to notice them in their most unqualified appearance, namely in what we have come to call 'modern representative democracy'. This manner of governing and being governed appeared first in England, in the Netherlands and in Switzerland, and was later (in various idioms) extended to other parts of western Europe and the United States of America. It is not to be understood either as an approximation to some ideal manner of government, or as a modification of a manner of government (with which it has no connection whatever) current for a short while in certain parts of the ancient world. It is simply what emerged in western Europe where the impact of the aspirations of individuality upon medieval institutions of government was greatest.

The first demand of those intent upon exploring the intimations of individuality was for an instrument of government capable of transforming the interests of individuality into rights and duties. To perform this task government required three attributes. First, it must be single and supreme; only by a concentration of all authority at one centre could the emergent individual escape from the communal pressures of family and guild, of church and local community, which hindered his enjoyment of his own character. Secondly, it must be an instrument of government not bound by prescription and therefore with authority to abolish old rights and create new: it must be a 'sovereign' government. And this, according to current ideas, means a government in which all who enjoyed rights were partners, a government in which the 'estates' of the realm were direct or indirect participants. Thirdly, it must be powerful—able to preserve the order without which the aspirations of individuality could not be realized; but not so powerful as itself to constitute a new threat to individuality. In an earlier time, the recognized methods of transforming interests into rights had been judicial; the 'parliaments' and 'councils' of the middle ages had been pre-eminently judicial bodies. But from these 'courts of law' emerged an instrument with more emphatic authority to recognize new interests by converting them into new rights and duties; there emerged legislative bodies. Thus a ruler, and a parliament representative of his subjects, came to share the business of 'making' law. And the law they made was favourable to the interests of individuality: it provided the detail of what became a well-understood condition of human circumstance, commonly denoted by the word 'freedom'. In this condition every subject was secured of the right to pursue his chosen directions of activity as little hindered as might be by his fellows or by the exactions of government itself, and as little distracted by communal pressures. Freedom of movement, of initiative, of speech, of belief and religious observance, of association and disassociation, of bequest and inheritance; security of person and property; the right to choose one's own occupation and dispose of one's labour and goods; and over all the 'rule of law'; the right to be ruled by a known law, applicable to all subjects alike. These rights, appropriate to individuality, were not the privileges of a single class — they were the property of every subject alike. Each signified the abrogation of some feudal privilege.

This manner of governing, which reached its climax in the 'parliamentary' government which emerged in England and elsewhere in the late eighteenth and early nineteenth centuries, was concurrently theorized in an understanding of the proper office of government. What had been a 'community' came to be recognized as an 'association' of individuals: this was the counterpart in political philosophy of the individualism that had established itself in ethical theory. And the office of government was understood to be the maintenance of arrangements favourable to the interests of individuality, arrangements (that is) which emancipated the subject from the 'chains' (as Rousseau put it) of communal allegiancies and constituted a condition of human circumstance in which the intimations of individuality might be explored and the experience of individuality enjoyed.

Briefly, then, my picture is as follows. Human individuality is an historical emergence, as 'artificial' and as 'natural' as the landscape. In modern Europe this emergence was gradual, and the specific character of the individual who emerged was determined by the manner of his generation. He became unmistakable when the habit appeared of engaging in activities identified as 'private'; indeed, the appearance of 'privacy' in human conduct is the obverse of the desuetude of the communal arrangements from which modern individuality sprang. This experience of individuality provoked a disposition to explore its own intimations, to place the highest value upon it, and to seek security in its enjoyment. To enjoy it came to be recognized as the main ingredient of 'happiness'. The experience was magnified into an ethical theory; it was reflected in manners of governing and being governed, in newly acquired rights and duties and in a whole pattern of living. The emergence of this disposition to be an individual is the pre-eminent event in modern European history.

III

There were many modest manners in which this disposition to be an individual might express itself. Every practical enterprise and every intellectual pursuit revealed itself as an assemblage of opportunities for making choices: art, literature, philosophy, commerce, industry and politics each came to partake of this character. Nevertheless, in a world being transformed by the aspirations and activities of those who were excited by these opportunities, there were some people, by circumstance or by temperament, less ready than others to respond to this invitation; and for many the invitation to make choices came before the ability to make them and was consequently recognized as a burden. The old certainties of belief, of occupation and of status were being dissolved, not only for those who had confidence in their own power to make a new place for themselves in an association of individuals, but also for those who had no such confidence. The counterpart of the agricultural and industrial *entrepreneur* of the sixteenth century was the displaced labourer; the counterpart of the *libertine* was the dispossessed believer. The familiar warmth of communal pressures was dissipated for all alike — an emancipation which excited some, depressed others. The familiar anonymity of communal life was replaced by a personal identity which was burdensome to those who could not transform it into an individuality. What some recognized as happiness appeared to others as discomfort. The same condition of human circumstance was identified as progress and as decay. In short, the circumstances of modern Europe, even as early as the sixteenth century, bred, not a single character, but two obliquely opposed characters: not only that of the individual, but also that of the 'individual *manqué*'. And this 'individual *manqué*' was not a relic of a past age, he was a 'modern' character, the product of the same dissolution of communal ties as had generated the modern European individual.

We need not speculate upon what combination of debility, ignorance, timidity, poverty or mischance operated in particular cases to provoke this character; it is enough to observe his appearance and his efforts to accommodate himself to his hostile environment. He sought a protector who would recognize his predicament, and he found what he sought, in some measure, in 'the government'. From as early as the sixteenth century the governments of Europe were being modified not only in response to the demands of individuality, but also in response to the needs of the 'individual *manqué*'. The 'godly prince' of the Reformation and his lineal descendant the 'enlightened despot' of the eighteenth century, were political inventions for making choices for those indisposed to make choices for themselves; the Elizabethan Statute of Labourers was designed to take care of those who were left behind in the race.

The aspirations of individuality had imposed themselves upon conduct and belief and upon the constitutions and activities of governments, in the first place, as demands emanating from a powerful and confident disposition. There was little attempt to moralize these demands, which in the sixteenth century were clearly in conflict with current moral sentiment still fixed in its loyalty to the morality of communal ties. Nevertheless, from the experience of individuality there sprang, in the course of time, a morality appropriate to it – a disposition not only to explore individuality but to approve of the pursuit of individuality. This constituted a considerable moral revolution; but such was its force and vigour that it not only swept aside the relics of the morality appropriate to the defunct communal order, but left little room for any alternative to itself And the weight of this moral victory bore heavily upon the 'individual *manqué*'. Already outmanoeuvred in the field (in conduct), he now suffered a defeat at home, in his own character. What had been no more than a doubt about his ability to hold his own in a struggle for existence, became a radical self-distrust; what had been merely a hostile prospect, disclosed itself as an abyss; what had been the discomfort of ill-success was turned into the misery of guilt.

In some, no doubt, this situation provoked resignation; but in others it bred envy, jealousy and resentment. And in these emotions a new disposition was generated: the impulse to escape from the predicament by imposing it upon all mankind. From the frustrated 'individual *manqué*' there sprang the militant 'anti-individual', disposed to assimilate the world to his own character by deposing the individual and destroying his moral prestige. No promise, or even offer, of self-advancement could tempt this 'anti-individual'; he knew his individuality was too poorly furnished to be explored or exploited with any satisfaction whatever. He was moved solely by the opportunity of complete escape from the anxiety of not being an individual, the opportunity of removing from the world all that convicted him of his own inadequacy. His situation provoked him to seek release in separatist communities, insulated from the moral pressure of individuality. But the opportunity he sought appeared fully when he recognized that, so far from being alone, he belonged to the most numerous class in modern European society, the class of those who had no choices of their own to make. Thus, in the recognition of his numerical superiority the 'anti-individual' at once recognized himself as the 'mass man' and discovered the way of escape from his predicament. For although the 'mass man' is specified by his disposition—a disposition to allow in others only a replica of himself, to impose upon all a uniformity of belief and conduct that leaves no room for either the pains or the pleasures of choice—and not by his numbers, he is confirmed in this disposition by the support of others of his kind. He can have no friends (because friendship is a relation between individuals), but he has comrades. The 'masses' as they appear in modern European history are not composed of individuals, they are composed of 'anti-individuals' united in a revulsion from individuality. Consequently, although the remarkable growth of population in western Europe during the last four-hundred years is a condition of the success with which this character has imposed itself, it is not a condition of the character itself.

Nevertheless, the 'anti-individual' had feelings rather than thoughts, impulses rather than opinions, inabilities rather than passions, and was only dimly aware of his power. Consequently he required 'leaders': indeed, the modern concept of 'leadership' is a concomitant of the 'anti-individual' and without him it would be unintelligible. An association of individuals requires a ruler but it has no place for a 'leader'. The 'anti-individual' needed to be told what to think; his impulses had to be transformed into desires, and these desires into projects; he had to be made aware of his power; and these were the tasks of his leaders. Indeed, from one point of view, 'the masses' must be regarded as the invention of their leaders.

The natural submissiveness of the 'mass man' may itself be supposed to have been capable of prompting the appearance of appropriate leaders. He was unmistakably an instrument to be played upon, and no doubt the instrument provoked the *virtuoso*. But there was, in fact, a character ready to occupy this office. What was required was a man who could at once appear as the image and the master of his followers; a man who could more easily make choices for others than for himself; a man disposed to mind other people's business because he lacked the skill to find satisfaction in minding his own. And these', precisely, were the attributes of the 'individual *manqué*', whose achievements and whose failures in respect of individuality exactly fitted him for this task of leadership. He was enough of an individual to seek a personal satisfaction in the exercise of individuality, but too little to seek it anywhere but in commanding others. He loved himself too little to be anything but an egoist; and what his followers took to be a genuine concern for their salvation was in fact nothing more than the vanity of the almost selfless. No doubt the 'masses' in modern Europe have had other leaders than this cunning frustrate who has led always by flattery and whose only concern is the exercise of power; but they have had none more appropriate — for he only had never prompted them to be critical of their impulses. Indeed, the 'anti-individual' and his leader were the counterparts of a single moral situation; they relieved one another's frustrations and supplied one another's wants. Nevertheless it was an uneasy partnership: moved by impulses rather than by desires the 'mass man' has been submissive but not loyal to his leaders: even the exiguous individuality of the leader has easily aroused his suspicion. And the leader's greed for power has disposed him to raise hopes in his followers which he has never been able to satisfy.

Of all the manners in which the 'anti-individual' has imposed himself upon Western Europe two have been pre-eminent. He has generated a morality designed to displace the current morality of individuality; and he has evoked an understanding of the proper office of government and manners of governing appropriate to his character.

The emergence of the morality of the 'anti-individual', a morality, namely, not of 'liberty' and 'self-determination' but of 'equality and 'solidarity' is, of course, difficult to discern; but it is already clearly visible in the seventeenth century. The obscurity of its beginnings is due in part to the fact that its vocabulary was at first that of the morality of the defunct communal order; and there can be little doubt that it derived strength and plausibility from its deceptive affinity to that morality. But it was, in fact, a new morality, generated in opposition to the hegemony of individuality and calling for the establishment of a new condition of human circumstance reflecting the aspirations of the 'anti-individual'.

The nucleus of this morality was the concept of a substantive condition of human circumstance represented as the 'common' or 'public' good, which was understood, not to be composed of the various goods that might be sought by individuals on their own account but to be an independent entity. 'Self-love', which was recognized in the morality of individuality as a legitimate spring of human activity, the morality of the 'anti-individual' pronounced to be evil. But it was to be replaced not by the love of 'others', or by 'charity' or by 'benevolence' (which would have entailed a relapse into the vocabulary of individuality), but by the love of 'the community'.

Round this nucleus revolved a constellation of appropriate subordinate beliefs. From the beginning the designers of this morality identified private property with individuality, and consequently connected its abolition with the condition of human circumstances appropriate to the 'mass man'. And further, it was appropriate that the morality of the 'anti-individual' should be radically equalitarian: how should the 'mass man', whose sole distinction was his resemblance to his fellows and whose salvation lay in the recognition of others as merely replicas of himself, approve of any divergence from an exact uniformity? All must be equal and anonymous units in a 'community'. And, in the generation of this morality, the character of this 'unit' was tirelessly explored. He was understood as a 'man' *per se*, as a 'comrade', as a 'citizen'. But the most acute diagnosis, that of Proudhon, recognized him as a 'debtor'; for in this notion what was asserted was not only the absence of distinction between the units who composed the 'community' (all are alike 'debtors'), but also a debt owed, not to 'others' to but to the 'community' itself: at birth he enters into an inheritance which he had played no part in accumulating, and whatever the magnitude of his subsequent contribution it never equals what he has enjoyed: he dies necessarily insolvent.

This morality of the 'anti-individual', the morality of a *solidarité commune,* began to be constructed in the sixteenth century. Its designers were mostly visionaries, dimly aware of their purposes and lacking a large audience. But a momentous change occurred when the 'anti-individual' recognized himself as the 'mass man' and perceived the power that his numerical superiority gave him. The recognition that the morality of the 'anti-individual' was, in the first place, the morality not of a sect of aspirants but of a large ready-made class in society (the class not of the 'poor' but of those who by circumstance or by occupation had been denied the experience of individuality), and that in the interests of this class it must be imposed upon all mankind, appears unmistakably first in the writings of Marx and Engels.

Before the end of the nineteenth century, then, a morality of 'anti-individualism' had been generated in response to the aspirations of the 'mass man'. It was in many respects a rickety construction: it never achieved a design comparable to that which Hobbes or Kant or Hegel gave the morality of individuality, and it has never been able to resist relapse into the inappropriate concepts of individuality. Nevertheless it throws back a tolerably clear reflection of the 'mass man', who by this means became more thoroughly acquainted with himself. But we are not concerned with its merits or defects, we are concerned only to notice it as evidence of the power with which the 'mass man' has imposed himself on modem Europe over a period of about four centuries. 'Anti-individuality', long before the nineteenth century, had established itself as one of the major dispositions of the modern European moral character. And this disposition was evident enough for it to be recognized unequivocally by Sorel and to be identified by writers such as Nietzsche, Kierkegaard and Burckhardt as the image of a new barbarism.

From the beginning (in the sixteenth century) those who exerted themselves on behalf of the 'anti-individual' perceived that his counterpart, a 'community' reflecting his aspirations, entailed a 'government' active in a certain manner. To govern was understood to be the exercise of power in order to impose and maintain the substantive condition of human circumstance identified as 'the public good'; to be governed was, for the 'anti-individual', to have made for him the choices he was unable to make for himself. Thus 'government' was cast for the role of architect and custodian, not of 'public order' in an 'association' of individuals pursuing their own activities but of 'the public good' of a 'community'. The ruler was recognized to be not the referee of the collisions of individuals but the moral leader and managing director of 'the community'. And this understanding of government has been tirelessly explored over a period of four and a half centuries, from Thomas More's *Utopia* to the Fabian Society, from Campanella to Lenin. But the leaders who served the 'mass man' were not merely theorists concerned to make his character intelligible in a moral doctrine and in an understanding of the office of government; they were also practical men who revealed to him his power and the manner in which the institutions of modern democratic government might be appropriated to his aspirations. And if we call the manner of government that had been generated by the aspirations of individuality 'parliamentary government', we may call the modification of it under the impact of the 'mass man' 'popular government'. But it is important to understand that these are two wholly different manners of government.

The emergent individual in the sixteenth century had sought new rights and by the beginning of the nineteenth century the rights appropriate to his character had, in England and elsewhere, been largely established. The 'anti-individual' observed these rights, and he was persuaded that his circumstances (chiefly his poverty) had hitherto prevented him from sharing them. Hence the new rights called for on his behalf were, in the first place, understood as the means by which he might come to participate in the rights won and enjoyed by those he thought of as his better-placed fellows. But this was a great illusion; first, because in fact he had these rights, and secondly because he had no use for them. For the disposition of the 'mass man' was not to become an individual and the enterprise of his leaders was not to urge him in this direction. And what, in fact, prevented him enjoying the rights of individuality (which were as available to him as to anyone else) was not his 'circumstances' but his character — his 'anti-individuality'. The rights of individuality were necessarily such that the 'mass man' could have no use for them. And so, in the end, it turned out: what he came to demand were rights of an entirely different kind, and of a kind which entailed the abolition of the rights appropriate to individuality. He required the right to enjoy a substantive condition of human circumstance in which he would not be asked to make choices for himself. He had no use for the right to 'pursue happiness' — that could only be a burden to him: he needed the right to 'enjoy happiness'. And looking into his own character he identified this with Security — but again, not security against arbitrary interference in the exercise of his preferences, but Security against having to make choices for himself and against having to meet the vicissitudes of life from his own resources. In short, the right he claimed, the right appropriate to his character, was the right to live in a social protectorate which relieved him from the burden of 'self-determination'.

But this condition of human circumstances was seen to be impossible unless it were imposed upon all alike. So long as others were permitted to make choices for themselves, not only would his anxiety at not being able to do so himself remain to convict him of his inadequacy and threaten his emotional security, but also the social protectorate which he recognized as his counterpart would itself be disrupted. The Security he needed entailed a genuine equality if circumstances imposed upon all. The condition he sought was one in which he would meet in others only a replica of himself: what he was everybody must become.

He claimed this condition as a 'right', and consequently he sought a government disposed to give it to him and one endowed with the power necessary to impose upon all activities the substantive pattern of activity called 'the public good'. 'Popular government' is, precisely, a modification of 'parliamentary government' designed to accomplish this purpose. And if this reading is correct, 'popular government' is no more intimated in 'parliamentary government' than the rights appropriate to the 'anti-individual' are intimated in the rights appropriate to individuality: they are not complementary but directly opposed to one another. Nevertheless, what I have called 'popular government' is not a concrete manner of government established and practised; it is a disposition to impose certain modifications upon 'parliamentary government' in order to convert it into a manner of government appropriate to the aspirations of the 'mass man'.

This disposition has displayed itself in specific enterprises, and in less specific habits and manners in respect of government. The first great enterprise was the establishment of universal adult suffrage. The power of the 'mass man' lay in his numbers, and this power could be brought to bear upon government by means of 'the vote'. Secondly, a change in the character of the parliamentary representative was called for: he must be not an individual but a *mandataire* charged with the task of imposing the substantive condition of human circumstances required by the 'mass man'. 'Parliament' must become a 'work-shop', not a debating assembly. Neither of these changes was intimated in 'parliamentary government'; both, insofar as they have been achieved, have entailed an assembly of a new character. Their immediate effect has been twofold: first, to confirm the authority of mere numbers (an authority alien to the practice of 'parliamentary government'); and secondly, to give governments immensely increased power.

But the institutions of 'parliamentary government' proved to have only a limited eligibility for conversion into institutions appropriate to serve the aspirations of the 'mass man'. And an assembly of instructed delegates was seen to be vulnerable to a much more appropriate contrivance – the *plébiscite*. Just as it lay in the character of the 'mass man' to see everyman as a 'public official', an agent of 'the public good', and to see his representatives not as individuals but instructed delegates, so he saw every voter as the direct participant in the activity of governing: and the means of this was the *plébiscite*. An assembly elected on a universal adult suffrage, composed of instructed delegates and flanked by the device of the *plébiscite* was, then, the counterpart of the 'mass man'. They gave him exactly what he wanted: the illusion without the reality of choice; choice without the burden of having to choose. For with universal suffrage have appeared the massive political parties of the modern world, composed not of individuals but of 'anti-individuals'. And both the instructed delegate and the *plébiscite* are devices for avoiding the necessity for making choices. The 'mandate' from the beginning was an illusion. The 'mass man', as we have seen, is a creature of impulses not desires; he is utterly unable to draw up instructions for his representative to follow. What in fact has happened, whenever the disposition of 'popular government' has imposed itself, is that the prospective representative has drawn up his own mandate and then, by a familiar trick of ventriloquism, has put it into the mouth of his electors. As an instructed delegate he is not an individual, and as a 'leader' he relieves his followers of the need to make choices for themselves. And similarly, the *plébiscite* is not a method by which the 'mass man' imposes his choices upon his rulers; it is a method of generating a government with unlimited authority to make choices on his behalf. In the *plébiscite* the 'mass man' achieved final release from the burden of individuality: he was told emphatically what to choose.

Thus in these and other constitutional devices and in less formal habits of political conduct was generated a new art of politics: the art,not of 'ruling' (that is, of seeking the most practicable adjustments for the collisions of 'individuals'), nor even of maintaining the support of a majority of individuals in a 'parliamentary' assembly, but of knowing what offer will collect most votes and making it in such a manner that it appears to come from 'the people'; the art, in short, of 'leading' in the modern idiom. Moreover, it is known in advance what offer will collect the most votes: the character of the 'mass man' is such that he will be moved only by the offer of release from the burden of making choices for himself, the offer of 'salvation'. And anyone who makes this offer may confidently demand unlimited power; it will be given him.

The 'mass man', as I understand him, then, is specified by his character, not by his numbers. He is distinguished by so exiguous an individuality that when it meets a powerful experience of individuality it revolts into 'anti-individuality'. He has generated for himself an appropriate morality, an appropriate understanding of the office of government and appropriate modifications of 'parliamentary government'. He is not necessarily 'poor', nor is he envious only of 'riches'; he is not necessarily 'ignorant', often he is a member of the so-called *intelligentsia*; he belongs to a class which corresponds exactly

with no other class. He is specified primarily by a moral, not
an intellectual, inadequacy. He wants 'salvation' and in the
end will be satisfied only with release from the burden of having to make choices for himself. He is dangerous, not on
account of his opinions or desires, for he has none, but on
account of his submissiveness. His disposition is to endow
government with power and authority such as it has never
before enjoyed. He is utterly unable to distinguish a 'ruler'
from a 'leader'. In short, the disposition to be an anti-
individual' is one to which every European man has a propensity; the 'mass man' is merely one in whom this propensity is
dominant.

IV

Of the many conclusions which follow from this reading of the
situation the most important is to dispose of the most insidi-
ous of our current political delusions. It has been said, and it is
commonly believed, that the event of supreme importance in
modern European history is 'the accession of the masses to
complete social power'. But that no such event has taken place
is evident when we consider what it would entail. If it is true
(as I have contended) that modern Europe enjoys two
opposed moralities (that of individuality and that of the 'anti-
individual'), that it enjoys two opposed understandings of the
office of government and two corresponding interpretations
of the current institutions of government, then for the 'mass
man' to have won for himself a position of undisputed sovereignty would entail the complete suppression of what, in any
reading, must be considered the strongest of our moral and
political dispositions and the survival of the weakest. A world
in which the 'mass man' exercised 'complete social power'
would be a world in which the activity of governing was
understood *solely* as the imposition of a single substantive
condition of human circumstance, a world in which 'popular
government' had altogether displaced 'parliamentary government', a world in which the 'civil' rights of individuality
had been abrogated by the 'social' rights of anti-individuality
—and there is no evidence that we live in such a world. Certainly the 'mass man' has emerged and has signified his emergence in an appropriate morality and an appropriate

understanding of the office of government. He has sought to transform the world into a replica of himself, and he has not been entirely unsuccessful. He has sought to enjoy what he could not create for himself, and nothing he has appropriated remains unchanged. Nevertheless, he remains an unmistakably derivative character, an emanation of the pursuit of individuality; helpless, parasitic and able to survive only in opposition to individuality. Only in the most favourable circumstances, and then only by segregating him from all alien influences, have his leaders been able to suppress in him an unquenched propensity to desert at the call of individuality. He has imposed himself emphatically only where the relics of a morality of communal ties survived to make plausible his moral and political impulses. Elsewhere the modifications he has provoked in political manners and moral beliefs have been extensive, but the notion that they have effaced the morality of individuality and 'parliamentary government' is without foundation. He loves himself too little to be able to dispose effectively of the only power he has, namely his numerical superiority. He lacks passion rather than reason. He has had a past in which he was taught to admire himself and his antipathies; he has a present in which he is often the object of the ill-concealed contempt of his 'leaders'; but the heroic future forecast him is discrepant with his own character. He is no hero.

On the other hand, if we judge the world as we find it (which includes, of course, the emergence of the 'mass man') the event of supreme and seminal importance in modern European history remains the emergence of the human individual in his modern idiom. The pursuit of individuality has evoked a moral disposition, an understanding of the office of government and manners of governing, a multiplicity of activity and opinion and a notion of 'happiness' which have impressed themselves indelibly upon European civilization. The onslaught of the 'mass man' has shaken but not destroyed the moral prestige of individuality; even the 'anti-individual', whose salvation lies in escape, has not been able to escape it. The desire of 'the masses' to enjoy the products of individuality has modified their destructive urge. And the antipathy of the 'mass man' to the 'happiness' of 'self-determination' easily dissolves into self-pity. At all important points the individual still appears as the substance and the 'anti-individual' only as the shadow.

Acknowledgements

Reprinted by permission from *Freedom and Serfdom: An Anthology of Western Thought*, ed. Albert Hunold. © 1961, D. Reidel Publishing Co., Dordrecht, Holland.

Redmond Mullin

States, Dissent and Constructive Disorder

A just and healthy society must include forces within it which provide alternatives to the state's provisions and which may contradict its policies. This is my argument here. It assumes, with John Locke and Tom Paine, that 'society' is larger than and antecedent to the state. It may be an Anglo-Saxon attitude. It is precious.

The other part of my argument is that if the real will and intelligence of a people are to be expressed, they must be able to speak and act outside the scope of government. This is a role for non-statutory agencies. Why? Because, expecting them to believe their claims, statistics and promises, meretriciously argued, governments increasingly treat their electorates as fools. Atop the pyramid of fools, its questions unanswered and its views ignored, is Parliament. There is no true democratic discourse. Politicians are motivated to serve their parties, for office and electoral success, not the common good. There is a pretence of listening to the public; but this 'listening' is the opportunism of politicians seeking favour. For our governments today, all of us are dumb. People have no voice, except as occasional, structurally manipulated voters (just think of Wales and the gerrymandering over the selection of London mayoral candidates). Critics of today's government, from left, right or centre, are ridiculed or vilified as the 'dark forces of conservatism', when they only wish to protest at a culture of change for change's sake—on basic issues, such as the health, education or judicial systems or on frivolities such as the Dome's vacuous tackiness. It is outside the governmental and political spheres that people can declare, argue and act on their ideals effectively. Was it always so?

'Society'; 'Nation'; 'State'

It here seems more useful to sketch a description of what may be meant by 'Society' or 'society' than to attempt a definition. We all have a sense of the meanings: people and peoples living and interacting together; with some main common interests; sharing physical and economic environments; with common internal and external threats; with some shared and many diverse cultures. A society has needs and expectations. These may differ within and between societies. In the primary way I am using it, 'society' has a regional, even local, aspect and may well include racial and multi-racial elements. 'Society' may be used of small units of population or of all the units which make up a 'nation'. 'Nation' and 'society' can be co-terminous but this is not necessarily so. There may be clashes between different parts of a 'nation' or of 'society'. There are special applications of words: 'nation' may be supra-national, as in the 'Nation of Islam'; and 'society' may reach across nations and societies, as in 'The Society of Friends'.

'The State' we know has assumed a number of roles: to legislate, to protect and to provide for those unable to provide for themselves. The state (after classical times) has evolved from the great Italian and Protestant cities and the period of mercantile growth from the sixteenth century onwards (when national banks, stock markets and armies emerged), through the Industrial Revolution and the period of revolution and Bismarckian reform in Europe when huge centralized states, some controlling large empires, became normal; with, in the background, the American United States emerging as a great, diverse, 'enlightened' world power. We now live during a period in which, deviously or directly, many states have tried to be all-powerful — a trend latterly continued by other means through the undemocratic institutions of the European Union. I concentrate in this chapter on two aspects of society: provision for the needy, and dissent (which is usually needed if state provision is to be reformed or replaced).

In the origins of what we call Western society there emerges confusion between what we designate as 'statutory' and 'non-statutory'. This confusion continues up to and beyond the Reformation and Enlightenment, the period during which our concepts of state and society congeal. It continues today.

Provision for the Needy

States and economies were relatively less developed during the Middle Ages than they are now; but some aspects of welfare provision were well advanced and their traces, for example at Holy Cross in Winchester, St Bartholomew's Hospital in London, Oxford and Cambridge Universities, survive today. Taxes, in England for funding French Wars and everywhere for the Pope's Peter's Pence, were usually resentfully paid. But a great engine for non-state fundraising, more effective even than our Lottery, was the market in salvation. Indulgences, which for a price reduced sinners' periods of torment in Purgatory before they qualified for Heaven, were used for a range of purposes: Masses for rich people's souls, sacred buildings, pilgrimages to profitable sites, paying off the Pope's debts to the Fuggers and other bankers or moneylenders (usury was banned by Canon Law). More significantly for my argument, indulgences attached also to welfare provision: housing the homeless; feeding the hungry; healing the sick; caring for the elderly; paying dowries for poor marriageable women; dealing with international crises, such as the ransom money for hostages and prisoners—particularly those captured by the Muslims during the Crusades; and also for infrastructure—roads, bridges and causeways.

This mixture of causes and beneficiaries was adequate in some places and at the same time partly chaotic. It reflected society's response to some needful priorities of those times, which had to be met by society complementing the emergent states. Then as now, it was necessary to limit and control the liability of society and state to fluctuating numbers of the needy.

In late antiquity there had also been an attempt to bring random poor relief under control. The early Christian churches had produced lists (*matriculae*) of the deserving poor, who were the only ones who should benefit. (The church's control of urban mobs in the fourth century helped them to power in the Empire.) In the period before and after Europe's Reformation, the same issues were critical and similar methods were used. One cause of crisis was common to both periods: the movement of huge numbers of the rural poor into towns, as wealth based on trade and commerce grew, demanding a waged, skilled and unskilled labour force. This situation had to be controlled. The towns in late Medieval Europe were centres for new ideas and therefore for Reformation and Counter Reformation, which leapfrogged each other in their religious doctrines and activities as well as in their welfare measures. This was also the period during which the Italian cities and the European nations were forming themselves into States as we understand them.

Social pressures forced Henry VIII in England, Calvin in Geneva and Zwingli in Zurich to control welfare provision. There were existing Guild or Common Chest organizations, many too pious for the Reformers, in most cities, usually providing for their members first and then for the needy generally. There was much mendicancy, involving the worthy poor as well as the Sturdy Beggars, who were deemed able to provide for themselves. Such random begging and activity (sometimes radical) threatened civil order. There were violent religious groups who ransacked the rich on the grounds: 'You are rich because we are poor' (a fourth-century British Pelagian). So the nascent states wanted to regulate what was happening. Henry VIII's Beggar's Act (1536) banned begging, penalized random philanthropy and tried to regulate provision: on specific Sundays, sermons were to be preached in every church demanding funds, to be followed up household by household by Elders who were to collect an appropriate sum from each. Similar measures were introduced by Zwingli and Calvin in Protestant Europe. There could be no offer of indulgences. The *Aumone General* in Roman Catholic France was similarly organized and even stipulated the weight of bread needed by each poor person. Only approved candidates would be eligible for aid. Statutory and non-statutory provisions were superimposed.

Jewish provision for its own societies, particularly in parts of Eastern Europe with large populations of Jews, operated for its own people and the *goyim*. For example, during the late seventeenth century in Poland there were meal tickets for the resident poor and for visitors and more fundamental provision of work and tools funded by levies proportionate to a community member's means.

There was a mixture of statutory, quasi-statutory, quasi-voluntary and voluntary provisions. They were aimed selectively at individuals and groups who were deemed at whatever time socially and economically needy. They were also aimed at actual or perceived threats, to particular societies or to emergent states. In England they have left an inheritance which, because of legal and social continuities here, includes some charities, hospitals, universities; the origins of our Trust (or Charities) Law; and prejudices about the deserving and undeserving in society and the limits to our liabilities towards them which still vex New Labour today.

Dissent

My other topic is dissent. There were dissenters throughout the Middle Ages. The Pelagians, Lollards, Albigenses, Hussites, Beghards were all social as well as ecclesiastical radicals, basing themselves on a 'pure' and 'primitive' interpretation of the Gospels. They were therefore deemed heretics, of interest to the Inquisitors and quite likely to be burned at the stake. They included some impassioned voices for the poor. Lollard and Hussite doctrines fuelled and survived the Reformation. The religious orders generally represented an approved protest against worldly values; but there were limits to their dissent. When the 'Spiritual' faction within the Franciscan order argued that Jesus had taught and practised absolute poverty they were investigated and condemned through their fellow friars, the Dominicans (a story finely illustrated in Umberto Eco's *Name of the Rose*). Nor was there freedom in the universities, where we would expect to find it. Unorthodox teachers and teachings were excluded and condemned. The thuggish, manipulative Bernard had Abelard excommunicated and exiled (1140). Highly relevantly to my theme, when in 1324 Marsilius of Padua argued in his *Defensor Pacis* that the state, based on the will and consent of the people, had primacy over papacy and church, he was promptly condemned and fled into exile. There needs to be a balanced judgment here. There were factions and supporters for dissenters. Marsilius had to flee but was protected by Ludwig of Bavaria. Abelard had to flee but was protected and defended by the powerful Abbot of Cluny, Peter the Venerable. In the epitaph he wrote, Peter described Abelard as a prince of learning, a uniquely special man: *Abelardus erat*; he was Abelard. Writing to the abbess Heloise, after Abelard's death, Peter said that, in heaven, she would be reunited with her lover; and he contrived their burial in the same grave.

Even after the Treaty of Augsburg (1555) settled the religious wars in Europe, there was no freedom in observance. Subjects adhered to their monarchs' faiths (*cuius regio eius religio*) and the charitable institutions tended to offer care selectively according to religious affiliation, Protestant or Roman Catholic. During the nineteenth century there were voluntary movements for reforms, many in England featuring the great Earl of Shaftesbury. From the late eighteenth century, there had been societies for major reforms, including the abolition of slavery. (Not until the late 1950s did non- proselytizing, charitable movements for developing countries become established in the West.) Yet still, during the nineteenth century, the Irish prostitutes and unmarried mothers of York would be cared for only if they assented to Protestant indoctrination and observance; while the phoney Doctor Barnardo and Cardinal Wiseman competed through litigation by creed as well as by kindness for their orphan or abandoned children. Perhaps only the Jews disregarded religion and proselytizing in the care they offered.

Modern States; Modern Voluntary Actions

With the Enlightenment (an imprecise term) other parts of our inheritance were introduced, as concepts of society and the state again became more potent, as they had been in Greece and Rome. There were, up to and after the Reformation, rich networks of non-state agencies providing for infrastructure as well as welfare needs. Their coverage was admirable but incomplete. Protestant organizations stripped these agencies of their most profitable income source, indulgences. Therefore more formal systems had to be introduced. Anyway the needs of states had become greater and more complex. With the introduction of printing, people and the societies they lived in became more self-aware.

Enlightenment introduced more radical concepts of society and the state, which had to reject or accommodate the roles of voluntary agencies. Anglo-Saxon values, reflected by de Tocqueville, and French Revolutionary ideals, embodied in French legislation, led to very different concepts and consequences.

One thing de Tocqueville admired in the United States, something inherited and re-nurtured out of England, was the burgeoning, thriving system of 'associations' which defined communities and societies, independently of the state or states. They were perceived by him as essential features of American democracy. In parallel, following Rousseau's doctrine, the French Constitution of 1792 had outlawed such initiatives: there should be no organizations independent of the state or refusing its policies.

Here are basic divergences of doctrines and practice crucial for the period ahead:

- May there be groups independent of the state, offering alternative views and provisions to its views and provisions?

- Should a state exclude, tolerate or encourage them? Within what degrees of tolerance?

Surely there is an impulse in healthy societies for people to contradict what is wrong, to challenge it, to provide alternatives? Surely states that deny this will not survive (although the Chinese regime does)? Descriptions and definitions here are fogged, confusing. It will be helpful to get back to descriptions.

No democracy has ever been perfectly tolerant and democratic. But absolute states do not permit, and even outlaw, the kinds of organizations and initiatives promoted here: those that offer alternatives, challenge policies, work for different futures. Those kinds of activities are uncomfortable for any state. Where the state is totalitarian — its provisions and policies ultimately definitive — there is no place for them. The non-governmental agencies may be:

- So weak, as in Russia, which never had a functioning civil society, they will not be allowed to emerge or will struggle to exist.

- So nationalistic, as in Hitler's Reich, they may be subverted by the state and subordinated to its policies and programmes (as with the Scouts and most charities there).

- Sufficiently independent (as in Poland, where independent organizations were fostered by the Roman church, with other negative consequences) that they can survive the totalitarian regime.

- In a temporary regime, as in Franco's Spain, or one sufficiently chaotic, as in Italy, that the independence of associations cannot quite be subverted.

I return to two themes here: religion and the academic institutions. It is now assumed in the West that there will be freedoms for both; and they interact at many points with the non-statutory interests. Of course, there has never been complete freedom for religions. Sects have persecuted each other, formally and informally, to this day. As in Northern Ireland, housing and job allocations as well as physical violence, even murder, have been used to exclude one sect, to promote another. In Ulster, excepting the Alliance Party, politics has been defined by sect. The 'Yes' Campaign, to win assent for a pan-sectarian Assembly, had to be voluntarily funded. 'No' had been organized and financed well in advance of the vote. Yet 'Yes' succeeded, backed by enlightened Irish, English and international supporters.

Before the Enlightenment, European universities taught the orthodoxies of the Roman Church. As a ghostly super-state, the Vatican still persecutes the great Latin American thinkers and activists for the poor and dispossessed: liberation theologians such as Boff and Sobrino. Did the Vatican tacitly collude with the CIA in the murder of Archbishop Romero, whose advisor was Sobrino, or in the assassination by government troops of Sobrino's university colleagues in Salvador? Where there is such persecution, informal society must intervene to provide what formal society has banned. (When an eminent Jesuit in Salvador was, on the Pope's command, excommunicated and expelled from the order, fellow Jesuits gave him the house they shared and asked his permission to remain there.) Very recently Lavinia Byrne, a devoted Roman Catholic, has left the religious order in which she had for years been a nun, because her book on a woman priesthood had been banned by the Vatican and she had endured virtual persecution by the Holy Office (a relic of the Inquisition).

This is not an irrelevant *excursus*. In our own, presumed liberal, society the state has reacted against what it has regarded as more awkward non-statutory initiatives. Margaret Thatcher wanted the Charity Commission to remove at least some of Shelter's charitable privileges, on the grounds that its attacks on housing provision and on their causes in statutory policies and instruments were 'political'. She also instigated an academic appraisal of Bradford's Department of Peace Studies, because they were critical of the government's defence and armaments policies. (This was then, I think, a unique state intervention in a UK university's affairs.) Both Shelter and the Department of Peace Studies were vindicated, the latter emerging with academic accolades, based on peer review. New Labour is no less dangerous. The European Commission is poised to enforce the view that all agencies should be subservient to the state. This may become a condition of EU membership, in or out of EMU. (On the latter, watch for the Government's contempt of the public in their arguments: will the focus be only on possible economic benefits; or on certain reductions in our autonomy and liberties, as more power shifts to the essentially undemocratic Council of Ministers, Commission and Central Bank?)

Voluntary Agencies and Funding are Necessary

According to my argument here the diverse roles of voluntary, non-statutory agencies within the state are essential. They are not luxuries. Without them, injustices in policies and provision will be unchecked. Society will stagnate. The stronger the state, the stronger the need for the voluntary agencies of civil society. They provide alternative realms for discourse and action — on the environment, civil liberties, forms of health-care and education, armaments and war. It is therefore essential that these agencies should function and be funded independently of the state. Their voluntary funding and the fundraising that supports them are necessary. It is in and around voluntary agencies, not political parties, that most people actively participate in and influence the societies in which they live.

State funding entails subservience, even in apparently objective fields such as research and education. The propaganda on genetically modified crops and foods has illustrated this. Dependence on non-statutory funding leaves the non-governmental agencies vulnerable. At least in principle, this too may be valuable, because it means that, year by year, they must prove their arguments for support and demonstrate their efficacy to the public. Active participation in their work — such as petitioning through Amnesty — is one way to affirm assent in their work. A gift is another form of affirmation, a vote for their survival.

That situation has generally been sound; but it raises new issues. Most developed countries allow tax relief on some gifts to non-governmental causes. These have been quite narrow in some countries, such as Sweden, where a few years ago the main charities argued that more generous concessions would encourage unworthy motivations for philanthropy. They have been generous in the USA, where there have been positive incentives for giving through the tax deduction; and very positive in the UK, which now has a mixed system, with minor concessions to donors who are higher-rate taxpayers and large concessions to the recipient agencies.[1] Tax concessions in the UK are not permitted for activities deemed 'political'; hence threats to Shelter and Oxfam and Amnesty's largely non-tax-benefited activity. My preference is for Lord Goodman's view that a definition of what is 'political' in this context should be confined to the pursuit of office or of party advantage.

It seems wonderfully, oddly enlightened that governments should, through the tax system, encourage organizations and activities, outside the formal systems, which may challenge, contradict, offer alternatives to their policies and provision. There are some in the USA who have argued that tax conces-

---

[1] New Labour has typically started to describe long-established tax rebates as 'donations' by the government. I fear that Gordon Brown's new encouragement of the voluntary sector and accompanying fiscal concessions may tend to enforce increased conformity and subservience. As this book goes to print, new concessions for donors and beneficiaries are being offered by the Chancellor. Beware of governments bearing gifts.

sions relating to charitable donations are a matter of rights. I cannot see that there is anything intrinsic to the charitable transaction which entails a tax concession. Nor is there anything intrinsic to a mortgage transaction which entails tax reliefs. What governments do depends on the kinds of behaviour they want to encourage — home purchase or philanthropy in these instances — and on what they deem morally right — which is more restrictive outside Anglo-Saxon cultures. Encouragement of philanthropy is a precious idiosyncrasy. It is part of an ancient tradition.

That does not mean that all is right with voluntary agencies funded through philanthropy. Private, corporate and state patrons can be equivalently compromising. There are honours in private patronage. There may be narrow personal or corporate purposes. These need not be harmful. The purchase of glory, honours or salvation can generate public benefits. They may also compromise a voluntary agency's integrity and distort its aims. There are perils here.

Other perils were identified by Marx and Foucault, amongst others: that strong and persuasive, non-statutory agencies may impose the views and interests of powerful minorities on communities and on society generally, by-passing and even subverting the policies of elected governments. Agencies such as Friends of the Earth and Greenpeace, because so popular and effective in promoting themselves, could be seen in this way. Even when they have, arguably, been fundamentally wrong — as with Brent Spar — their views have prevailed. They are assumed right on GM issues by *Today* programme interviewers. Greenpeace even claimed to have a mandate for its invasion and destruction of private property. There are perils here? Are there also perils that voluntary and statutory agencies both suffer from institutional entropy, which blurs their founding idealism, confusing their actions and aims?

Yes, but they are benevolent perils. States and societies are flawed, imperfect things. Utopia means — and is — No Place. Voluntary, non-statutory bodies and the regimes that contain them will be imperfect, flawed. But surely this is desirable? Perfect systems and regimes are tyrannical, absolute, inhuman, dumb. The non-statutory universe is in parts ossified, misguided and in many of its parts challenging and creative. It should be constructive, dangerous, skilled. It is the way in which societies organize and reorganize and change themselves. Its financial vulnerability has its response in the public's affirmation, through their gifts. This provides for an essential independence from governments. The voluntary agencies force democratic governments to reappraise policies, to adjust or introduce provisions and to enter into genuine discourse. Within voluntary bodies, minority cultures are enabled to survive. Factional interests are given scope. They are essential to the chaos of any healthy society.

Michael Johnson

'Dumbing Up': The Consequences of Permanent Revolution in the Civil Service

This article appears when civil service reform is once again high on the public agenda, in the wake of a report to Prime Minister Tony Blair by the assembled heads of UK civil service departments.[1] Has there been a time since the end of the Second World War, a cynic might ask, when the UK civil service was *not* being reformed and restructured? This article tries to disentangle the main strands in that continuous process of modernization and reform. It will reach uncomfortable conclusions about the impact of accelerating change on the service's performance of what is still — nominally, at least — its core function of analysing and formulating policy, and of providing independent-minded advice to ministers.

First, what do we mean when we talk about the British 'civil service'? This article uses the most commonly accepted definition, meaning the officials who are employed to carry out the central functions of government in the United Kingdom, including its executive functions. The civil service does not extend to the public sector as a whole, that is it does not cover the armed services, police, local government workers, health service or teachers.

During the last three decades this service has undergone profound changes in its structure and working practices. The

---

[1] *Civil Service Reform*, a report to the Prime Minister from Sir Richard Wilson, Head of the Home Civil Service. Cabinet Office, December 1999.

reasons are partly its own necessary response to economic, social and technological developments, and partly decisions taken by elected politicians in pursuit of their own priorities.

The reduction in civil service numbers by nearly 40%, from a peak equivalent to 751,000 full-time workers in 1976 to 463,000 as at April 1998,[2] is only the most visible of those changes. There have been far-reaching changes both in the internal procedures and management of the service and in the relationships between civil servants and the politicians they serve. A sharp distinction has been drawn between the policy-making and the executive functions of government. Most executive functions, such as management of government properties, procurement, companies registration, patents and trademarks administration, the issue of passports, licensing of vehicles and drivers, road construction and maintenance and veterinary services, are now carried out by the self-contained agencies which have been set up under the *Next Steps* programme. Most of those agencies are still formally located within central ministries and subject to ministerial control, but they have discrete budgetary and performance objectives which are modelled on private-sector procedures and can be separately monitored. Of the current total of about 460,000 civil servants, no fewer than 356,000 work in agencies or under *Next Steps* conditions. That leaves only some 100,000 now working, largely in policy-making functions, under more traditional civil service terms.

For convenience, this article will further narrow its discussion of the civil service in three ways.

- It concentrates on the home civil service. It leaves out of the account the Foreign and Commonwealth Office and the diplomatic service, because of the special nature of their work.

- It focuses on the senior civil service, that is broadly officials from the level of Section Head (in pre-reform parlance, the grade of Principal) upwards. Contact with ministers is not confined to the senior grades, but it is those grades which carry out the core functions of policy formation and briefing.

---

[2]   Source: *The Civil Service Yearbook*, HM Stationery Office, 1999.

- It does not consider the impact of the devolution in 1999 of certain functions from Westminster to administrations in Scotland and Wales. The central administrative structures of the United Kingdom and those which serve the Scottish Parliament and the Welsh National Assembly are bound to diverge over time. At the time of writing policy differences had already started to appear, for example over agricultural support and student fees; but it is too early to discern any trend.

Next, we need to confront two basic questions. What in the modern world is—or can be—the function of government? What are the respective roles in government of the elected politicians and of the civil service which serves them?

To the first question the straightforward answer is that even though the policy environment and the tools for information and analysis which are available to governments have changed beyond recognition during the last generation, basic political requirements have not. Any government is a coalition of diverse interests, even within a single party. However, to be credible it has to rest on a coherent set of political principles. To these it must add a realistic understanding and appraisal of national and international conditions, and the willingness to adapt its policies and objectives in the light of external developments.

The vast expansion of the information sources now available can greatly assist the process of rational policy-making. Paradoxically however, instant communication, ever-intensifying media pressure, and legitimate public demands for more open government also mean that policy decisions are increasingly taken as a rushed response to public and lobby pressures. The late Lord (William) Armstrong, who was Head of the Home Civil Service under the Heath Government in the early 1970s, mused in a television interview after his retirement on how greatly the real power of governments is limited by external factors. In the last twenty years the economic and technological changes on which he was reflecting have been greatly accentuated. Yet the same factors which progressively reduce the power of governments (globalization of the economy and of business, the instant availability of information through the Internet and broadcast media) simultaneously encourage national populations to demand that those same governments take instant positions and find instant solutions.

In answer to the second question, the political responsibilities of ministers have not essentially changed in two centuries. Ministers are answerable to the Crown as the source of legitimate authority in the Government of the United Kingdom; to the constituents who elect them; to their supporters (and their opponents) in Parliament; and to the wider public interest, which includes the country's international relations and responsibilities.

As regards the civil service, the *New Encyclopaedia Britannica*, 15th Edition, contains what looks like a classic definition:

> The civil service is a professional body of individuals employed by the state in an administrative capacity. Ideally it is a non-political body whose members serve in the military, constabulary, ministerial or diplomatic branches of government. Civil servants are generally regarded as experts in public affairs and administration and are often utilized as neutral advisers by those responsible for state policy. Although the role of the civil service is not to make official decisions, it can assist in their implementation.

These words reflect the principles which were introduced into the British civil service by the Northcote–Trevelyan reforms of 1853,[3] namely the recruitment by competitive examination and on merit alone of an impartial and professional administrative structure which serves the government of the day without having its own political agenda. However the inclusion of the word 'ideally' gives the game away: no civil service can function as impartially as this purist statement describes. Officials cannot be involved in the formation by politicians of state policy, or implement official decisions, without being implicated in politics. In Britain, this is particularly so in the early year or two of a new government, especially if there has been a change of party, when the prime

---

[3] Sir Charles Edward Trevelyan and Sir Stafford Northcote: *The Organisation of the Permanent Civil Service*, 23 November 1853, Parliamentary Papers 1854, xxvii.1.

concern of incoming ministers is to implement the promises in the party's election manifesto.[4]

Furthermore, in democratic states there are many different models for the interrelationship between politicians and officials. In the United Kingdom senior officials have traditionally had direct access to ministers to proffer and discuss policy advice, and have been the principal source of that advice. In continental Europe, the model is usually for the minister to be surrounded by a personal 'cabinet' of political associates and friends, through which advice from the permanent officials is filtered. In the United States, a change of Administration entails changes in appointments quite far down the executive ladder, so that the whole administration is in effect politicized.

Orthodox opinion in Britain still articulates the traditional definition, or something close to it. According to Sir Richard Wilson, the current Cabinet Secretary and Head of the Home Civil Service:[5]

> The challenge for us is to give the best advice about what can and what cannot be done, and then do our level best to deliver what can be done really well...[The Prime Minister] is clear about what he wants to achieve and I am clear that we need to be an excellent organization. But how we translate that into action is something that I and my permanent secretary colleagues are responsible for.

How therefore does the modern civil service work in practice? As suggested above, we must look at two different categories of change that have been happening during the last three decades: first of all, changes brought about within the service itself (as a natural management response to changes in the priorities of governments and public administration, in social attitudes and in technology); and secondly, change imposed as a result of decisions at the political level.

On the managerial and organizational level, the civil service has had throughout the post-war period to adapt to technical

---

[4] Politicians can be slow to learn. In October 1999 a junior Health Minister used the broadcast media to challenge openly a High Court decision that tobacco advertising could not be banned, not on legal grounds but because it was contrary to the Labour Government's election manifesto.

[5] Interview in the *Financial Times*, 29 September 1999.

and social developments like any other large organization. It has been rather good at this. It was transformed during my 35 years of service from a humane but elephantine structure, designed for wartime conditions which required it to be all things to all men and to have an answer to everything, to a much fitter, more responsive but also more selective organization. Because the government no longer seeks to intervene in or to be expert in every area of the economy, it has had to accept that there are areas of activity, such as in day-to-day relations with industry, where much of the former expertise of departments has been lost.

In more recent years it has been technological developments, above all information technology (IT), which played the biggest part in generating internal change in the civil service. As well as hugely expanding the available database and speeding reaction times, IT reversed what had been a long-standing upward drift in the level of responsibility for policy work (a reverse also linked with the senior staff cuts of the 1990s). An intelligent junior officer who knows his subject can now produce briefing for a minister which looks every bit as good as the work of senior officials, because he uses the same technology. Computer-literate ministers can log into their department's database and delve into a topic without waiting for official advice. How different from my own early years in the Board of Trade in the 1960s, when only officers of Assistant Secretary rank and above had typewriters with pica-size typeface and supplies of the heavy blue paper on which ministerial briefs had to be typed!

The old concept of a uniform civil service with a single grade structure across all central departments has gone. In the past the rule was that a person with the intellectual attainments to reach a grade such as Principal, Under-Secretary or whatever, ought to be able to do any job graded at that level, and that accordingly each grade should have a single pay-scale. Having uniform pay scales (linked with the expectation of a centrally-planned 'career move' within a few years) also made it possible to persuade able people to take the less attractive jobs. However the growing range and technical complexity of many civil service jobs has undermined the concept (which was always more theoretical than real) of the omnicompetence of civil servants at the various grades.

Nowadays there is a move towards grading (and even titling) jobs individually; and to allocate them on a more transparent basis through competitive advertisement within and across departments and, in the case of the most senior and demanding posts, increasingly through public advertisement. The expectation is that people will stay in jobs longer, and when they move it is generally because they have applied for and got a post somewhere else in the service. For practical purposes, centralized posting and career planning no longer exist.

Some of the most important actual or potential civil service changes are a response both to economic circumstances and to initiatives by politicians. Since 1995 senior civil servants have been required to sign individual contracts. Previously they never had anything more than a letter of appointment, but they enjoyed a high level of employment protection, meaning that once an official was 'established', dismissal was impossible except for dishonesty or other disciplinary offences, or for gross incompetence. The new contracts are mostly in standard form and reflect the conditions under which civil servants were previously working. However this change was originally designed by the previous Conservative Government as a first step in placing civil servants on a footing more like that of managers in the private sector, to keep people who are in post on their toes, and to ease the movement of people into slots that suit them best. It was meant to facilitate the recruitment of qualified managers from the private sector (for which reason contracts for outside recruits to senior posts tend to be limited to five years), and to ease the movement of civil servants into the private sector. Following the return of Labour in 1997 the Conservatives' intention of putting all civil servants on time-limited and individually-negotiated contracts was temporarily shelved in favour of other priorities, but even so the concept of an established civil service has effectively been abolished.

The Conservative Government had also started a move towards negotiation of salaries job by job, to reflect the move away from the idea of official omnicompetence. Not surprisingly this change proved very sensitive. The former labyrinthine structure of salary scales within the service has been simplified, but the task of matching pay rates to the individual job has still not gone much beyond the award of extra salary increments to people who are identified through the internal reporting system as performing particularly well, and special bonuses for good performance in unusual (meaning exceptionally difficult) circumstances.

Turning to the developments which have been exclusively politically-inspired, the traditional UK model for relations between ministers and civil servants has been in a state of change for three decades. The process started with the introduction of a few political advisers by the Labour Administration under Harold Wilson in the 1960s, most prominently Wilson's own political secretary Marcia Williams (later Baroness Falkender). In the early 1970s Edward Heath also felt the need for a source of advice to counterbalance the regular departmental structure. He set up the Central Policy Review Staff in the Cabinet Office. This was however not so much a channel for political advice as an expert think tank composed of both outsiders and insiders, the latter including some of the cleverest young people from Whitehall itself. During the Labour Governments of the 1970s and the early days of Margaret Thatcher, there was a marked growth in the appointment and use of political advisers: but these still tended to number only one or two per department, plus one or two at 10 Downing Street.

Under Thatcher, progressively more stress was placed on the obligation of the Whitehall machinery as a whole, including the civil service, to implement the policies of The Government rather than of government in general: Thatcher's oft-quoted question 'Is he one of us?' applied mainly to her political associates and ministers, but it could also extend to senior officials, and it blighted the careers of some of them.

The use of outside political advisers in government has been carried further by the Labour Government of Tony Blair. Actually, under his Administration the numbers of such advisers have not increased very much. They still stand at about two per Cabinet minister. However there is a much expanded Policy Unit at 10 Downing Street, and under Labour the influence and public prominence of individual advisers is markedly greater, together with their ability, accidentally or by design, to land their ministers in public controversy.

In parallel, there have been marked and widely-reported changes in the pattern of decision taking at the political level. As recently as 20 years ago the publicly-maintained principle was that all decisions of the Government were made collectively by the Cabinet. The fact that many decisions were delegated to subordinate committees of ministers was, if not formally denied, at least never publicly admitted, and officials were not allowed to acknowledge openly that Cabinet Committees existed. Under Margaret Thatcher a trend developed of key decisions being taken not even by ministerial committees, but by informal groups of ministers. This downgrading of collective decision taking was to some extent reversed under John Major (because his political position in the Conservative party and above all in Parliament was so much weaker than Thatcher's); but it is once again being carried forward under Blair. It is reported that important decisions are increasingly taken, not through the conventional structure of the Cabinet and Cabinet Committees, with facts, arguments and recommendations being sifted and balanced beforehand through the supporting structure of interdepartmental official committees, but by small groups of like-minded ministers acting primarily on the guidance of political advisers.

Underlying this trend is the perennially equivocal relationship of politicians and civil servants. Relations of trust, confidence and friendship often grow up between ministers and the permanent officials who serve them. But the relationship can equally lead to suspicion and mistrust, particularly where ministers receive analyses and advice which are unwelcome — perhaps at odds with cherished party principles or with manifesto commitments. In 1964 some senior members of the first Wilson Government came to office convinced that following 13 years of continuous Tory government, the civil service must be against them (from my personal observation at the time, I have always been convinced that the exact opposite was true). A similar counter-productive attitude was again evident when Labour returned to office in 1997.

Meanwhile during both the Thatcher and the Major years the Conservative Government followed a determined programme of reducing the size of the public sector. Principally this involved privatization of most of the nationalized industries and services, but it also involved the massive proportionate reduction in the size of the civil service which is referred to above, and a sustained determination, through public statements and private briefings, to downplay the role of the public sector, including the civil service. I was present at an internal meeting in the Department of Trade and Industry in the early 1990s when Michael Heseltine, then President of the Board of Trade, said flatly that the private sector could do anything better than the public sector. Later on, as Deputy Prime Minister, Heseltine pushed through the policy of reducing the senior civil service, over the years from 1993 to 1996, by about one-third across the board — without, of course, reducing civil service responsibilities or workloads to match. So it is not surprising that, overall, relations between politicians and civil servants have soured.

The package of reform proposals announced by Sir Richard Wilson in December 1999 is designed to carry all these processes — both internally-generated reform and the civil service's response to political pressures — much further, and very fast. Public sector reform is a high priority of the Labour Government, and during 1999 we were repeatedly told through media briefings that Tony Blair was displeased with what he saw as slow progress. The Wilson proposals embody a determined effort by the assembled Permanent Secretaries of Whitehall to respond to that political pressure.

Accordingly, the proposals commit the civil service to six 'key themes':

- stronger leadership, with a clear sense of purpose;

- better business planning from top to bottom;

- sharper performance management;

- a dramatic improvement in diversity;

- a service more open to people and ideas, which brings on talent; and

- a better deal for staff.

Individual departments should, by the time this article appears, have prepared action plans to implement these principles. The overall aim is to provide better-researched and more widely-based solutions to problems, stronger leadership training within the service (particularly for a select number of especially high fliers); and detailed business planning. There will be rigorous performance appraisal at all stages and all levels, new pay systems much more closely related to individual performance and results, and a vague commitment to a 'better balance between work and private life' (which presumably means trying to reduce some of the current levels of overwork which are indicated below).

Renewed efforts are to be made to broaden recruitment and to increase the role of women and ethnic minorities. From the point of view of this analysis a particularly important commitment is that by 2005 two-thirds of all senior civil servants should have had experience outside the service. There is to be extended and more flexible use of early retirement schemes. Action on all these objectives is subject to deadlines, mostly by dates before the end of 2001, with results in some cases expected over a five-year period.

The Wilson Report remembers to make a nod in the direction of the traditional duty of civil servants to 'act with integrity, propriety and political impartiality, and select on merit', and to put first the interests of the public. Nevertheless these proposals, whatever their intrinsic merits, are likely to intensify the already widespread sense among officials that the Labour Government's reform agenda derives not merely from administrative necessity, but also from a widespread suspicion — if not outright rejection — of what is perceived as a conservative administrative culture. Sir Richard Wilson's *Financial Times* interview implied that the basic function of the civil service is now the execution of policies handed down from the political level. His new proposals strengthen that impression.

Nothing in this analysis is meant to suggest that new developments in the civil service, or in the decision-making procedures of government, should be resisted *per se*. Change in response to technological and social developments is inevitable. Elected politicians have every right to review how policies are made and decisions taken, and it is not surprising if a new government feels that a long-established bureaucracy does not react quickly enough.

Some of the sensitive points in the political/official relationship which are discussed above can be argued both ways. For example, departmental officials may think that the Policy Unit at 10 Downing Street interferes unduly with the policy-making process, in particular by injecting strictly political concerns before the interdepartmental spadework has been thoroughly done. An alternative view is that by getting involved in the early stages of Whitehall policy making, the Unit actually assists the process of discussion and compromise, and the eventual acceptance of recommendations by Ministers. On another point, it can be argued that if ministers' political advisers take a higher public profile, that is helpful because they can relieve the permanent officials in departmental Press Offices of some of the more equivocal political aspects of presenting government policy.

What is more questionable is the apparent downgrading of the role of Parliament in policy making, at the same time as the Government feels increasingly obliged to respond to pressures from the highly-organized but usually unelected special interest groups who are nowadays included within the broad description of 'civil society'. In the name of 'transparency' these interests have every right to be heard. The question is through what channels, and whether their contributions add to or indeed confuse the accepted consultative processes of government.

Turning to the position of civil servants in the broader context of the national economy and labour market, it is understandable that like most other workers they should no longer expect to have a job for life. Of course, over the years the service tolerated many thousands of people, particularly in the more junior grades, who did not deserve to enjoy job security at all. Nowadays the reduction of numbers, the hiving-off or privatization of many functions and new inefficiency procedures have removed most of such people, as well as the 'sump' functions into which they could formerly be shunted and forgotten. No-one should regret that.

However in operational terms there are already serious disadvantages to the present practice of allocating officials to posts on the basis of advertisement and application, and these may be further accentuated as the new proposals for wider recruitment, more short-term secondments and individually-negotiated employment terms are implemented.

First, departments no longer have the routine ability to move people when they get stale in a job or do not live up to their initial promise. The proposal to make more use in future of early retirement schemes is designed as one means of tackling this problem, but early retirement is a blunt weapon and will be expensive. At the same time many competent people who would benefit from experience in a wider range of jobs, but who tend not to be the first choice of interview panels, may not realize their full potential or offer the service as much as they could. Procedures designed to increase the flexibility and technical competence of the civil service may thus have the perverse effect of building back into it a serious inertia in staffing.

A second particular disadvantage is that it may be harder to attract the more able people into the less appealing jobs, because once they are there they could find themselves stuck. Paradoxically, it might in the end be necessary to pay higher rates to get decent people into less intellectually satisfying jobs than for the better-quality posts.

Third, systematic career planning has been abandoned. Special ways are still found of bringing on the brightest people — they always were — and Wilson's new proposals promise to accentuate the selection of high-fliers. But in general the service-wide preoccupation with developing the talents of individuals has waned. It is left to people to seek their own personal and career development through a mixture of self-generated job changes and attendance at training courses.

A fourth, and more generalized, downside is that civil servants no longer feel 'secure' in their jobs in the way that they used to: not just materially secure, but also secure intellectually. Even senior officials will now have to look over their shoulders at career prospects, at the chances of getting a contract renewed (if it has a limited term), or of getting selected for a better-paid or more attractive job. Ten years ago I could feel easy in giving a minister advice which I knew he would dislike, but which I believed to be correct. He had every right to reject it, but I did not have to compromise my analysis in submitting it. One must question whether civil servants in their new conditions are going to be able to insist on independence and rigour of mind.

Up to now the civil service reform process, whether internally or politically generated, has also shown important elements both of modishness and of time-lag. To illustrate the first, there has been a tendency to try to transplant into the public service management principles and structures which are fashionable in the private sector, regardless of whether they fit or not. Thus twenty years ago, 'management by objectives' (MBO) was the plausible cry, and thousands of expensive hours were spent training civil servants (including myself) in it. MBO could indeed apply in the routine management of a predictable flow of work of a uniform type, but not to higher-level policy making tasks where even the best-defined performance objectives were regularly derailed by a political crisis, or even by a tricky Parliamentary Question. Sooner or later the UK will once again have a government which dominates Parliament less than Blair's 1997 administration. One dares to ask how proof the better business planning promised in the Wilson report may then be against the demands of the political establishment.

To illustrate the second, a few years ago the civil service adopted the principle of 'delayering', effectively the removal from the senior official structure of the whole of the former Under Secretary grade. Just at that time, many industrial companies were finding that the financial savings from their own delayering of their staff were outweighed by the loss of middle management and (particularly) planning capacity. There is at least a chance that the Ministry of Agriculture's reaction—and that of ministers who depended on its advice—to the BSE crisis would have been less lamentable had not the upper ranks of that department recently been so thinned out in both numbers and capacity.

Then there is the question of overwork. Not only did the Conservatives fail to match delayering with a commensurate reduction in departmental workloads, but the change of government in 1997 naturally involved a massive programme of new legislation. Anecdotally, most officials will say that they are working excessive hours; or, just as importantly, that increased political pressures and reduced reaction times mean that they cannot use efficiently the hours that they do work. In answer to a survey conducted in July 1998 by the Association of First Division Civil Servants, 42% of the senior civil service said that they were working 11 hours or over per week more than they were paid for (that is the equivalent of an extra one and a half standard working days). The percentage had declined a year later to 29%, but the number who then claimed to be working between 6 and 10 hours extra per week had increased in proportion. The broad conclusion is that the senior civil service is still heavily overworked, at a time when many members feel that their skill and advice are under-valued.

An important question raised by the Wilson proposals is whether, apart from their objective of aligning civil service management practice with modern standards, they will provide a serious answer to some of these problems. Clearly they are intended to do so. But paradoxically the process of improving management in the civil service tends to reduce the independent policy-making and advice function of even those officials who remain in what are designated as policy posts. The Wilson proposals, with their stress on business planning, ceaseless performance appraisal and 360-degree feedback (that is, from below as well as from above) for senior managers, look likely to bring about a process which might be character-ized as 'dumbing up': where civil servants have ever-increasing supplies of information for the equitable and transparent dis-charge of the management functions which increasingly dom-inate their jobs, but less and less time or independence of mind to think constructively about what the governments whom they serve ought actually to be doing.

There is one very important factor which these days pro-foundly affects the work of United Kingdom ministers and civil servants and which I have not yet mentioned: namely, membership of the European Union. Important areas of policy and law are effectively set and controlled at the level of the Union, such as trade policy, industrial standards, agriculture, the regulation of financial services, and many aspects of trans-port. It is also safe to say that no significant area of the work of any central government department today remains unaf-fected by EU law.

All this impacts on the work of both politicians and officials in two ways which look contradictory. On one hand, so much law and regulation is now decided at the EU level — according to the demonology of the Eurosceptics, 'imposed by

Brussels' — that much of the government process in the UK is effectively devoted to implementing EU laws, further accentuating the executive function of much of the British government machine.

On the other hand, policy and legislative decisions in the EU are taken jointly by responsible ministers from all the member states in the Council of Ministers. The proposals which are placed before ministers for decision do not emerge from the blue or spring fully-armed from the capricious head of some Brussels bureaucrat: they have always been exhaustively worked out at official level beforehand, between the Commission and all the member states.[6] The negotiating process in Brussels demands a high level of both strategic and tactical skill — higher in many ways than the demands of a purely domestic policy-making process. When policy or legal proposals are on the table in the EU, officials must first agree with their ministers what are the UK national objectives; then judge the likely objectives and probable negotiating tactics of the other member states; define the range within which a solution acceptable to the UK might lie; then go, often repeatedly over a long period, to Brussels to negotiate for a solution which preserves the essentials of the UK national position while recognizing the legitimate aims of the other member states; expend much time and effort along the way on diplomacy and building alliances with the Commission and sympathetic member states; and finally justify the resulting solution to their own ministers, prior to political-level discussion in the Council.

Once the Council has taken its decision, the implementation of the new law or regulation has to be within the confines of EU law, even if it is the UK national authorities which are responsible for its execution. To that extent, as already noted, the UK government's scope for initiative is reduced. But at the earlier legislative stage, and perhaps paradoxically, the procedures at the EU level require a sustained effort of thought and negotiation over a timescale which these days is rarely available in domestic policymaking. In this way EU membership

[6] For a detailed practitioner's description of how this process works, see: Michael Johnson, *European Community Trade Policy and the Article 113 Committee*, Royal Institute of International Affairs, London, 1998.

actually places a heavier load of responsibility on UK ministers and officials in the matter of policymaking; and inasfar as it is the officials who bear the brunt of negotiations in Brussels, operating within the EU helps to restore a measure of the responsibility which has been ebbing away from the civil service at home.

Of course there never was a Golden Age of civil service independence, of perfect rigour of analysis and purity of political and administrative principle. Although under the staffing procedures previously operated by departments the adverse impact on individual careers of personal animosities was offset by a more impartial system of centralized personnel reporting and posting, poor personal relationships still blighted the careers of some people. Ministers who disliked the advice which they were given might not have been able to get the officials sacked, but they could still get them moved to other work. People who were adept at playing the system could rise to the level of their own incompetence and beyond. Centralized career planning was certainly not effectively carried through at all levels: despite repeated government commitments to the principle of career development and a series of expensive training schemes, rational staff and career planning were regularly knocked sideways by some new political crisis, a new policy initiative, or the decision of an incoming government to restructure Whitehall ministries or establish new ones overnight.

In short, the civil service is a juggernaut. It is still too large and diverse for any generalization about its conditions and standing to be uniformly valid. It covers a huge variety of tasks which are equally difficult to manage whether one tries to impose a uniform structure, or opts (as now) for discrete and individually tailored models. It therefore takes time to reform and redirect.

On balance, however, there are strong grounds for arguing that while the many changes of recent years have undoubtedly improved the management of the civil service beyond recognition compared with the post-war years, they have at the same time combined to erode the position of the individual civil servant in a British government department, both in terms of personal job security (which must have at least an indirect impact on independence of mind) and in the extent of influence which can be exerted on policy formation within the new domestic political structures created by the Thatcher and Blair Governments. It is too early to say that the civil service has become an essentially executive rather than a policy-making structure, or that the Northcote–Trevelyan principles of recruitment and promotion on merit have been abandoned; but disquieting trends are visible, and the Wilson proposals of December 1999 do little to allay that disquiet.

Domestically, policy objectives have always been laid down, and properly so, by the elected representatives; but in recent years decisions have increasingly been taken by processes which sidestep or reduce the careful sifting by officials which remains essential to rational policymaking. Instant national and global communication means that any government is now subject to sustained pressures from lobby-groups and single-interest campaigners. The politician's natural desire to please and to respond to a perceived social, moral or economic problem leads increasingly to policymaking by knee-jerk reaction: two random recent examples are the Conservative Government's hasty and unenforceable Dangerous Dogs Act, and Tony Blair's 1999 pledge on television (rapidly watered down) to ban hunting with dogs. I do not argue, of course, that in all such cases the decision of ministers would necessarily be different if the issues were thoroughly tested through traditional civil service processes of analysis. However there would be a better chance that all the aspects of a case would be taken into account in a more rational and orderly way. Meanwhile, and *pace* Sir Richard Wilson, an over-worked, overmanaged and less personally-secure civil service is less well placed to be heeded when it points out to the politicians the likely disadvantages of their actions.

None of this constitutes a crisis in British public administration. In many respects the civil service still works enviably well, and with impressive commitment. No-one argues that it should not stay abreast of the best in current management practice. But the implications of current trends for the quality and consistency of policymaking in the United Kingdom are worrying. That remains so despite the stimulating and beneficial challenges presented by policy formation and diplomacy within the EU. According to orthodox British constitutional theory, it is Parliament which provides the checks and balances which restrain and discipline the actions of the executive. However the orthodox definition no longer holds good where there is a massive government majority in the House of Commons, where it appears more important for ministers to be 'on message' than to respond to Parliamentary concerns, and where political decision-making, whether by Conservative or Labour Governments, increasingly becomes a sandwich of political opportunism with a filling of knee-jerk populism.

Until recently, the existence of an independent—or rather non-party political—civil service in the United Kingdom has, however imperfectly, provided a further check and discipline on the politicians. The independence of that service is being progressively eroded, just when we may find that we need it more than ever.

Dominic Hobson

Government as Business, or Let's Play Shops!

I t is commonplace to describe the age we live in as one bereft of any system of ideas. As the epic contest between two mutually antagonistic ways of life recedes into history, neither tradition nor reason has succeeded ideology. The political institutions which linked the present to the past — monarchy, Parliament, judiciary — are being bypassed or undermined. History itself is being re-written as apology. Technology occupies the space once reserved for reflection and inquiry, and principle has yielded to pragmatism. But where ideas fail, technique flourishes. Business, the most practical of all the disciplines, has now become the model for modern government. It suits the temper of the times. Business, with its disrespect for established ways of doing things and its insatiable appetite for novelty, appeals to politicians interested not in justice or liberty but in efficiency. The political coalitions which dominate the age — Majorism, New Labour, Clintonism, *Die Neue Mitte* — are doctrines whose only principle is expediency. For them, facts are for spinning, and ideas are of interest only for their psephological appeal. This is an age whose governing elites believe that politics is a form of brand management, and that governments can be run like businesses.

These are odd beliefs, perhaps peculiar to an age of professional politicians, who lack experience of business and the limitations of business techniques. But their effectiveness, in a modern media-driven democracy, is undeniable. Voters, no longer trapped by class or ideology, can be treated like shop-

pers. Government press officers are no longer the dry distrib-
utors of fact, but 'spin doctors' who look to place flattering
stories about the Government in the newspapers. The corporate public relations departments of fast moving consumer
goods companies have filled the pages of *The Grocer* and
Cosmopolitan with similar material for decades. New Labour
psephologists monitor the reaction of the voters to every twist
and turn of Government policy, just as companies have used
opinion polls and focus groups to measure consumer reaction
to their products and services. 'If you are running a company
nowadays – suppose you are running Marks and Spencer or
Sainsbury,' mused the Prime Minister in a revealing interview
he gave a few weeks after taking office, 'you will be constantly
trying to work out whether your consumers are satisfied with
the product they are getting. I don't think there is anything
wrong with government trying to do that in the same way.'

In fact, there is a great deal wrong with it. New Labour
thinks it can avoid difficult choices about the role and limits of
the state by making government less like government and
more like business. But government is different from business.
It is driven by policy as well as judged by results. Unlike a
company, the primary role of the state is political and juridical,
not economic or commercial. Companies provide tradable
goods and services which consumers purchase willingly out
of their own income. Governments provide non-tradable
goods and services which taxpayers purchase unwillingly out
of expropriated earnings. In the marketplace, companies allocate resources to activities which are profitable. In government, resources are allocated by politicians (who seek votes,
the support of interest groups and influence with the media)
and civil servants (who seek fresh career opportunities, bigger
budgets and more subordinates). Unlike companies, which go
bankrupt if they fail to produce goods and services at prices
which consumers are willing to pay, ministers and officials
can distribute payments, contracts, subsidies, laws, regulations, tariffs and other measures without risking financial failure. Government, unlike business, is immortal. Business is a
competitive activity; government is a coercive one.

The distinction is important: it is why the Third Way is a
chimera. Just as the economic policy of Old Labour Governments was based on the belief – first detailed by Tony

Crosland in 1956 in *The Future of Socialism*, the intellectual handbook of Old Labour—that public corporations and private companies were indistinguishable in every respect but ownership, the New Labour Government is convinced that efficient and effective public services are merely a matter of re-organization and better management. There is an instinctive resistance to the idea that an extended order of any kind can arise spontaneously and maintain itself without anybody being in charge. In the case of the marketplace, this resistance is fortified not only by a distaste for the inequalities which result, but by a contempt for the degree of redundancy involved. To the uninitiated, capitalism appears wasteful as well as unjust. At the heart of the case for economic planning lies the belief that disinterested professionals can—by gathering knowledge, analysing it rationally, and setting themselves appropriate targets—achieve better results than mere entrepreneurs responding to price signals in an apparently chaotic marketplace.

For 40 years, from the 1940s to the 1980s, politicians and civil servants ran the nationalized industries on the basis of this conceit. The three great White Papers on the management of the nationalized industries (published in 1961, 1967 and 1978) laid down a variety of techniques and objectives by which prices were to be matched to costs, and subsidies for socially desirable services (like rural post offices and branch lines) were to be contained. As late as 1981, the Central Policy Review Staff argued that the performance of the nationalized industries could be transformed by the setting of 'strategic objectives'. A year later, the nationalized industries exchanged lists of objectives with their sponsoring departments. In retrospect, it is hard to understand why the idea of the rational and disinterested bureaucrat was taken so seriously for so long. The self-interest of ministers, civil servants and nationalized industry managers—to say nothing of their staff, who were absent or on strike almost as often as they were at work—is a large part of the explanation of the failure of nationalization. Unlike private companies, which are at constant risk of failure or take-over, nationalized industries could overpay workers, overcharge or undercharge customers, squander capital and shun innovation, sure in the knowledge that the taxpayer would always enable them to survive. Paper targets are not the same as financial incentives. As Patrick Hutber, the former City editor of the *Sunday Telegraph* pointed out at the time, you cannot turn a donkey into a zebra by painting stripes on its back.

Since the privatization of industry started in earnest in November 1984, with the sale of the first tranche of shares in BT, nobody has disputed the truth of Hutber's Law in the case of the nationalized industries. Unfortunately, every other part of the state machine is still in denial. Sir David Wright, the former ambassador to Japan recently appointed head of British Trade International — or BTI, the joint Foreign Office–Department of Trade & Industry trade promotion vehicle established earlier this year — explained in October that his aim was to make trade promotion 'more business-like, and more like business'. Paraded as an early example of 'joined-up government' under New Labour, BTI is actually the latest in a long line of initiatives designed to make Whitehall more business-like. Three in four civil servants no longer work in traditional departments but in one of nearly 150 Executive Agencies, which mimic companies in every respect — save shareholders. They have balance sheets and profit and loss accounts, and are run by boards of directors headed by a chief executive. Even traditional government departments now fix budgets for three years ahead, assess costs as well as revenues, and prepare balance sheets. There is talk of introducing to central government a corporate governance regime of the kind Big Business has imposed on itself to allay public disquiet about Fat Cattery in the boardroom.

Ironically, there is no better example of the futility of stripe-painting than corporate governance. The corporate governance section of the average annual report now itemizes boardroom remunerations in loving detail, charts how they were approved by multiple committees, and lists the myriad rules and regulations with which they comply. But nothing has changed: boardroom pay is higher than ever, and rising still. Directors may be ticking the boxes, but they are not changing their behaviour. Indeed, the outcome is perverse: massive awards have acquired a legitimacy they previously lacked. The same syndrome is apparent throughout the public sector, where officials of all kinds are now managing to targets. The chief executives of Executive Agencies make sure that at least nine and a half out of ten of the targets they set can always be met. Teachers, set demanding objectives by the Department for Education and Employment, have learnt how to meet them by lowering the standards of testing and examination. Health officials, instructed to reduce the number of people awaiting surgery or hospital admission, have found many ingenious ways to remove patients from the waiting list. Doctors, charged with testing and re-testing the professional competence of colleagues, have created a labyrinthine structure of training and examination to fool the official inspectors. Dons, offered money for students and published work, have increased their intake of undergraduates and their output of paper.

A similar pattern is observable in the regulated industries, where the Government has also sought to achieve public policy objectives by stripe-painting and target-setting. BT and the gas, water and electricity companies have found it easy to hoodwink the regulators on prices by denying them information on the scope for improving efficiency. The railway franchise holders can meet apparently stiff targets by adjusting timetables or running fewer trains. The truth is, there is only one way to stop companies exploiting consumers: competition. Regulation is at best a temporary expedient, designed to contain prices while competitors establish themselves (as they are now doing in telecommunications, gas and electricity). Naturally, regulators are reluctant to accept their own demise. Despite fierce competition in several industries, none has disappeared. They have all ventured into new areas, like the quality of service and the scope of competition, which were not part of their original remit. Unfortunately, the New Labour Government is encouraging their ambitions. It sees regulation not as a temporary alternative to competition, but as an effective alternative to re-nationalization. Ministers are already using regulators to promote a variety of political enthusiasms, from increased investment to environmental protection.

This is a reminder that government attempts to manipulate behaviour are worse than pointless. They are almost invariably perverse in their effects. Even before New Labour identified regulation as a form of interference without ownership, the regulated industries had themselves sought to escape price control by diversifying into unregulated activities, usually with disastrous results. Similarly, the decline in educational standards is a direct result of the attempt to raise them. This is the paradox of almost all forms of government intervention. The textbook examples are seat-belt and helmet laws, which have increased road fatalities by encouraging drivers to go faster, so killing more motorcyclists and pedestrians. The vast inflation of financial services regulators is less well-known. In the early 1980s, the London financial markets were regulated by a handful of officials at the London Stock Exchange. Today, a giant state bureaucracy of 1,800 lawyers, armed with a budget of £177 million, is needed to do the same job. What is more, every firm needs a complement of compliance officers to understand and follow their diktats. Yet this army of regulators failed to prevent the greatest financial failure of the century (Barings) and its greatest financial scandal (pensions mis-selling).

Regulations are not harmless. Like taxes, they impose costs. As costs rise, output and employment fall, and prosperity is reduced. The overall cost of government attempts to improve on the verdict of the marketplace has yet to be calculated. But if the American experience is typical, the annual cost of compliance is massive—equivalent perhaps to half the size of the total tax take, or £125 billion. (If the consequent loss of output is taken into account, the figure is higher still.) Alive to the growing chorus of complaint, both the Major and the Blair governments promised to reduce the regulatory burden on the private sector. It is an ambition which they have yet to fulfil. Regulators earn their living by regulation, and can enhance their status and income only by devising new regulations. They are aided and abetted by ministers (who cannot allow any accident or mistake to happen twice) and multi- nationals (who find regulation a useful way of restricting competition). To that extent, the decision of the Major government to subject all new government regulations to a cost/benefit analysis by other civil servants, read like the plot from an episode of 'Yes, Minister'. The real alternative— self-regulation—is never considered. Yet it works, and avoids the costs and the moral hazards of excessive regulation. A railway company has no interest in economies which cause fatal accidents, or a food manufacturer in making dangerous products. Accidents and fatalities damage the reputation of the company, lose it business, and so cost its shareholders money. That fear of loss is a far more effective deterrent to corner-cutting than any amount of box-ticking, which merely provides an alibi in the case of disaster.

Every shopper is familiar with this process. 'It is not from the benevolence of the butcher, the brewer or the baker that we expect our dinner', as Adam Smith famously put it, 'but from their regard to their own interest. We address ourselves not to their humanity but to their self-love.' Two centuries after the publication of *Wealth of Nations* and in spite of daily confirmation of the truth of this observation, there is still an instinctive resistance to the idea that self-interested behaviour can have socially beneficial results.

A century of democracy has also encouraged the belief that there is a political or legal cure for every social ill. Today, getting money matters more than defending freedom, and few care whether it comes from work, the DSS, litigation or the National Lottery. Ignorance about the scale of taxation and public expenditure is widespread: most people on £30,000 a year would be surprised to learn that they are better off than 92 per cent of taxpayers. This explains why opinion polls consistently record large majorities in favour of more public spending; it is assumed that someone else will pay. Parliament will not enlighten them. It is at present a cipher, useful only as an excuse to convene new parliaments in Brussels, Cardiff and Edinburgh, where the growing class of professional politicians and empire-building officials can create new sinecures for themselves and their friends. (Animated debates were held by the Welsh and Scottish parliaments over what Members should be paid.) Popular newspapers, in past generations a valuable corrective to the self-regard of the political classes, are now too absorbed in the system to question its morals. Counter-productive legislation and regulation—against dangerous dogs, sex pests, hand guns, railway accidents, and beef on the bone—invariably originate in some tabloid newspaper campaign.

This is the culture of modern government: the State, like a food manufacturer or a department store, is in business not only to satisfy the wants and needs of the voters but to anticipate them as well. Paradoxically, the effect on the standard of living is invariably deleterious. Every tax or regulation has its counterpart in a private or commercial decision delayed, distorted or aborted. Throughout the twentieth century, and especially since the Second World War, the immense productivity of modern capitalism has masked this State-sponsored prodigality. The corporations also equipped the governing classes with the ideal alternative to taxing and regulating the voters directly. Rich, malleable and often unpopular, companies have collected income tax, National Insurance contributions, VAT and excise duties painlessly and efficiently for decades. Business insulated politicians from the costs, but not the benefits, of their actions.

Until recently, there was little prospect of any alteration which favoured taxpayers rather than tax-eaters, but there are now some grounds for hope. One is the 'black' economy. The best guess is that this unspoken revolt of the over-taxed is now equivalent to between 8 and 15 per cent of the national income, or £75-130 billion. Another hopeful sign is the growing power of information technology. In a service-dominated global economy, cheap computer power and even cheaper telecommunications are shrinking the number of transactions which can be captured and taxed by the Inland Revenue or the Customs and Excise. The tax base of national governments is shrinking already, increasing competition between countries to cut their rates of taxation, and shifting the burden from corporate intermediaries to people themselves. But the most hopeful sign of all is the attitude of the young. They recognize modern democracy for what it is: a quinquennial jamboree to decide which group of placemen and charlatans will spend their money over the next five years. Unlike the generations who fought for New Jerusalem between 1939 and 1945, or for free love and abortion-on-demand in the 1960s, politics is for them neither noble nor useful. Rather, like all forms of intermediation, it is an obstacle to self-realization. They are equally distrustful of cartelized, paternalistic, institutionalized forms of capitalism. Thanks to a mixture of information technology, the illusory nature of an efficient state and the inextinguishable human urge to freedom, theirs could well be the first generation of consumers to enjoy the privileges — wealth, freedom, knowledge — which were once the preserve of monarchs and barons. They will truly live, as kings once did, 'of their own'.

Interview with Ravi Shankar

Ivo Mosley

IM: You are in an unusual position, in that you have enjoyed great popular success, for instance performing at many pop festivals in the sixties and seventies, while you also underwent a rigorous classical training. Having read your autobiography, I know you were having a very wild and exciting time in Europe in your late teens before you decided to go back and study Indian classical music. So what drew you to undergo a rigorous and very disciplined traditional training?

RS: India at that time was so secluded, it was not like it is today. India is nowadays as modern as everywhere else — people who are educated read the same things as people in the West. In fact, they read it two hours earlier, because of the time difference! What I am trying to say is, in those days there was definitely a big gap, a cultural gap. So when I think how at that young age I wanted to go back, I am amazed at my own self! It was some strange pull that brought me from all this wonderful life in the West. What brought me back was the religious and spiritual aspects, which run through Indian music.

I believe very strongly that it is important to hold on to our traditions, which have been passed down so beautifully through the ages. There is a shattering contradiction in everything that we are facing now, it is very disturbing. I am personally in favour of the old manners but young people tell me we have to move on. When I listen to the music of my own daughter, for instance, I see the traditions are alive. Yet at the same time she is not totally at one with me — she has full knowledge of what is happening today.

IM: She has, as well as being modern, a knowledge of the tradition......

Yes, because of having grown up with me, and through making music with me. But it is like walking on a tightrope; if she wants, she can keep her balance, that depends upon her. But all this has made me realize that the world has now become one big family. On one side everybody knows a little of everything, but not deep enough. You know? Not deep.

IM: A lot of young people nowadays feel the same kind of yearning that you felt for a tradition, but traditions are hard to find now. Lyrics of pop music are very depressed and despairing and nihilist. I wonder if that's because in a very commercial world, everything is treated as a commodity, an enjoyment, not as a discipline...not as a demanding thing...

The older people are also responsible for it, because they are making money. Houses, magazines, all these fashions, all this distribution of drugs. It's not the young people, it's those horrible people, who are much older; they want to make money and exploit the whole situation. They are teaching them all the new fashions, so that they want to put on new things, you know, always for them to be attractive. I think the biggest crime is to encourage this. But that has become something everybody knows about, but as long as money is flowing in...

IM: So there's a feeling of the old behaving irresponsibly towards the young....

Exactly! And we are blaming or criticizing the young people, but at the same time we are providing them with negative things, you know.

IM: Do you see a special role for a high and demanding culture? Does it fulfill any special function? Does it provide thoughtfulness, or hand on important truths?

I have been told again and again by different people in different countries that they have found so much through the music that I give them. This has made me happy of course, but I have not been able to analyze it fully. Is it peace of mind just for a moment, or for the one or two hours of listening? Is it a spiritual experience? I could work just for that, you know! Without sermons, giving any talks; because there are enough wise people, swamis and very interesting people who can really talk and give them peace of mind or whatever advice they need. But through sound only, no words, no songs...it is amazing...which proves that I have been lucky to acquire a little of the music which has that power.

IM: I noticed in your book you used the word ' sacred' quite a lot. Do you feel what you have to give has something to do with Man's relationship with God?
It is really very strange because, in effect, you don't know which word to use, 'God' or some power...it can be occult also, you know, power of minds...magicians, many yogis can use this power of mind over matter, so it can be channeled through any medium. A painter, maybe, can have that within whatever he does, can bring out a certain feeling to the person who sees it. Or the same thing with a great writer; some have that magic, you know, you just read two lines and something happens to you...how do you explain that? It cannot be just the language, because those works might have been written by other people also. It's like Fritz Kreisler — in just one note he can produce in people tears in their eyes. I have witnessed that myself in my travels. Kreisler — why is it that some people are masters, and they can do anything, especially mastery over virtuosity; but some people can have just one simple note; they can touch something in you? And that's a hard thing, you know!

IM: Something I've been very interested in is the contrast between Indian music and Western music. I remember something you said about John Coltrane...you admired his music tremendously, but there was a disturbing element in his music. Whereas Indian music seems to build up a creative and passionate intensity, Western music and art, generally, seem to want to incorporate the bad and destructive sides as well. Sometimes they make something good out of that, but sometimes it just becomes bad and destructive. Do you think that is a fair point?
Yes. In early times, until Bach's period, Western music had some connection with the Church and some relationship with religion. After that there was more emphasis on composed music and symphonies...then twelve tone and so on, and now music from the avant-garde: It's like architecture, you see,

now it is such pain, it hurts the eyes! The old architecture, it had something that pleased you, whether Indian or Egyptian or wherever.

When I started, myself, about forty-five years ago, there was no understanding or appreciation of Indian music and I started explaining to people that we try to meditate through music, we start with that feeling. And gradually we build up...like growing in age, tenderness, we develop the beauty, the sensuous or romantic aspects and then there comes that beautiful climax; it excites people also, like any music does, it is entertaining. But we never started with the excitement. We always build up from what is very slow, serene. In the beginning, it was very difficult for Westerners to appreciate that.

Now in the West—and I see the younger generation especially—they don't want to go to Wagner opera, they don't want to go to symphonic music or classical music and I'm amazed by that; being born here, having grown up here, they do hear a lot of classical music, but they don't want to listen. They have their own rock, pop and all kinds of different protest music, they are also doing violent music because of their anger, their unhappiness. So it starts from the violence, from the anger. And yet at the same time they have such interest in listening to music from other parts of the world, especially Indian music.

IM: So they are looking for something outside of their own tradition...
There are many wonderful composers, like Philip Glass, who are taking their inspiration from Indian music, or Middle Eastern music, or Balinese music, or from the Amazon or Australia. So there must be something they are trying to find.

IM: You have done a lot of work bringing together musicians from different cultures. Do you feel that when cultures meet they can produce great and profound music?
I do feel that and that's why I started with Yehudi Menuhin, a great friend of mine, and I am sorry that he has left us. Just two weeks ago I did two new pieces. I wrote many pieces, completely Indian, based on Indian raga, in Indian style, nothing Western, but I did it in a way which gives a glimpse of all the different, structured patterns of our music. And the musicians

loved it! So that proves that if we seriously want to know we can find something.

And for many years, a lot of Indian musicians have taken from the West. But they have tried to ape, not really learn seriously; they take a phrase from the cha-cha-cha, or from rock, pop, metallic rap, they take all kinds of things. Some of them have tried to do symphonic sounds with a lot of harmony and chords, to make it very dramatic and it hasn't worked very well, though the common man likes it, they like the lighter side of it. So, what is the conclusion? Do you have to be culturally yourself to appreciate tradition?

I have always asked why is it that the common man cannot appreciate Shakespeare? Why do you have to be at some level of education to be able to understand Goethe? On the other hand, I believe also in the theory that a true thing that is simple can have more power. Have you noticed how Shakespeare is becoming popular again through films? And this is the word, 'simplicity'! When things become complex, everybody cannot take it.

IM: Can a worldwide culture that appeals to everyone be a profound culture?
This whole new idea of globalization and mixed culture.... I don't mind it, so long as we don't kill the individual culture. Because see how sad it is; great Egyptian culture, Greek, Roman, so many others...even with Chinese culture, you now have only museum pieces, beautiful things from 5,000 years ago. They show every rock; but what is China today? What is Egypt today? What is Greece today?

We in India are the lucky ones...in India, tradition is still a living art. Whether in music, or dance, or artifacts or whatever, it hasn't stopped. Everywhere else it is only museum pieces. Tourists can see 5,000 years of these mind-boggling things, but what about today? The people, they don't seem to be at all concerned! That, also, is something about which I am frightened. People can always make friends across cultures, and do new things, but we mustn't kill our own. Whatever remains wonderful in Western culture should be kept, and the same with every different culture.

*IM: Moving from culture to morality; people associate globaliza-
tion with greater freedom from traditional morality. In your autobiography, you describe the demands of being a travelling celebrity
musician, how you felt you were unable to give enough time to your
wife and family. But now celebrity has been glamorized, and everyone wants to be like that.*

Royalty, rich people, aristocrats, famous artists will always be
able to have the life of gods. I guess society excuses them,
because they have given something to society, otherwise they
would have been hanged for what they do, like any other normal person!

But morality changes in different places. A thing like female
circumcision, which is a normal thing in Africa or Muslim
countries, now it is being fought against. You know, all the
Middle Eastern countries openly keep little boys, and they are
not charged with molesting young people, that seems to be
natural for them. But now, with globalization, all these things
will be criticized and controlled. So this a very difficult issue,
really. We find changes in different countries over what is censored, like on television or film. So this whole thing…unless
you only live in one country, and never travel, and follow the
rules and regulations of that country, it's very difficult.

*IM: So do you think that globalization is a form of American and, I
suppose, English cultural imperialism?*

Americans certainly have the upper hand now, with their
Coca-Cola, their burgers, their way of life, the way they talk,
everything, even music.

Again it comes back to money. Of course, there are a lot of
good things—computers and other useful new inventions. At
the same time, lots of negative things are also being put forward. No-one can stop it; that's the whole thing now…no-one
can stop anything!

*IM: Have things changed with affluence, with everyone wanting to
be rich?*

Yes, and why not? But if you think of the olden days, at least
the poor knew how to budget, the middle class knew, the rich
knew…at least they could adjust. Now, it is very difficult; the
poor man doesn't want to live the way he is living, the middle
class doesn't want to either. The minimum always gets higher

and higher. Everybody wants to have a television, a fridge; minimum requirement. But it is nothing like a minimum, because it grows more and more.

IM: So affluence has brought on some of these troubles?
I think so. As they say in our mythological literature, this is typical *maya* or a sign of Kali yuga. This is such a destructive time…gradually going to death, you know. With the spirit of acceptance in the olden days, it was terrible, people suffered. But, you know, mentally they had taken that as their fate, and that kept them at least more at peace. I don't say that is good; but today I don't think anyone is satisfied.

IM: So after the Kali yuga, do you get regeneration?
No. We are going through that period in the cycle of history. I cannot tell you exactly how long—but they do have calculations—exactly how many years. But it goes from bad to worse, and then there will be that final explosion or destruction and then again it will start. That is always the journey; you know, the mythic journey. So it looks that things are all getting so scary. But I think we who think about it, can contribute something to healing, at least. We should try out anything, even if it may only be a drop in the ocean.

IM: I wanted to ask you a few questions about the sixties. First of all, you had the satisfaction of enabling people to understand Indian music. Then, when you heard it being played on all kinds of pop music records, did you feel cross?
Initially I was, naturally. Because I had that strong feeling, that it is not right. It is like hearing the violin or cello, if you hear somewhere in Africa they are making a strange scratching noise. You have been used to the traditional sound of the violin, the way it should be played. You would feel uneasy wouldn't you, it is the natural thing. So I, having lived my life with sitar and Indian music, I did feel cross; but gradually, I understood. That this too shall pass, this too shall…you know the Chinese saying? And it did.

   In the field of pop and rock, they always want new things, new change. It is one of those commercial things. Everybody is thinking all the time how to do something new. A little bit of bell, a little bit of this or playing sitar or anything; anything which is new. Now, of course, they have the technology, they don't need any instruments; they can produce weird sounds, nice sounds, beautiful sounds electronically. Everybody's trying. So this is something which can't be stopped, because it has a whole commercial life to it—and out of that, sometimes you hear beautiful things. Sometimes I hear something outstanding. But then you see, again, most of this is gimmick. So it doesn't bother me any more. But it did initially.

IM: About politics in art or in music; do you think that politics should keep right out of.........
Absolutely! I have never been able to carry placards, although I've appreciated people like Paul Robeson or Joan Baez, who had an urge to do that. But I personally feel that this is so momentary, what you are fighting against, it is something that won't be there for long, that's my feeling, so why worry? It is better to give a little happiness, a little peace to people.

In music now, many fantastic talents are working, and I have been very impressed by them. But, as I said, there are many levels of listening. Sometimes it gives you pleasure just to hear; it could be muzak! Or it could be something which excites you, or even something which gives you a lot of happiness. But the thing which disturbs me about modern music is the loudness—all these concerts are now becoming so loud, too amplified. Loudness is what makes the young people very excited. And that excitement can be dangerous, I think, because physically they are provoked, and their anger, which they have in them, becomes more dominant. That seems to be the main thing in rock or music festivals, you know rock, pop, techno, whatever.

IM: Are you hopeful for the future?
I'm an optimist by nature, really, and I've seen so many things come and go, and at least musically I feel very hopeful. Who can say? Things can happen like what happened in Kashmir, or Kosovo, or someone might get crazy and drop a nuclear bomb. So you never know. But still I think we should look at life hopefully—people like you who are conscious of it, and thinking about it and writing about it.

Philip Rieff

The Impossible Culture:
Wilde as a Modern Prophet

I shall begin by quoting at length from Edward Carson's[†] cross-examination of Wilde during the first of the three trials when Wilde was still plaintiff in that ruinous case of libel he brought against the Marquess of Queensberry. Then we shall see at once the quality of Wilde's wit, his view on certain aspects of culture and how far we have come towards Wilde's view in the three-quarters of a century since he became something less than a martyr and more than a victim.

Wilde: I do not believe that any book or work of art ever had any effect whatever on morality.

Carson: Am I right in saying that you do not consider the effect in creating morality or immorality?

Wilde: Certainly, I do not.

Carson: So far as your works are concerned, you pose as not being concerned about morality or immorality?

Wilde: I do not know whether you use the word 'pose' in any particular sense.

Carson: It is a favourite word of your own?

Wilde: Is it? I have no pose in this matter. In writing a play or a book, I am concerned entirely with literature—that is, with art. I aim not at doing good or evil, but at trying to make a thing that will have some quality of beauty.

Carson: Listen, sir. Here is one of the 'Phrases and Philosophies for the Use of the Young' which you contributed: 'Wickedness is a myth invented by good people to account for the curious attractiveness of others.' You think that true?

Wilde: I rarely think that anything I write is true.

Carson: Did you say 'rarely'?

Wilde: I said 'rarely', I might have said 'never' — not true in the actual sense of the word.

Carson: 'Religions die when they are proved to be true.' Is that true?

Wilde: Yes; I hold that. It is a suggestion towards a philosophy of the absorption of religions by science, but it is too big a question to go into now.

Carson: Do you think that was a safe axiom to put forward for the philosophy of the young?

Wilde: Most stimulating.

Carson: If one tells the truth, one is sure, sooner or later, to be found out?

Wilde: That is a pleasing paradox, but I do not set very high store on it as an axiom.

Carson: Is it good for the young?

Wilde: Anything is good that stimulates thought in whatever age.

Carson: Whether moral or immoral?

Wilde: There is no such thing as morality or immorality in thought. There is immoral emotion.

Carson: Pleasure is the only thing one should live for?

Wilde: I think that the realization of oneself is the prime aim of life, and to realize oneself through pleasure is finer than to do so through pain. I am, on that point, entirely on the side of the ancients — the Greeks. It is a pagan idea.

Carson: A truth ceases to be true when more than one person believes in it?

Wilde: Perfectly. That would be my metaphysical definition of truth; something so personal that the same truth could never be appreciated by two minds.

Carson: The condition of perfection is idleness: the aim of perfection is youth?

Wilde: Oh, yes; I think so. Half of it is true. The life of contemplation is the highest life, and so recognized by the philosopher.

Carson: There is something tragic about the enormous number of young men there are in England at the present moment who start life with perfect profiles, and end by adopting some useful profession?

Wilde: I should think that the young have enough sense of humour.

Carson: You think that is humorous?

Wilde: I think it is an amusing paradox, an amusing play on words.

Carson: What would anybody say would be the effect of *Phrases and Philosophies* taken in connection with such an article as *The Priest and the Acolyte?*...

Wilde: Undoubtedly it was the idea that might be formed that made me object so strongly to the story. I saw at once that maxims that were perfectly nonsensical, paradoxical, or anything you like, might be read in conjunction with it.

Carson: After the criticisms that were passed on *Dorian Gray*, was it modified a good deal?

Wilde: No. Additions were made. In one case it was pointed out to me — not in a newspaper or anything of that sort, but by the only critic of the century whose opinion I set high, Mr. Walter Pater — that a certain passage was liable to misconstruction, and I made an addition.

Carson: This is in your introduction to *Dorian Gray:* 'There is no such thing as a moral or an immoral book. Books are well written or badly written.' That expresses your view?

Wilde: My view on art, yes.

Carson: Then, I take it, that no matter how immoral a book may be, if it is well written, it is, in your opinion, a good book?

Wilde: Yes, if it were well written so as to produce a sense of beauty, which is the highest sense of which a human being can be capable. If it were badly written, it would produce a sense of disgust.

Carson: Then a well-written book putting forward perverted moral views may be a good book?

Wilde: No work of art ever puts forward views. Views belong to people who are not artists.

Carson: A perverted novel might be a good book?

Wilde: I don't know what you mean by a 'perverted' novel.

Carson: Then I will suggest *Dorian Gray* as open to the interpretation of being such a novel?

Wilde: That could only be to brutes and illiterates. The views of Philistines on art are incalculably stupid.

Carson: An illiterate person reading *Dorian Gray* might consider it such a novel?

Wilde: The views of illiterates on art are unaccountable. I am concerned only with my view of art. I don't care two-pence what other people think of it.

Carson: The majority of persons would come under your definition of Philistines and illiterates?

Wilde: I have found wonderful exceptions.

Carson: Do you think that the majority of people live up to the position you are giving us?

Wilde: I am afraid they are not cultivated enough.

Carson: Not cultivated enough to draw the distinction between a good book and a bad book?

Wilde: Certainly not.

Carson: The affection and love of the artist of *Dorian Gray* might lead an ordinary individual to believe that it might have a certain tendency?

Wilde: I have no knowledge of the views of ordinary individuals.

Carson: You did not prevent the ordinary individual from buying your book?

Wilde: I have never discouraged him.[1]

Wilde correctly said: 'A great artist invents a type, and life tries to copy it, to reproduce it in a popular form, like an enter-

---

[1] See *The Trials of Oscar Wilde*, ed. H. Montgomery Hyde (London: W. Hodge, 1948), pp. 122–4.

prising publisher.' He also agreed that 'literature always anticipates life'. Nowadays, the type Wilde created, not least in himself, has been reproduced in very popular form. I like to think that Wilde would have despised all the cheap reproductions of his prophecy, especially among the young. Perhaps Wilde might have agreed that there should be limits, not on a great artist's invention of a type but, rather, on the enterprise of reproducing it in popular form. Certainly, Wilde was suspicious enough of the ways in which new character types are commercially exploited and, in their success, cheapened almost to the point of contradiction.

Can invention and reproduction really be separated? I suppose the imaginative invention of a type and its reproduction are inseparable from the cultural process of choosing a pastoral guide for the conduct of life. This supposition on the changeable character of human types in any society specifies the power of art, even as Wilde wanted to use it—and even as others, at least since Plato, have wanted to censor precisely that power.

There are no neutral powers in the permanent war of culture. In his own way, representing the ordinary and established hypocrisies, Carson knew he was attacking one of the great commanders of the forces subverting his culture. Now Wilde's subversive spirit has been made obsolete by the cheap and massive reproduction of that spirit throughout the educated and televisioned strata of Western society. It is the Carsons, now, who are on the defensive. But Wilde can never win. For he imagined an impossible culture, one inhabited by consummate individualists, freed from the inherited inhibitions necessary, at least until our own time, to culture itself. As a guide through the future maze of choices, leading nowhere but attractive in his activity of choosing, Wilde named a type he imagined opposing all conformities: the 'artist'. In certain great artists of the past and present, including himself, Wilde found intimations of a future at once socialist (universally rich) and free (universally expressive). This artistic dream is, perhaps especially in advanced technological societies, more revolutionary than the dream of Marx.

For Wilde, the artist is the true revolutionary figure. Only the artist is fit to play the role of guide in the next culture. He is fit because 'he expresses everything'. Wilde italicized that sentence. The artist, radically different from any revolutionary figure preceding him, precisely by his special freedom to express everything, plays the prophetic role in Wilde's entertainments. Indeed, in the artist, revolutionary and entertainer merge.

Nothing is more contemporary than Wilde's imagination. Almost a century after his time, young revolutionaries in advanced industrial orders conceive themselves more artists than proletarians: their aim is to express everything.[2] But here the resemblance between Wilde and his epigones begins to fade. These latter-day epigones are, mainly, failed artists, relying on their assertions of freedom to express everything rather than upon the wit, grace and reticence with which Wilde believed everything should be expressed. Yet, precisely as failed artists, his successors follow Wilde in asserting the primacy of the artist as a guide to the next culture. What separates them from Wilde may be fatal to their art but vital to their success in a society increasingly uncertain about what it will, and will not, permit. Indeed, some confuse this uncertainty with civilization itself.

In every culture, guides are chosen to help men conduct themselves through those passages from one crisis of choice to another that constitute the experience of living. Once criteria of choice are established, guides are often self-chosen. Shamanry becomes hereditary; priesthood becomes an institution of those who would be ordained. The bandwagon effect operates in every culture. Men enjoy best those roles in which they can exercise an authority which is not their own and yet does not belong to the people they guide. Power may come out of the barrel of a gun; but authority comes out of the projection — and introjection — of ideals.

The rank-and-file members in idealizing institutions of guidance used to be called 'laities': laities were those who listened to whatever the mouthpieces of idealizing institutions had to say. A crisis in culture occurred whenever old guides

[2] In America, the allegiance of these young revolutionaries has shifted from proletariat to black *Lumpenproletariat*, because in blacks they believe they see a culture even less inhibited than their own parental one. I consider the Negroes, at least in the young white artist's understanding of them, by far the most powerful influence in contemporary American culture.

were struck dumb, or whenever laities began listening to new guides—new, because they encouraged their laities to do what theretofore they had not done (and not do what they had done). The crisis of modern culture adds something new to the history of such crises: the defensiveness and guilt of those who now know that they have nothing to say is compounded by the ascendancy of those who say that there should be no guides. Wilde is one of those permanently putative guides, ordained by his art, who have helped our culture advance beyond its unsuccessful Protestant phase in which every man would have been his own priest.

In the next culture there are to be no priests, not even secular ones; we are not to be guided—rather, entertainment, stimulation, liberation from the constraints drawn around us by narrowing guidelines become the functional equivalents of guidance. Where creeds once were, there therapies will be. Oscar Wilde was a brilliant herald of therapeutic culture when, near the turn of the century, the promise of it seemed dazzling. Neither the design nor implications of Wilde's heraldry are obvious to the naked eye. Wilde entertains so well that a guest at one of his feasts of words may easily forget these pleasures have a purpose beyond entertainment. The philistines wanted only entertainment, to be reassured by him in an amusing manner; and Wilde used his talent to entertain, precisely in his most popular plays, such as *The Importance of Being Earnest.* It is in his best essays that he tried to achieve the other purpose of art, which is not to entertain but to insinuate alternative prophecies of how men ought—and ought not—to act; and to make these insinuations at a level of character deep enough to help transform a culture. Plato was the first to acknowledge the seriousness and power of art in the transformation of character and society. Wilde denied this penultimate power only when he was in the public dock; there he defended the purity of art in a vain effort to save his life from the vengeance of philistines. But the philistines, who had him cornered, knew almost as well as he the power of art and its differences from entertainment. As entertainer, Wilde threatened nothing; only as an artist was he a threat to established culture. There is pathos in the separation of Wilde's talent as an entertainer from his genius as an artist; that genius appeared more in his life and essays than in his plays. He was a relentless performer, intent mainly upon himself and the impression he made. It was only upon those who knew him that Wilde made his greatest impression. We who come long after his performances are left with his supreme talent as an entertainer. But there is that other side of Wilde: his subversiveness as an artist.

A culture survives the assault of sheer possibility against it only so far as the members of a culture learn, through their membership, how to narrow the range of choices otherwise open. Safely inside their culture — more precisely, the culture safely inside them — members of it are disposed to enact only certain possibilities of behaviour while refusing even to dream of others. It is culture, deeply installed as authority, that generates depth of character; indeed, 'depth' is an edifying word for the learned capacity of rejection and acceptance. Members of the same culture can expect each other to behave in certain ways and not in others.

As culture sinks into the psyche and becomes character, what Wilde prized above all else is constrained: individuality. A culture in crisis favours the growth of individuality; deep down things no longer weigh so heavily to slow the surface play of experience. Hypothetically, if a culture could grow to full crisis, then everything could be expressed and nothing would be true. To prevent the expression of everything: that is the irreducible function of culture. By the creation of opposing values[3] — of ideals, of militant truths — a seal is fastened upon the terrific capacity of man to express everything.

Priesthoods preside over the origins of a culture and guard its character. If they did not preside, then a culture could be established without the mixed blessing of authority. A priest is whoever guides men by teaching them truths, or ideals. Sociologically, a truth is whatever militates against the human capacity to express everything. Repression is truth. God is not love, except as he is authority. When Wilde declared himself against authority, he did not know how he weakened what he was for: love. Authority will not be separated from love. To be

---

[3] 'Values': whenever I hear the word, I reach for my pillow. It is a poor, misleading word and belongs to a marketing culture. In order not to expand the argument with my search for a better word, I beg leave to use 'values' sparingly in this essay.

for love and against authority is a paradox upon which no institution, socialist or otherwise, can be built.

Wilde tells a different story. In a culture without authority — Wilde called it 'socialist' — the artist would teach each man, even the least talented, how to become more like himself. Freed by technology from labour, and by socialism from bondage to private property, each man would become what he can be: an individual, enjoying his own life, not degraded by poverty, not absorbed by possession. Imagine: not an art which has become popular, but a populace become artistic. We would entertain ourselves; self-entertainment is the final human autonomy.

> Is this Utopian? A map of the world that does not include Utopia is not worth even glancing at, for it leaves out the one country at which Humanity is always landing. And when Humanity lands there, it looks out, and, seeing a better country, sets sail. Progress is the realization of Utopias.[4]

We will have to tease out this new kind of prophet, the artist as every man who would inhabit Wilde's Utopia — until he spies a better country.

Certainly, the new prophet will be more witty and less serious than any who came before him. This is not a small point towards the understanding of Oscar Wilde. The artist is he who can take all God-terms lightly. Because Wilde's new prophet possesses the comic spirit, he is self-possessed — as no other man has been before him. The alternative to self-possession is to be possessed by some God-term.

By 'God-terms' I mean values that forbid certain actions and thereby encourage others. 'God-terms' express those significant inhibitions that characterize us all within a culture. They are compelling truths. To take God-terms unseriously, while admitting their existence, seemed to Wilde the main, saving 'pagan idea'. Wilde put himself entirely on the side of the pagans, against Jerusalem, because he knew that the terms in which our particular God was conceived could exist only so long as they limited the capacity of man to express everything;

[4] Oscar Wilde, *The Soul of Man Under Socialism and Other Essays* (New York: Harper Colophon), p. 246.

the 'pagan idea' was treated, in the nineteenth century by a small group of supremely talented European minds, as the refusal of this limit.

That Wilde had a most inaccurate notion of any actually pagan idea is beside the point. Like others gifted with revolutionary imaginations, Wilde meant by 'pagan' some ideas that lie considered would release men from their impoverishing inhibitions. To believe that man is the supreme being for man — supreme even over those primordial powers to which real pagans submitted — this is a subversive idea of modernity without precedent in any 'pagan' culture. Like Marx, or Nietzsche, Wilde is a very modern man. What characterizes modernity, I think, is just this idea that men need not submit to any power — higher or lower — other than their own. It is in this sense that modern men really believe they are becoming gods. This belief is the exact reverse of the truth; modern men are becoming antigods. Because, as I have said earlier, the terms in which our God was conceived can exist only so long as they limit the capacity of man to express everything, our old God was never so uninhibited as young man. Our God was bound, after all, by the terms of various covenants.

Thus, we can imagine all too easily Wilde's parody priesthood of de-inhibitors pitted against the repressive elites left over from the God-terms and institutions of the past. In Wilde's time, the struggle was still unequal; and Wilde himself has been considered a martyr in the struggle. That martyrdom, the trials and jail sentence, was due less to the repressive elite of English culture, which was more than willing not to have its hand forced, than to Wilde's own imperfect artistry. He intruded deeply into a struggle of son against father — Bosie Douglas against the Marquess of Queensberry — without realizing what it was about. More important, Wilde may have been led into the fatal step of prosecuting Queensberry for slander (the Marquess was naive enough at first to accuse Wilde merely of posing as a homosexual with his son) by his own sense of guilt. A more perfect artist of life should have been able to shatter the connection between guilt and culture. But the repressive culture was still sufficiently alive inside Wilde, I think, to destroy him when he blundered into a direct confrontation with its official inhibitions. Wilde lost his personal battle, in 1895, the moment he went to court against his own knowledge (not admitted to his lawyers) that he was a practicing homosexual. That battle lost, Wilde's side appears now to be winning the war, even in the courts.

* * *

In the history of Western culture, churchmen have played the leading role of pastoral guide. By Wilde's year of success and wreck, 1895, all except the obtuse understood that the clergy had lost whatever sense of direction they once may have had. The office of guide, the most important in any culture, was vacant. Why should not literary men, artists, scientists try to step in? Wilde commended this seizure of moral power. Such a seizure was in no way bizarre or out of the question; the modern political struggle appears to urban sophisticates an enlargement of their own personal struggles over distributions of the privileges amid deprivations that determine differences of style.

Of course, at the turn of the century, many churchmen were still unaware of their default. Ibsen's Pastor Manders is an immortal characterization of a guide upon whom it never dawns that he has nothing to say. Mrs Alving twice appealed to him as her figure of authority only because her own conversion to the art of life is bookish, a matter of idle chatter; deep down she still submits to the old authorities. Oswald is doomed by the fact that he is her son, the child of a destructively fictionalized past. The culture that Ibsen denounces so heavily, and that Wilde dismisses so wittily, must be called neurotic. But Wilde, and his circle, are products of that very culture. They are examples of posh bohemia, deviant entertainers whose subversive attitudes can be at once supported and denounced by the philistines in imperial cities. Posh bohemians become a pseudo-elite, easy to sacrifice and replace if they go too far out of line and forget that they are not really heralds of a new culture but entertainers of a society in search of kicks.

What has changed since Wilde's time? First, the artist has become a popular type, reproduced now in massive numbers among the young in Western societies. Second, the philistines are less self-confident and more easily persuaded that the bohemian life-style is something more than shocking enter-

tainment, exhibitions intended chiefly for their embarrassed
pleasure. The philistines can now read *The Soul of Man Under
Socialism* more sympathetically than in Wilde's time. Even so,
he remains the kind of figure who attracts philistine hostility
precisely by asserting a near relation between artistic genius
and deviancy.

Not only respectable philistines feel hostility to those who
challenge their established sense of limit, particularly on the
range of allowable deviancy. Prostitutes danced outside the
Old Bailey and lifted their skirts in mock salutes, when Wilde
was convicted. Were they mocking Wilde alone? The respectable philistine prosecutors of Wilde might well avert their
eyes; they too were being mocked, I think, for reaching up to
the talent of their own most celebrated entertainer and
destroying him for a deviancy he had kept quite private.[5]

A culture in control needs first of all to preserve that control
by not reaching its legal arms too far into the labyrinths of private life. The guardians of any culture must constantly protect
the difference between the public and private sectors—and
encourage forms of translation between the two sectors; that is
the meaning of ritual in all traditional cultures. Wilde never
advocated his private deviancy through his public art, as is
done nowadays. On the contrary, stage Bunburying masks
and transforms very different home truths. Wilde dealt bril-
liantly with the relations between art, lying and truth (see his
duologues on 'The Decay of Lying'). It is the stage honesty of
his successors that makes them failed artists. Their failure to
realize the superiority of stage Bunburying, in all its forms, is a
subversion of art itself and inadmissable in any culture. By
their failure to respect the rights of privacy and its sovereign
deceits, respectable philistines have played into the hands of
the new revolutionaries who, unlike Wilde, use honesty to
oppose culture itself. For the very life of every culture
depends upon its powers to mask and transform private
motive into something very different, even opposite, when it
appears in public. In this sense, art, including Wilde's art,

[5] Wilde was punishable under a Bill that almost casually included a section
which created as a new offence indecencies between male persons in public
or private. The clause making deviant behavior in private an offence had
become law only in 1886.

ought to function as an equivalent in modern culture of our lost opposing values. Art should be expressive and repressive at the same time. This, after all, is what is meant by sublimation.

In Wilde's time, as a side effect of their humourless insistence upon honesty, the philistines (this was what Wilde called the great propertied public) had created a high-mindedness that they mistook for culture. In this kind of culture, with the space between public and private sectors of feeling too narrow, anything of beauty was likely to give its viewer a case of what Wilde once called the 'Protestant jumps'.[6] Early in his life, Wilde determined to escape high-mindedness. The philistines, even those who called themselves socialists and engaged in good works,[7] were his natural enemies. The one difficulty with this ethic of escape is that it has become so easy; it can be achieved without the slightest talent. To be an escape artist without talent contradicts the meaning of art, installs things that are ugly as equal with anything beautiful and smashes up those structures of conformity from which alone art can emerge. This helps us understand why all those failed artists among the contemporary culture revolutionaries shout as one of their favourite words, 'Smash'. On walls everywhere in Western societies, graffiti invite us to smash this and smash that—solemn calls to an iconoclasm undignified by the slightest hint of alternative achievements of public meaning. Our young revolutionaries might learn from Wilde the real worth of wit. His genius lay in doing away with both the solemnity and incipient violence of serious argument. What should a free man, an artist, do when he is arguing against authority as such? Wilde's wit and good humour, his style, are the essence, not the ornament, of his case.

Under the needling of such wit, under those comic revelations of the Tartuffery of ideals that come from the best writers of the nineteenth century—Marx, Freud, Nietzsche, Wilde among the more strictly literary—we moderns have fled all

---

[6] *The Letters of Oscar Wilde*, edited by Rupert Hart-Davis (New York: Harcourt, Brace and World, 1962), p. 30.

[7] The highest-minded socialists have also been philistines; the Webbs, and other fighters for humanity in the abstract, come most easily to mind.

militant ideal conceptions of our own character; those conceptions once supplied bridges between the private and public
sectors of our experience, without abolishing the difference.
On the contrary, a bridge of militant ideals functioned to
establish and maintain the difference between what is private
and what public, although the price was certain necessary tensions, now variously called 'guilt', 'alienation' and other current curse words. Against those separations of public and
private, installed inside ourselves as our good name, we once
learned to fear even the faintest dispraise and willingly put up
with a diet of admonitions as our earliest form of moral nurture. Personality was identified with an idealized image of
itself.[8] Wilde was an early modern opponent of militant ideal
conceptions of the self, despite the fact that by such conceptions the private and public sectors of experience are kept discrete and in order, the one a transformation of the other. That
order cannot be established, as art or society, if no dialectic of
translation occurs between private motive and public experience. Without thereby eliminating what is an eternally renew-
able difference between culture and morality, the point at
which they meet and become inseparable is wherever a transformation of private motive occurs. A culture that does not
moralize is no culture at all.

Militant ideals are not another name for public poses; if they
are that, then they become the outward and visible signs of
some private hell. A transformation forbids what would otherwise be allowed. A deceit, so far as the joke is not on the
deceiver, allows precisely what it would forbid. Tartuffe was a
poseur, immediately comic, at least to maidservants and theatre audiences. But not all poses are comic. Kurtz, for example,
made 'civilization' mean 'exterminate the brutes'. The best
way to read every cultural translation is backwards, from public experience to private motive. Thus read — backwards — too
many translations evoke laughter, if only in order to avoid
tears. Wilde chose laughter. As a guide, his artist is deliber-

---

[8] In contrast, modern children are often educated early in a rejection of
authority and hear little about themselves except praise. At the same time,
militant ideal conceptions of character are mocked as injurious to the
creative potential of the child. This revolution in childrearing has occurred
mainly among the educated classes in Western societies.

ately intended to suspend belief; he must ensure his own harmlessness.

To emphasize the harmlessness of the new man, Wilde shifted from the artist to the more traditional image of the child. In his greatest essay, *The Soul of Man Under Socialism*, Wilde offers for our guidance both the artist and the child.

> It will be a marvellous thing — the true personality of man — when we see it. It will grow naturally and simply, flower-like, or as a tree grows. It will not be at discord. It will never argue or dispute. It will not prove things. It will know everything. And yet it will not busy itself about knowledge. It will have wisdom. Its value will not be measured by material things. It will have nothing. And yet it will have everything, and whatever one takes from it, it will still have, so rich will it be. It will not be always meddling with others, or asking them to be like itself. It will love them because they will be different. And yet while it will not meddle with others, it will help all, as a beautiful thing helps us, by being what it is. The personality of man will be very wonderful. It will be as wonderful as the personality of a child.[9]

This is one of Wilde's more sentimental passages. Nothing in it hints how human personality can stabilize its ambivalences except by installing oppositional ideals. Wilde's sentimentality derives from the ancient logic of so-called antinomian thought: if nothing is prohibited, then there will be no transgressions. But in point of psychiatric and historical fact it is *no*, rather than *yes*, upon which all culture and inner development of character depend. Ambivalence will not, I think, be eliminated; it can only be controlled and exploited. Ideal self-conceptions, militant truths, are modes of control. Character is the restrictive shaping of possibility. What Wilde called 'personality' represents a dissolution of restrictive shapings. In such freedom grown men would act less like cherubic children than like demons, for they would disrupt the restrictive order of character and social life.

---

[9] Wilde, *The Soul of Man Under Socialism*.

Anyone who so disrupts a restrictive order is performing a demonic function. Just such disruptions seemed to Wilde the mission of the artist. The main, sociological question is never whether such disruptions occur but only whether they occur in the public or private sector of behaviour. Wilde understood this difference between public and private disruption; we must understand the difference between public and private therapies — and, moreover, understand the dynamics by which every powerful private therapy tends to become public. In public the art of Bunburying meant one thing: in private it meant quite another.[10] Like any pastoral guide, the artist is a bridge between the private and public sectors of a culture. Therefore, by Wilde's implicit argument, the artist becomes a dangerous and necessary figure — dangerous because he disrupts the established order by casting doubt upon it, necessary because through such doubt progress occurs towards another mode of expressiveness.

We are now better placed to understand the precision of Wilde's wittiest and most famous interpretation of himself. André Gide had asked him how it happened that Wilde had failed to put the best of himself into his plays. Wilde replied: 'Would you like to know the great drama of my life? It is that I have put my genius into my life — I have put only my talent into my works.' Wilde understood that in the established society this was an inversion of the energies appropriate to the private and public sectors. In our culture, any man who exercises a genius for intimacy is bound to find it becoming public and therefore scandalous; he may be rewarded by public martyrdom. If some rare individual should be cursed with genius, then the safe course, in any society, is to put that genius into work, while reserving his talent, which can reassure friends and entertain associates, for living. So Kierkegaard arranged his life, after all, in the critical case of his genius versus Regine. In this way are preserved the sacred distances between desires and their objects. Ordinary men will rarely tolerate, except occasionally in politicians or prophets, a steady confusion of

---

[10] Just as in public the word 'artist' might mean one thing and in certain private circles another. In one of Wilde's circles, the word 'artist' also meant homosexual; 'renter' was yet another term Wilde used with the same meaning.

the public and private spheres. Yet it is precisely men who aspire to confuse the public and private sectors, putting genius into their lives, that become putative guides towards a different way of life. Following Weber (but with Freud's help) we now title such men 'Charismatics'. This merely argues the uncharitable character of charismatics, for they will not leave people alone in their privacies. Western society is again crawling with would-be charismatics; and they have a readymade audience. With all their experience of default among candidates for the office, ordinary men still crave guides for their conduct and not merely guiding principles. Abstractions will never do. God-terms have to be exemplified in order to be taught; or, at least, vital examples must be pointed to and a sense of indebtedness (which is the same as guilt) encouraged towards the imitation of these examples. Men crave their principles incarnate in enactable characters, actual selective mediators between themselves and the polytheism of experience.

Until recently it seemed true that without imitations of compelling characters *character* itself could not develop. Morality abhors impersonality. In this sense, so far as science develops through a transfer of truths impersonally, there can be no such cultural phenomenon as a scientific morality. In science, a truth ceases to be ideal and militant. Wilde had some premonitions of the dissolving effect of science upon culture and, as an artist, declared the amity of art and science — and both with socialism. Only under this triumvirate — art, science and socialism — could the New Man exist as anything more than an occasional rebel sport of the world as it is. But under the triumvirate of art, science and socialism Wilde looked forward, with a messianic smile, to a culture of many truths, none of them set up as ideal and none militant. In this way, authority as such — not merely this or that authority — would be defeated.

There are counter arguments. What Wilde dismissed as mere imitation of authority, as well as authority itself, may turn out to be the one way necessary to decide questions of internal development; culture must always come to each man with certain claims ready-made, to set deep within him answers that can prevent disorganizing questions from arising. To conceive of an individualism that 'does not come to a man with any claims upon him at all' destroys the established meaning of culture. Wilde could accept this destruction because he conceived of authority as completely external, like the cross he had heard of being carried through the streets of Jerusalem by some madman imitating Jesus. That madman seemed to Wilde to be acting out all 'lives that are marred by imitation'.

Wilde's attack on all authority is too easy. When authority becomes so external, then it has ceased to be authoritative. The heaviest crosses are internal, and men make them so, so that, thus skeletally supported, they can bear the burden of themselves. Under the sign of this inner cross, a certain inner distance is achieved from the infantile desire to be and have everything. Identification is a far more compelling concept of authority and includes imitation. True individuality must involve the capacity to say no, and this capacity is inseparable from the genesis of no in authority. A man can only resist the polytheism of experience if his character is anchored deeply enough by certain God-terms to resist shuttling endlessly among all.

Wilde uses the traditional, God-term-determined rhetoric of the inner life against the inner life itself. The logic of Wilde's opposition to all authority depends upon his prototype of a new prophet, the artist. He imagined himself and others, each with his sovereign calm, self-centred, submitting only to the authority of experience — never predisposed by the experience of authority. By the grace of his opposition to militant truths Wilde helped lead an aesthetic movement away from the dominance of inwardness and towards an externalization that works against all our received conceptions of character. The genius of modernity is in Wilde's cleverness. That genius is only now being caricatured by a culture which produces revolutionaries who are less oppressed proletarians than failed artists.

The history of the struggle to fill the vacant office of guide to what men may not and may do has taken a remarkable turn. There are powerful movements which proclaim some version or other of the doctrine that the new guiding character must make his presence felt only in order to abolish himself. By virtue of his essays Wilde belongs in the pantheon of this movement.

Of course, there are larger figures in the pantheon. But they are faced in the same direction. Nietzsche's future philosopher, as a humourist, is not far from Wilde's artist. The New Man for whom Marx was so impatient, and without whom the revolutionary process that he found in the hands of the unprincipled bourgeois could not be complete, is another near relation to Wilde's artist. Freud made a different and more cautious case in the character of the therapist, who is inseparable from his theory. I shall review the Freudian case briefly, for the background lighting it casts upon the Wildean case of the artist as our New Man.

For Freud, the power of decision over the internal redevelopment of a crippled, or arrested, individuality could be acquired, or extended, in that last phase of therapeutic suffering which constitutes the psychoanalytic relation. In correct Freudian time, after necessarily protracted resistances against his own opportunities, a patient should become able to seize on the opportunity presented by the fact that the sources of his suffering are evaginated. Those sources are uncovered precisely in the patient's relation to the analyst. In the resolution of the transference, certain internal guides lose their authority and the patient therefore becomes that much freer to be his own guide. The analyst played a virtually silent critic without whom a patient could not recreate his own character, at last to say something on his own behalf. Psychoanalysis may be viewed as much a branch of moral letters made over into a unique process of therapy as it was of medicine.

But, with all his interest in the relation between case and collectivity, Freud never made therapy a model for culture. On the contrary, therapy can be understood as the model for anticulture. Precisely here is the tension between Freudian therapy and his theory of culture, of which authority, incarnate in character, is a necessary part. Freud never dreamed that his genius would be used to assert a culture in which there would be no figures of authority against whom youth could react and thus achieve their own sense of the limits that define any truly human existence. Such a dream, if he had it, would batter against Freud's own colossal creation of himself as a figure of authority locked in immortal combat against his final rival, Moses.

Wilde shared with the other most sensitive spirits of the late nineteenth century what is now public knowledge: that whatever makes authority incarnate in our culture is no longer available to it. No creed, no ramifying symbolic of militant truths, is installed deeply enough now to help men constrain their capacity for expressing everything. Wilde understood that internalizations from an earlier period in our moral history no longer held good. Western men were sick precisely of those interior ideals which had shaped their characters. The New Man has no choice except to try and become a free character. Viewed from within any among the precedent cultures of commitment, the character of the New Man must be anti-credal. Wilde's artist is another version of the anti-credal character around whom other, more notable heralds of the future have announced their designs. No less than Marx's New Man, Wilde's artist is anti-credal because he too is conceived to live free from ideals. All the most important revolutionary movements of our culture, including the Marxist, represent various strategies of attack upon the inwardness of the Western character. They are efforts to evaginate those militant truths, functioning mainly as inhibitions, around which men learn to negotiate their elaborate dodges towards pleasure. Freud, Marx, Nietzsche, Wilde: these are some of the chief evangels associated with new ways towards the realization of self.[11]

A new way has to be shown, at least until laities are so practical in it that they can find the way for themselves. But contemporary culture is in such a turmoil of new ways that none of them can show to advantage. The field is too crowded. Even more in the era of anti-creeds than of creeds, prophecy and deviant performance have become closely related and lucrative arts. Where individualism is so highly prized, charisma can be reproduced cheaply and becomes a highly profitable product. Wilde reckoned that, until the advent of socialism, full expressive individuality could occur only 'on the imaginative plane of art'. He reckoned without the cultural effect of

---

[11] New ways, in order to appeal the more readily, can be supported by intimations from an ambivalently rejected past. Wilde considered Jesus as a forerunner, rather as Marx considered the utopian socialists. This branch of literature once came under the rubic 'apologetics'.

the mass media — and without an alliance of art with the most philistine commercialism. Bohemia is more posh than ever, and more inclusive, in a society that will buy everything. The revolutionary arts are now mass entertainments.

By standing the artist 'outside his subject', Wilde tried to make the artist revolutionary in a less easily corrupted manner. Such a lack of identification with his subject implies that the artist is a very special kind of personality. In Wilde's conception, the dissent of the artist becomes a kind of deviance. It is because he is detached from his subject that the artist can be trusted to defy authority. Such a mistaken conception of the relation between dissent and deviance permitted Wilde to indulge in some very sentimental writing, about criminals as well as artists. It helped him locate the revolutionary animus in psychological rather than social relations.

This is not to dismiss all thought on the psychological origins of revolution. The animus of all revolution may well be summed up in one passage from Marx, where he invokes that 'revolutionary daring which throws at its adversary the defiant phrase: "I am nothing and I should be everything" '. No phrase could be more defiant, and none could better express the infantile unconscious — if the infantile unconscious could express itself. But animus is not action. The artist who stands outside his subject is himself a subject. He is neither nothing nor everything, but, like all other men, a significant something. Culture is a tremendous articulation of compromise between equally intolerable feelings of nothing and everything.

The claim of the artist to express everything is subversive in one especially acute sense: the claim to express everything can only exacerbate feelings of being nothing. In such a mood, all limits begin to feel like humiliations. Wilde did not know that he was prophesying a hideous new anger in modern men, one that will render unexcited, peaceable existence even more utopian than before.

To criticize Wilde's prophecy of the soul of man under socialism is not to defend a dying culture. Indeed, men who aspire to express everything can exist only in a culture grown so superficial that it can no longer perform its proper preventative functions. A culture that penetrates deeper into the interior, creating its own interior space rather than growing ever more disposable, is not made to order. Professors do not renew a culture. The sources of renewal are no less irrational than the sources of revolutionary death sentences against it. We can only wait and see which character will dominate the future: the credal or anti-credal.

Wilde would have had the future liberate itself from the authority of the past. But, in the absence of sustaining opposition from its credal parent, the anti-credal character compounds for its own defeat, as Wilde's did; that character, instinct in his and all comic art, proved tragic to the life.

Near the end of his life, Wilde reaffirmed its aesthetic justification: 'Whatever is realized is right'. His homosexual realizations had a pyrrhic air about them. From the affair with Lord Alfred Douglas rose a miasma of ugliness. Wilde's laudations of the paederastic glory that was Greece, its pedagogic eros, bore little upon his relations to homosexual prostitutes. His feastings with those 'panthers', as he called them, appear to have been nothing like Plato's *Symposium*, in which he must have read, expertly in the original: 'diseases of all sorts spring from the excesses and disorders of the elements of love'.

On his own report, Wilde's homosexual affairs were lowering. Low life mocked high art. Wilde transgressed in life against the one god-term, Beauty, to which he would have remained faithful. We Pharisees of culture know the world is justified neither morally nor aesthetically. Yet we need trouble no more than Wilde about Leviticus 18:22, or any other of those sacred commands to disobedience from which we may acquire our own compassionate understandings of faithlessness. Wilde's homosexuality is condemned by his own aesthetic, which he took too seriously, as if it were his true religion.

In his great confession, *De Profundis*, Wilde almost realized what had 'lured' him from the 'beautiful unreal world of Art...into the imperfect world of coarse uncompleted passions, of appetite without distinction, desire without limit, and formless greed'. His aesthetic justifications of life scarcely survive their translations into life.

Asked how he endured prison, Wilde's riposte plunged deeper than any other he ever delivered: 'I was buoyed up with a sense of guilt'. That sense true, it is more spiritual than legal; it is more trustworthy than ego; it is more profound than reason. If shallowness is the supreme vice, as Wilde believed, then his true guilt began in the clever insolence of his approach to art as if it were supreme reality. The most insolent and contemporary of cleverities must follow: an approach to life as if it were an endless choice of styles; modes of fiction contrived by any with wit enough and will for such contrivances.

Tragedy reminds us that true condemnations of the self cannot be pronounced by the self alone. I shall end by quoting two sentences that may be taken to constitute Wilde's verdict upon his life as a work of art. Taken one after the other, they show a movement inevitable as that in a tragedy.

> What the paradox was to me in the sphere of thought, perversity became to me in the sphere of passion.

> Everything to be true must become a religion.
> (70: 1b)

Endnote

† Edward Henry Carson, QC (1863–1928), later Lord Carson. Carson had been Wilde's contemporary at Trinity College, Dublin, in the '70s and probably shared a general reluctance to take Queensbury's defence. The case taken, he attacked, through Wilde's art, the doctrine of life celebrated in that art.

All three trials of Oscar Wilde were of a man who 'stood in symbolic relations to the art and culture of my age'. Knowing himself to be a 'symbolic figure', always on stage in a life representing the art of brilliant comedy, Wilde rightly took as the vital issue his justification of life as an aesthetic, rather than moral, phenomenon.

Edward Carson too was a symbolic figure. The philistine barrister represented life justified as a moral phenomenon. With the instinct of a great advocate, Carson took aim at Wilde's artistic acceptance of all experiences. That acceptance required a tone of subtlety and nuance, a nobility of manner that would limit the danger of moving in strange perspectives. The tone of Wilde's homosexual affairs, not least with Queensberry's son, Lord Alfred Douglas, appears ignoble. Lord Alfred was a bad actor and made ugly scenes. In the Bosie affair Wilde found no brilliant comedy; rather, 'a revolting and sinister tragedy...stripped of that mask of joy and pleasure' behind which he saw, too late, the horror of that carnality we, with him, have learned to call 'hatred'.

Through Carson's questions we may see represented articulate old suspicions of the truth of masks that have all but lost their voice in our culture. Carson stood square for those external sanctions and sacred commands that Wilde would not admit: unadmitted even as necessary fictions of limit upon his search for modes of 'self-realization' so fresh that they aspired to self-creation. For all his cold questioning, the victorious philistine kept a merciful sense of fair play. 'Cannot you let up on the fellow now?' Carson asked Sir Frank Lockwood, the Solicitor-General. 'He has suffered a great deal.'

So far as he realized himself in the Wilde affair, Lord Alfred Douglas, too, rises to the rank of a symbol. It was from this nemesis that Wilde suffered the hatred of father figures complicit in 'the love that dare not speak its name'.

Suppose Wilde's love life, with both sexes, exemplified a law in which this self-proclaimed 'born antinomian' believed: the enlightened modern law of continuity, rather than opposition, between evil and good. Then might 'all men kill the thing they love'. It was under this profanation of 'thou shalt not kill' that Wilde became the victim of his lover and, in turn, Constance Wilde became his victim.

Acknowledgements

This article first appeared in *Salmagundi* 58-59 (Autumn 1982–Winter 1983): 406-26.

Robert Brustein

When Political Correctness Becomes Dumbocracy

O ver 150 years ago, Alexis de Tocqueville wrote in his study of Democracy in America:

> I do not believe that it is a necessary effect of a democratic social condition and of democratic institutions to diminish the number of those who cultivate the fine arts, but these causes exert a powerful influence on the manner in which these arts are cultivated...The productions of artists are more numerous, but the merit of each production is diminished...In aristocracies, a few great pictures are produced; in democratic countries a vast number of insignificant ones.

These Delphic notations, inscribed after a visit to America in the early years of the Republic by a foreigner who is still among the most prophetic commentators on American life, in effect defined the problems that serious or high culture would henceforth encounter in an increasingly massified and industrialized society. What Tocqueville prophesied was that among the things a political democracy might have to sacrifice to egalitarian needs would be a civilization of real importance. American culture, in his view, would become flooded with insignificant forms of expression, genuine works of art being rare and often unacknowledged, and artistic standards would be determined not by the intrinsic quality of the art but rather by the intrinsic size of the audience. Put another way, the evolution of American culture would be based on a continuing tension, and later on a state of hostility, between the minority

expression called high art—subscribed to by a decreasing
number of 'fastidious consumers'—and what constituted the
culture of the masses.

Tocqueville, though an aristocrat himself, was highly partial to the new political experiment being tested in the US. But
he yearned for a system that could join a democratic politics
with a meritocratic culture. He correctly saw that, without
access to the civilizing influence of great artworks, the voting
majority in this country was bound to remain benighted. Only
art and education could provide the synthesis needed to
evolve a more enlightened and cultivated electorate. There
were times when this synthesis looked achievable. In the nineteenth century, certainly, high art and popular culture seemed
to coexist in healthy if often separate compartments. Not only
were Hawthorne and Emerson traded in the same bookstalls
as penny dreadfuls but travelling troupes performed Shakespeare, albeit in bowdlerized form, attracting wildly enthusiastic audiences from the most primitive frontiers (so indeed
did Oscar Wilde on his famous lecture tour across America).

Even in our more embattled century, high art and popular
culture managed to enjoy a brief honeymoon. Certainly serious American artists in the first half of this century drew great
infusions of energy from indigenous American forms, as did
their counterparts in Europe. Of course the channels of
exchange have flowed the other way as well. Neither fashion
nor advertising would have produced many original ideas
had they not been able to loot the iconography of high art. No
sooner does a visual artist emerge in America than his or her
advances are instantly appropriated by Madison and Seventh
Avenues. Similarly the history of the movies would have been
sadly different had studios not been in a position to feed off
contemporary literature and theatre; and popular music
would have been similarly impoverished had it not been able
to feed off jazz. So intimate were the relations between high
and popular culture, in fact, that it was sometimes difficult to
determine whether an artist like Andy Warhol belonged more
to bohemia or suburbia, whether his true home was the Factory or the creative department of a fashionable advertising
firm. Similarly such respected figures as F. Scott Fitzgerald,
William Faulkner, Nathanael West, among many other American writers—not to mention expatriate Europeans such as

Bertolt Brecht and Aldous Huxley—spent almost as much time huddling in script conferences in Hollywood as bending over their writing desks.

The interdependence of popular and high art in America had both positive and negative effects. One obvious advantage was economic. The commercial system subsidized a lot of needy artists whose customary royalties would have been too meagre to pay for their typewriter ribbons. It is true that the same system often distracted these artists from their legitimate work, though not so much as commonly assumed. Fitzgerald wasted his time writing third-rate movies like Winter Carnival, but his motion picture studio experience also inspired a fine if unfinished Hollywood novel, *The Last Tycoon.* It can be argued that working with such popular forms as the detective novel, science fiction and film noir screenplays provided a stream of energy that kept high culture hard-boiled, vigorous and vital. Still, the relationship between the artist and the commodity culture was always uneasy and it soon began to curdle, partly through the efforts of a number of highbrow intellectuals who regarded the participating artist as a sellout or, worse, a collaborator in a mass art that was leaving a brutalizing imprint on American minds.

The fear that popular culture would absorb high art had always worried social commentators, from Tocqueville on. But that fear intensified during the culture wars of the '50s. Then, such crusading highbrows as Dwight Macdonald began protesting the power of 'Masscult' and 'Midcult' to debase and overshadow 'High Cult' (note how even Macdonald's terms were infected by the mass media, reflecting the glib clipped style of *Time* magazine where, along with other intellectuals like James Agee, he made his living). At the same time increasingly vocal opponents of the highbrows, usually representing the supposedly 'value-free' social sciences, were defending middle and mass culture as more democratic; and more democratic it was, if you measured culture by statistical instead of qualitative criteria—namely the incidence and popularity of the commodities consumed by the mass public.

To be sure, a democratic art was always the dream of great poets like Walt Whitman. But it was somehow easier for a nineteenth-century artist to imagine 'Democratic Vistas' without relinquishing his belief in artistic standards. That balance is more difficult today. The culture wars of the '50s, raging in such periodicals as *Partisan Review* and *Commentary*, not only planted wedges between high, middle and popular culture, it also resulted in a hostile backlash against serious art and the critical intellect.

This eventually spread to include the whole construct of Eurocentric civilization and its 'dead white male' artists and intellectuals, as they are now scornfully identified. We had entered a time when competing special-interest groups were beginning to clamour for recognition of their own forms of cultural expression, often identifying both traditional and avant-garde art as 'elitist' (the populist epithet that was henceforth to control the terms of this debate). The charge of 'elitism' was hurled not only against the wealthy consumers of art but also against its often penniless creators, thus confusing patronage with talent, class with taste, economic status with artistic vision. You were 'elitist' if you created works of art and you were 'elitist' if you bought them. Love of art was perceived in some quarters as equivalent to being indifferent to suffering, inequality and injustice. No wonder so few people were willing to come to the defence of elitism.

These implications of callousness (and, more specifically, of racism) caused a major retreat—the surrender of many of the standards and values that make a serious culture possible. I do not mean to suggest that inspired artists are no longer able to function in America, but rather that what was once a hospitable climate for their work has turned mean and indifferent. Native talent may be as abundant as ever, but never in memory has it been so inadequately evaluated, published, produced, disseminated and supported.

Although the ongoing war on culture originally had economic causes related to the recession, its thrust has now become mainly political. Forces opposing the high arts advance by means of a three-pronged incursion—from the right, left and centre of the political spectrum, all claiming endorsement from the majority.

The attack from the right exploded with full force after President Bush appointed John E. Frohnmayer as chairman of the NEA. It was then that controversial grants to Robert Mapplethorpe and Andres Serrano, among others, aroused the fiery wrath of such conservative bullies as North Carolina senator

Jesse Helms, who took the position that the government should not fund any artistic work offensive to the majority. Such was Helms's power that he even persuaded Congress to impose content restrictions on grantees in the form of a new obscenity clause that all applicants were obliged to sign, though a successful class-action suit by Bella Lewitzky temporarily resulted in the provision being struck down as unconstitutional (unfortunately the Supreme Court recently overturned that decision).

The attack from the politically correct left proved just as disturbing in its way as that from the right-wing minions of moral correctness. It is significant that both sides claimed the endorsement of the democratic majority. For the right, this usually meant those clean-cut Americans who celebrate Thanksgiving in Norman Rockwell paintings and sip vanilla sodas in Thornton Wilder plays. For the left, the majority was represented not by churchgoing Anglo-Saxon patriots but rather by those previously excluded from the cultural banquet, a diverse mixture of racial, sexual and ethnic constituencies summed up in the catchwords 'multiculturalism' and 'cultural diversity'.

Now there is no question that intercultural exchange has been a source of great artistic refreshment. Cultural diversity is responsible for much that is vital and original in our culture. Multicultural grants have helped to increase the visibility of deserving minority artists, especially in artistic institutions, which is a highly welcome move. But frequently awards have been made on other than artistic grounds, as if there were different standards for people of different colours, sexes and ethnicities. Such awards are less a form of patronage than of patronization, reflecting not so much a love of art as a passion for social engineering. As H.L. Mencken has written, 'Every third American devotes himself to improving and lifting up his fellow citizens, usually by force; the messianic delusion is our national disease.' Trying to compensate for the failures of society in an area least suited to be an avenue of social change, namely the arts, the cultural bureaucrats began to threaten hard-won achievements for the sake of evangelical gestures.

Ironically, the popular phrase associated with this process, 'political correctness', has recently lost most of its currency, having been bombarded with ridicule from all sides of the political spectrum. These broadsides may have succeeded in destroying political correctness as a phrase, but not as a sentiment. It has resurfaced, more powerful than ever, under the rubrics of 'cultural diversity' and 'multiculturalism' or, to use the White House slogan, 'representing the true face of America'. Whatever you call it, PC in extreme form is dedicated to a programme not unlike that of the unlamented cultural revolution by the Peoples Republic of China—replacing an 'elite' system with a 'populist' agenda through egalitarian levelling. Chairman Mao's little red books now take the form of little black books by a variety of authors—including dictionaries of euphemisms advising us how to identify various members of minority groups without hurting their feelings (pale penis people, namely white males living or dead, are not assumed to have feelings worthy of consideration). Such glossaries may seem ludicrous, but their impact on uninhibited expression can be menacing. Even more threatening is the related effort to proscribe offensive ideas, censor improper books and syllabi, and cleanse the culture of independent thought. In the movie *Invasion of the Body Snatchers*, people possessed by alien forces identify all those still left human by bugging their eyes, pointing their fingers and issuing horrible guttural sounds from their throats. This strikes me as a good description of the way those dissenting from political correctness are now being treated in the arts and humanities.

This crypto-Maoist process is a heritage of the sixties. Many, if not most, of today's PC leaders were active members of the New Left 25 years ago. The radical students who once occupied university buildings over the Vietnam War are now officially occupying university offices as professors, administrators, deans, and even presidents. Having helped to promote increased enrolment by minority students, a desirable goal, they are now responding to the inevitable consequence: increased demands for new departments, beginning with black and women's studies, and then extending to virtually every 'oppressed' minority in the land. Meanwhile, today's students assume the old roles of the newly tenured radicals, using '60s methods to achieve their ends—protests, sit-ins, occupations, shouting down speakers, shutting down universities. At the University of Pennsylvania, for example, a group of black students expropriated an entire run of a student newspaper to protest at a 'racist' article, while at the University of California, Berkeley, Chicano students went on a hunger strike until officials granted their demand for a department of Chicano studies.

Some of these new departments have proved extremely useful additions, opening up interesting new areas of research. Others have been created less to increase knowledge than to increase power and presence. This exposes the most serious consequence of PC in the university, which is the growing politicization of academic life, usually at the cost of scholarship and learning. On the pretext that everything is political and always was, courses are created for no other purpose than to redress past injustice and validate minority claims. It is not surprising that hitherto ignored people should desire more information about their history and culture, not only in order to inform themselves but to educate others. Yet the need to increase self-esteem has developed malignant side effects, leading, for example, to conditions of self-segregation where hard-won advances in civil rights have been vitiated by separate classrooms, exclusive dormitories and sequestered dining facilities.

In this politicized atmosphere, some members of the PC professoriat will not hesitate to use fabricated or skewed research in order to consolidate feelings of racial or gender superiority (the 'sun people–ice people' theory and the current myths about the intellectual influence of 'black' Egypt on Periclean Athens are only two examples). Just as historical fact is manipulated for racial purposes, so the issue of free speech becomes selective. PC professors and students can protest at speakers such as Colin Powell for his position on gays in the military and in the same breath cite the privileges of free expression to defend the campus presence of notorious anti-Semites like Leonard Jeffries. (Some fellow-travelling academics—notably Stanley Fish of Duke University—are even in favour of chucking the First Amendment altogether if it doesn't promote social equality or conform to PC thinking.)

PC restrictions in the field of knowledge are as demoralizing as the insults to truth, history and civil liberties. The multiplication of special studies and special departments has made it possible for minority students not just to be better informed about their own culture, but to go through college without learning about anything else. What Christopher Lasch called 'the culture of narcissism' has now found its politically-approved form. Students learn by looking in a mirror and studying themselves; and what they see has got to be 'positive images' — no example of non-Caucasian brutality, or instance of female misbehavior, is allowed to upset the historical melo-drama of minority victims and white male oppressors. It goes without saying that the university exists not to confirm what you desire to believe or believe already, but to extend the reach of your mind into areas of ignorance. Yet gays want to learn about the virtues of being gay, blacks study their own role models, and women search for instances of gender dis-crimination throughout the history and literature of the West (replacing the witch-hunts of the seventeenth century with twentieth-century warlock hunts).

PC's narcissistic agenda begins early, particularly in the schools. In a number of states, most notably New York, the basic subjects required for advancement in society are being replaced by a 'Rainbow' curriculum more preoccupied with inspiring self-esteem and promoting tolerance than with teaching reading or writing. The time is nigh when eight-year-olds will have more knowledge about Native American totem rituals than about the multiplication tables, and will be better informed about how to apply a condom than about the rules of grammar. In a recent newspaper cartoon, two little girls are walking down the street. One of them says, 'My friend has two mommies,' and the other replies, 'How much is two?' The skills with which young people advance are being smothered in a wash of feel-good civics lessons, as if achievement were produced by self-esteem and not the other way around.

In culture the problem is, if anything, more acute. If there was a time when intellectuals could fight for social justice and high art simultaneously, when it was possible to study both Trotsky and Joyce (or both Marx and Wagner, like Shaw in the British Museum), that time is no more. Today we are being asked to choose, in the belief that 'elite' culture (the dismissive phrase for the entire Western tradition) is simply another instance of white male oppression. 'Multiculturalism' — in its true sense the fertilization of one culture by another — has become a process for promoting exclusive 'life-styles' and endorsing struggles for artistic supremacy.

Culture wars are nothing new. What is novel about 'multi-culturalism' is the effort of its practitioners and publicists to demolish what little remains of high culture in America. Just as rock and hip-hop stations on FM radio often drown out the weaker signals of NPR's classical programming, so the multiculturalists, using a variety of political means and aesthetic arguments, try to drown out the weaker signals of high art. Although this is represented as another form of equal opportunity, popular or mass culture has, by definition, never wanted for audiences or acclaim in America — or money for that matter (popular recording artists are now among the highest paid in the land). The branding of serious art as 'elitist' is simply another power ploy to promote supremacy by hoisting popular culture into the lofty niche formerly reserved for more complicated, profound and discriminating work.

This is being done in a variety of ways, but primarily by trying to demolish our traditional standards and values. Just as all objective academic research is now labelled 'political', a secret means of exalting Western civilization over that of the Third World, so the very idea of 'quality' is assumed to be racist, a conspiratorial method of excluding popular and folk artists from serious consideration. In the multicultural aesthetic all values are relative — only high art is subject to absolute judgment, as a pernicious form of 'Eurocentrism'.

The Clinton administration revealed 'the true face of America' by orchestrating an inaugural entertainment wholly inspired by Hollywood and Tin Pan Alley (even Kathleen Battle was obliged to sing a popular song), by commissioning an inaugural poem by a writer of modest talents, obviously chosen because she was an African-American woman, and by otherwise behaving less like an appointments agency examining qualifications than a casting agency looking for types ('Get me a black female lawyer for the part of Assistant Attorney General!'). The 'true face of America', apparently, is shaped with obsessive attention to colour and gender, and those who fail to use these palettes are stigmatized for racism or sexism even when their works have popular appeal.

Many of the same quota systems and populist demands are now being imposed on the serious arts by the cultural bureaucrats who control their fate. In their humanitarian effort to increase the number of minorities in companies, audiences, board rooms and repertoires, the minions of political correctness have succeeded in imposing personnel restrictions on not-for-profit arts groups very similar to the content restrictions being sanctioned by Jesse Helms and his moral myrmidons. Both have totalitarian implications. Those who do not conform to the required aesthetic cleansing are sent not to labour camps, as in Stalinist Russia, but rather to an economic gulag where they are starved of resources. But the result is similar, and so is the disgusting Orwellian technique known as 'sensitivity training', where people are asked to confess to unconscious racism and brainwashed of any thought diverging from current ideological conformity. It is a pitiful development indeed when some of the very same agencies responsible for the great resurgence of high art in this country between the '60s and the '90s are now preparing the way for its extinction.

Are these politically-correct methods improving the lot of minorities? Yes, I suppose they are to some extent. While the dropout rate among black college students remains inordinately high, the numbers of African-Americans entering the middle class through law, business, education and medicine has increased dramatically. Black, female and Latino artists have also been multiplying, and while many insist their work can only be judged by black, female and Latino critics (more evidence of narcissism), some are impressive by any standards. One hopes, as their number and standing increase, that minority artists will come to be regarded as belonging to a fraternity of creative people rather than to any special class, gender, race or group.

Chekhov once wrote: 'Great writers and thinkers must occupy themselves with politics only in order to put up a defence against politics.' By this, he meant that (1) it was the writer's obligation to contest narrow interpretations of reality, and (2) that art provided one of the best alternatives to what Orwell was later to call 'the smelly little orthodoxies that are nowadays contending for our souls'.

The treatment of minorities in the US, though far from perfect, is as good or better than that of any nation in the world. Yet there is more protest and complaint here than in any nation in the world. You cannot clear your throat without hurting somebody's feelings, or cough without wounding someone's self-esteem. This accounts for the spread of vigilante organizations, not just monitoring hateful actions but vetting speech for evidence of anti-Semitism, sexism, racism, ageism, lookism or homophobia. Are our skins so paper-thin that words and names have such power to inflict lasting damage? I hear Nietzsche's advice ringing in my ears: 'Life is hard to bear, but do not affect to be so sensitive.'

One of the worst side-effects of political correctness is the way it chokes the aesthetic atmosphere. Simply put, it's boring. The politically correct are almost invariably humour-impaired, finding racist or sexual insults even in the most innocuous jokes. The phrases they use to describe these imagined slights eventually have a numbing effect on everybody's senses but are so contagious they become a substitute for thinking. Left-wing scholars and journalists, quick enough to charge other people with racial stereotyping, riddle their own prose with PC clichés. Language is used as a form of incantation by people who respond to any original idea as a dangerous form of deviance.

Finally there is the threat to the high arts from the middle spectrum, more accurately the middlebrow arbiters of culture, the watchdogs who bark at anything not immediately accessible to the middle-class public. With artistic standards being controlled by media critics, many of them incompetent, and publication and production controlled by publishers and producers hypnotized by the bottom line, the possibility of sustaining high culture in our time is becoming increasingly problematical. As more and more material tries to compete for the lucrative middle ground, serious culture becomes an economic and cultural irrelevance. Serious bookstores are losing their franchise; small publishing houses are closing shop; little magazines are going out of business; nonprofit theatres are surviving primarily by commercializing their repertories; symphony orchestras are diluting their programmes; classical radio stations are dwindling; museums are resorting to blockbuster shows; dance is dying. Only opera is increasing its audience.

In the preface to *The Liberal Imagination*, Lionel Trilling quoted Goethe's remark that liberals have no ideas, they only have sentiments. Obviously little has changed in the intervening years. What has changed is the virtual monopoly on ideas by the conservative camp. Trilling had cautioned liberals to take as their motto, 'Lord, enlighten thou my enemies', seeing intelligent opposition as the only way to develop a sensible body of liberal thought. He did not foresee a time when the opposition would dominate thinking while liberals sat impotent, mired in sentiment or paralysed with guilt.

The growing library of books on PC suggests that liberals may at last be awakening from their long slumber. It is incumbent on us now to spur the liberal imagination further before the darker forces in our society initiate a reaction that none of us wants. An important way to start is by recognizing that equality of opportunity is not the same as equality of achievement. We must support and facilitate the entry of minority groups into the mainstream, but not by tolerating comforting lies and debased standards. It is neither racist nor sexist to believe that some individuals are more beautiful than others, some more intelligent, some more brave, and some more talented. It is only racist and sexist if we believe those qualities exist because of (rather than regardless of) race, sex, class or religion. Both the politically correct and their reactionary opponents share that position, the one by denying the past, the other by denying the future.

The incorrigible tendency by right, left and centre to muddle culture and politics has had the result of altering the terms of the cultural debate. The traditional arguments between 'High Cult' and 'Masscult' could not be heard today; serious and popular culture no longer coexist in their separate compartments. The once proud and confident highbrow has fled the field, pursued by a hail of arrows shaped in the form of epithets, while the serious artist finds it harder and harder to resist the pressures of popular taste. Is Tocqueville once again confirmed in his belief that a meritocratic art is not indigenous to a democratic society? He is certainly right that the relationship will always cause tensions. Each age chooses different weapons for its war on the serious arts, but the nature of the war remains the same. What should really worry us is the resolution of that war in the total collapse of high culture. It is not the proper way to celebrate American pluralism. It is not what the Founding Fathers envisioned when they conceived the American Republic. It is not a healthy sign for American democracy.

Anne Glyn-Jones

Sensationalism in Modern Entertainment

Civilizations rise and fall, wax and wane. Historians seek
parallels, debating whether similar dynamics are at
work, and if so what they are. Are they implacable determi-
nants beyond human influence, or can we, by identifying the
forces of change, enable a society to grasp the nettle of its own
decay and 'change the course of history'?

One of those who believed he had unravelled the key to
social change was the Russian social historian Pitirim Sorokin,
expelled by the Bolsheviks from his post at St Petersburg University and permitted, after a sojourn in prison, to go into
exile. He settled ultimately in America, where he founded
Harvard's Department of Sociology. Through the 1920s and
1930s he was, with the aid of numerous researchers in Harvard and Prague Universities, compiling the statistical data on
which his massive four-volume *Social and Cultural Dynamics*
was based. It was published during the Second World War,
and made little impact except among academics, the Western
World having at that time more pressing preoccupations. The
Sociology Departments that began to burgeon in the 1960s
were largely uninterested, being heavily Marxist-orientated,
or concerned with the sort of short-term localized analysis of
immediate social problems (crime, racialism, poverty *etc.*) that
attracted government research grants.

The half century since Sorokin wrote has vindicated his
prophecies and thus gone far to validate his claim to have pin-
pointed the dynamics underlying social change. Post-Marxist
Russia, in particular, is showing an interest in its erstwhile

son, most recently by the convening, in February 1999, of international symposia on Sorokin both in Moscow and in St Petersburg.

Sorokin's analysis stretched from Babylon and the Nile to modern America, taking in the evolution of Europe on the way. He did not examine Indian, Chinese, Latin American or Arab civilizations in any depth, which leaves open the possibility that his thesis has not the universal validity he claimed for it, a contingency that he admitted but considered unlikely. For the civilizations he did examine, he claimed that there was a recurrent pattern.

In 1996 I published my own interpretation of his work, updating his analysis to our own time and limiting my canvas to just four civilizations, Ancient Greece, Ancient Rome, Medieval Christendom, and modern England since the Reformation. Put very briefly, Sorokin treats humanity's search for truth as the bedrock of his theory. What is to be believed, what is to be trusted? What follows from these beliefs? In the early phase of a society, when vulnerable people live in great insecurity, fearing the forces of Nature and feeling themselves dependent for survival on Unseen Powers, they are deeply religious. The transcendent world of the gods is seen as of greater significance than this world. Truth is what is revealed, in dreams and visions, to priests and shamans; it is passed on in ancestral wisdom and enshrined (when the society becomes literate) in sacred texts. The art of such a society is indistinguishable from worship—there is no secular portraiture for instance, only ikons, or symbols; no drama but worshipful rituals. Architectural wealth is concentrated on temples, literature celebrates the deeds of the gods and expounds the conditions on which their continued benevolence depends.

Questing minds, particularly as time and experience produce improved and less threatening living conditions, begin to explore the material world with which we are surrounded and of which we are a part. Philosophers question (as Socrates did) the dictates of authority, and in their search for certitude fasten (as Aristotle did) on the evidence presented to the senses as of paramount validity.

As the best minds turn their attention to the physical, material environment, from theology to what we call 'science' and the classical and medieval peoples called 'natural philosophy' (*i.e.* the study of the natural world), huge dividends are reaped in terms of humanity's capacity to manipulate its environment. By the late fourth century BC, with the translation of mathematical speculation into mechanical engineering, Greeks were experimenting with the five basic constructional tools of wheel, lever, pulley, wedge and screw. By imperial Roman times bridges, dams, piped water (almost universal except in the poorest tenements), glass windows, under-floor heating, mass-produced textiles, domestic utensils and basic foodstuffs such as bread and oil were available, not only in the Roman heartland, but also in benighted northern colonial outposts like Britain.

For a time respect for both material and spiritual realities co-exist. There is loyalty to old beliefs, there are doubts about the reliability of sense-experience as the sole repository of knowledge. Descartes felt impelled to devote a large part of his philosophic treatise to proving the existence of God, for only in the sure confidence of a God who did not set out to deceive, he felt, could we dare have confidence in the evidence apparently present to our so-easily-deluded senses.

But with increasing evidence of the sheer effectiveness of the empirical, materialist approach comes an attitude of mind which not only regards observation and ratiocination as incontrovertible, it feels impelled to dismiss as at best irrelevant, at worst dangerous, all other sources of knowledge (*e.g.* intuition); and not merely to sideline but also to destroy traditional faith. There are a variety of motives, including resentment at the political power structures which traditional religion reinforced; a noble-hearted desire to free humanity from the superstitious terrors inculcated by conventional beliefs (*e.g.* in hell and judgment); and of course in some cases a simple preference for a life untrammelled by moral inhibitions. Whatever the motivation, there comes a time when any conviction not derived from the scientific criteria of observation and quantitative measurement ceases to be regarded as intellectually respectable.

The termination of an ethics based on revelation and authority (such as the Ten Commandments) challenges moral philosophers to produce a substitute ethical code, and they have striven to rise to the challenge. Epicureans and Stoics in the ancient world, Rationalists, Utilitarians, Humanists,

Marxists over the years since the Renaissance have sought to replace Revelation with Reason (the French revolutionaries even re-dedicated Notre Dame to the Goddess of Reason).

For small numbers of educated people the prescriptions of the philosophers have proved adequate, and adherents of rationalist codes of conduct have advocated, for more than 2,000 years, that an intensive programme of education in good citizenship is called for if mass acceptance of altruism and self-discipline is to be achieved. Unfortunately (and Polybius, a Greek historian of the second century BC, is only one of many observers to make the comment), in the absence of religious commitment, exhortation and even indoctrination appear unable to restrain society's more self-destructive impulses. Proposals for amended training in citizenship flood the educational press. Meanwhile, even before the collapse that followed the demise of the Soviet Union, its Marxist Prime Minister was (in 1989) inviting the World Council of Churches to avail itself of *perestroika* to collaborate in stemming the rising tide of crime, alcoholism and hooliganism engulfing the USSR. There is a precedent for such an aspiration — following the rise of Methodism in the eighteenth century, and the nineteenth-century religious revival associated with Evangelicalism and, later, the Oxford Movement, there was a notable improvement of conduct in England, observed in, for instance, diminished drunkenness and domestic violence as well as a reduction in crime in general. Incredibly, crimes of violence actually declined in nineteenth-century England, in spite of population increase—from 1,700+ in mid-century to 1,400+ at the end (the 1997 figure was nearly 350,000).

Late Greece, in particular before the Roman conquest in the second century BC; late Rome, especially in the third and fourth centuries AD; the late Medieval period, particularly the fourteenth century; all show rising levels of urban and rural crimes such as theft, assault and vandalism, increasingly involving violence—to combat which weapon-carrying by civilians and the establishment of vigilantes become legally permissible. Macho conduct on the streets does not, however, translate into a willingness to serve in the armed forces of the state—all three societies were by the end principally reliant on mercenaries for their defence. Contemporaries comment on the universal worship of wealth and comfort. There are reports of a breakdown in standards of sexual conduct, divorce and abortion widespread in Rome where 'chastity is proof only of ugliness', and both in the Empire and in the late Medieval period there is concern about venereal disease, a concern culminating, so far as Christendom is concerned, in the syphilis pandemic of the late fifteenth century. In both classical civilizations there is, at the time of their demise, a catastrophic failure of reproduction, though whether voluntary (greed and hedonism?) or involuntary (lead poisoning? venereal disease?) is not known. The population collapse that occurred across Europe in the fourteenth century is usually ascribed solely to plague rather than to empty cradles.

In today's Europe empty cradles are perhaps the most striking symptom of our incipient demise. In no Western European country is the indigenous birthrate at replacement level, in some it is far below (this does not, of course, translate into declining populations as the vacuum is immediately filled by immigration). But the other hallmarks of decline are also plentifully evident, even to the recent decision, in default of adequate recruits, to incorporate Gurkhas into below-strength elements of the British Army.

Closer, perhaps, to general awareness is the mounting lawlessness of our society. Even when (harried by insurance companies) burglar alarms, metal screens and locking devices secure homes, shops and cars and thus deter theft and burglary to an extent that is reflected in a reduction in the overall crime statistics, crimes of violence and sexual crimes continue the increase that has been inexorable for the past 50 years. In 1940 just over 5,000 violent crimes were recorded, by 1961 the figure was over 17,500, of which some 2,000 were robberies, *i.e.* theft with violence (the 1930 figure was 217), and by 1997 the total for violent crime stood at 347,100, with robberies at over 63,000 — increases that have persisted whatever the economic conditions or the political persuasion of the government. Rapes, numbering 240 in 1947, totalled over 6,000 by 1997. Even the probable greater reluctance to report rape in the earlier period cannot negate so huge an increase. Disruptive conduct at school has led to mounting numbers of permanent exclusions, totalling over 12,500 by 1996-7, with thousands of teachers attacked and one in eight schools annually set on fire.

A number of horrific murders perpetrated by minors on vulnerable old people have frightened and, until we became inured, shocked the public, but no crime so disturbed people as the abduction and murder, in 1993, of the toddler James Bulger by two ten-year-olds. A feature of that tragedy was the suggestion that the boys had been influenced by their fondness for 'video nasties', in particular *Child's Play 3*, which one of the perpetrators was suspected of having seen. This leads to the hugely illuminating topic of the arts as mirrors of society's values. Sorokin pursued this topic in detail, especially in regard to painting, but he largely neglected the theatre (except as an aspect of literature). My study concentrated particularly on dramatic entertainment. Is the theatre 'a mirror', as Shakespeare called it, 'held up to Nature'? Or does it have its own dynamic, is it (as many of its exponents firmly hope and believe in the context of politics, while denying it in the context of personal conduct) a burning glass, influencing the evolution of society's values?

In the early period of a civilization, drama like the other arts is an aspect of worship. Greek drama evolved out of the choral celebrations of the death and resurrection of Dionysus, the god of wine, fertility and renewal. Not until the sixth century BC was there so blasphemous an interpolation as direct impersonation of the gods, and it was an innovation that shocked old-time participants in the rites. From the sixth century BC tragic drama developed, with the institution of prizes at the festival for the best play, and over the next century winners included such hallowed names as Thespis (who first introduced dialogue into the choral celebrations), Aeschylus, Sophocles and Euripedes. By Euripedes' time, subtle changes were occurring. The music was less austere, more alluring and popular, and the drama was shifting from the exploration of life's mystery, the relationship of humanity to the gods, the great issues of justice, retribution, death and mercy, to a focus on human beings in all their frailty, with a particular concentration on individual hatreds, jealousies and rages that began to pander to melodrama and *grand guignol*. (Light relief was afforded by comedies, but like the tragedies they were only performed in the context of religious festivals.)

The Golden Age of Greek drama occurred before wealth and technology had advanced to the point at which the stone theatres whose ruins we admire today had been constructed. There were revivals of Golden Age dramas, but of the new works staged, posterity rated none worth saving. Within the next century a wholly secular drama developed, not requiring the formality of masks, dispensing with the choral element entirely, notoriously irreverent and permitting women to act, thus introducing novel opportunities for the exhibition of feminine charms. At first these productions (so-called mimes, though the description does not in the classical context imply absence of speech) appear to have been vignettes rather than sustained stories, 'turns' of a music-hall type perhaps. The theatre was becoming a place of entertainment rather than of instruction or worship, and soon touring companies had freed themselves from the limitation of performing only at official religious festivals.

Horrific though the topics covered in the old tragedies had been, in presentation there were powerful restraints, violence being almost invariably reported rather than enacted. (Aristotle in particular condemned the crassness of any attempt to portray violent death directly to the audience.) In the new drama there were no such inhibitions, indeed a collapsing dagger was invented to enhance verisimilitude. Sex and violence now moved centre stage, indeed the taste for violence resulted, by the second century BC, in seats for spectators being erected round the altar at which Spartan youths were traditionally scourged in a rite of passage signifying their courageous graduation to manhood. A new type of performer, the 'pantomime', a male solo dancer, now took the Greek world by storm, wordlessly enacting stories from Greek mythology with marked concentration on those with the most erotic possibilities, Leda and the swan, Danae and the shower of gold, Pasiphae and the bull *etc.*

The Roman republic's first essay into drama began with the importation of Etruscans to perform a solemn ritual of song and dance at a religious festival in the fourth century BC. No further development seems to have occurred until they encountered the Greeks of southern Italy in the Punic wars of the third century, whereupon Greek slaves were permitted to translate and stage the old Greek tragedies at Roman religious festivals. The Romans were wary. Their own playwrights began to write and stage patriotic histories of the great leaders of Rome's past, but there was a frivolity about Greek theatre that Roman republicans distrusted. Put bluntly, Rome was a martial nation, and in their eyes the Greek theatrical troupes were a bunch of nancy-boys. It was not until the first century BC that the first permanent theatre was constructed at Rome, and that was only by the subterfuge of incorporating a temple in the upper storey, thus making it blasphemous for the Senate to require demolition.

Meanwhile, the evolution of Roman drama pursued a fast-track version of the Greek. The mime actresses were prostitutes (for many decades they were only allowed to perform at the Floralia, the prostitutes' festival), and by imperial times their prices and addresses were being read out from the stage. The plays in which they performed had one main theme: adultery, and as Ovid was to point out the theatres in which they performed were splendid venues for lechery and seduction. Sexual liaisons were illustrated on stage with an explicitness that led the magistrates of more puritanical cities (Marseilles for instance) to ban mime performances, and after the spread of Christianity congregations were constantly enjoined to stay away from the theatre, indeed actors, impresarios and drama coaches were all ineligible for baptism.

But it was not just the endless sexual shenanigans that brought late Roman theatre into disrepute, not only with Christians but with patriotic pagans as well. There was another source of distress. Tragedies, with all their grim exploration of human suffering, had dropped from the repertoire and been replaced with displays of suffering that dispensed with any meditation or analysis, focusing on violence entirely for its own sake. The appeal of the amphitheatre soon outstripped that of the theatre, indeed all over the classical world, as may be seen to this day, architectural alterations were made to render the old theatres appropriate venues for fighting men and wild animals.

Early Roman drama had been as fastidious as early Greek in not portraying violence directly to an audience, indeed in the second century BC, by which time Greek material had become much more sensational, translations from Greek for Roman audiences omitted some of the more violent scenes in the Greek originals. In this as in other respects Roman practice rapidly outpaced Greek. In the first century BC there began the staging, for public entertainment, of gladiatorial fights previously practised only as an occasional funeral rite. As well as displaying the prowess of professional fighters, the occasion was used to stage public executions in which the condemned were sent into the arena unarmed to be butchered either by animals or by fellow criminals temporarily armed for the purpose until they, in their turn, were sent in defenceless. Some of the Christian divines preached that the very act of enjoying the suffering of others was in itself sinful, irrespective of whether it left the viewer progressively more calloused. Gladiators, their trainers and patrons, were, like members of the theatrical profession, debarred from baptism.

In the early Empire the idea occurred of intensifying dramatic sensationalism by dispensing with imagination altogether, and portraying violence not only in lurid simulation but in grisly actuality. Condemned criminals, who were in any case going to be executed, were cast in the roles of characters due to undergo death or mutilation—and the play was enacted in brutal reality. Small wonder that for many centuries after the Roman theatres closed (whether from penury or official disapproval is a moot point) there was no secular theatre in Christendom. In fact a gap of a thousand years separates the closure of the Roman theatres from the first English purpose-built theatre, which opened in 1576 (to serve the company later joined by young Will Shakespeare).

Dramatic performances had returned several hundred years before the Theatre (as the new building was officially called) opened, and once again religion was the matrix. In the tenth century, celebrations of the Easter morning Mass introduced the novelty of four priests (or monks) enacting the scene in the garden when the three Marys approach the empty tomb. Out of this simple and wholly liturgical beginning developed the half millennium of Passion and Mystery plays. At first, as among the ancient Greeks, mere mortals were considered unfit to portray supreme divinity, such characters as God, Christ or the Virgin Mary being represented by lights or ikons. But increasingly the plays took the naturalistic rather than liturgical path, switching, for instance, from the Latin of the liturgy to the vernacular of the people, introducing non-scriptural characters, and anchoring the portrayals in contemporary actuality with realistic stage props and gags such as a stage donkey depositing turds on its triumphant entry into Jerusalem. The Church gradually lost control of the occasion, pageant wagons took the scenes out of the church and all across town, and lay performers replaced the priests and monks formerly responsible for the presentation. An evolution familiar from the Classical theatre soon became apparent. The Old Testament was combed for sensational episodes with sexual or violent potential, guttings and disembowellings disgorging buckets of entrails from the pork butchers to satisfy audience demands for sensationalism, and actors playing such vulnerable roles as Judas or Christ at genuine risk of suffering real harm in the interests of realism.

Post-Reformation Protestantism never repeated the worshipful phase of the theatrical cycle, though it did, in the complete closure of the theatres during the Commonwealth in the seventeenth century, echo the detestation in which early Roman and early Christian societies had held the profession. Modern secular theatre has gone through various vicissitudes, including a long dalliance with obscenity and violence which made it a highly controversial activity in the 80 years following the Restoration of Charles II (at which time women were first accepted onto the English stage). The much stricter censorship introduced in 1737 (and effective for over 200 years), though provoked primarily by political considerations, met with widespread approval, and the greater restraint thereafter shown may account for the fact that by Victorian times theatre-going was becoming a respectable middle-class activity. By the twentieth century, however, writers were chaffing at the thematic straightjacket within which they were confined. In campaigning for an end to censorship, finally achieved in the Theatres Act of 1968, it was controversial ideas, not female flesh, that most of them were seeking to expose—indeed George Bernard Shaw is on record as ridiculing the very idea that an end to censorship would result in public acts of indecency; and another ardent campaigner, A.P Herbert, lamented (*à propos* '0 Calcutta') that 'our efforts seem to have ended in a right to represent copulation, veraciously, on the public stage'.

The appetite for novelty, for pushing the boundaries of taste ever one step further (which Sorokin had identified as typifying a society governed by the goal of sensual gratification) soon impelled theatre, film, TV and video productions along a path of increasingly explicit portrayals not merely of sex and violence, but of every possible exploration of perversion (de Sade became a favourite author), blasphemy and gratuitous violence. Actresses became used to the routine requirement for them to appear nude, and the actors' union, Equity, had to intervene with regulations to protect actresses from extreme sexual harassment at auditions. Shakespeare was not merely re-interpreted, he was re-written to heighten horror and pitilessness. The revival by Peter Brook of the gruesome *Titus Andronicus* (not thought worth staging for at least 150 preceding years) set a fashion not only for frequent fresh productions, to the point when the play developed a cult following and ceased to distress audiences, but also for a regurgitation of one after another of the cynical Jacobean revenge dramas, bristling with contempt for humanity. Public appetite grew by what it fed on, extra scenes of violence were added by producers to authors such as Brecht. Modern dramatists, adherents of the Theatre of Cruelty and the Theatre of the Absurd, vied with one another to stage increasingly stark diatribes at the futility and absurdity of faith, hope or charity in a world in which God was irredeemably dead and human beings grotesque and/or repellent.

Film producers, liberated by trick photography from the limitations imposed by live performance, excelled themselves in explorations of rape, sadism, torture and murder. By the 1970s, before control of videos had been imposed, so-called 'snuff' movies were said to include actual murder in a sexual context. No-one, at least in Britain, has been found guilty of their production, but there are paedophiles in British prisons whose crimes include the filming of activities with boys whom the police believe (but were unable to prove as the bodies were not found) died as a result of their treatment. 'Snuff' movies were certainly in circulation prior to the 1984 Act controlling video distribution, and indeed were reputedly one of Fred West's favourite recreations.

Depiction of violence, particularly against women, has worried the censors. Though the theatre has been virtually unregulated since 1968, films and (since 1984) videos have had to be categorized according to their suitability for different age groups. The current authority is the British Board of Film Classification. For TV, the Independent Television Authority and the BBC's Board of Governors are the responsible authorities, and there also exists the Broadcasting Standards Authority to whom complaints can be addressed—it is not within their remit to initiate any critique of broadcast material, they act only on receipt of a complaint. If they agree with the complainant they have no powers other than to compel the offending channel to broadcast their adjudication, but they cannot prevent the originators immediately re-broadcasting the offensive material—a somewhat toothless tiger in fact.

Virtually every civilization draws the line somewhere as to what may be said or portrayed in public. In the ancient civilizations censorship was imposed largely for political reasons. The Church maintained its own standards as best it could during the Middle Ages, though towards the end its sanctions, such as banning performers from Church property, were not very effective. The Tudor court swiftly established its authority over the secular theatre in the sixteenth century, and though blasphemy and obscenity featured in the control exercised, so far as the magistrates were concerned it was the suspicion of sedition that most readily provoked the heavy hand of the law and lay behind the tighter regulation of the 1737 Act.

The power to act on such topics as sex and violence has been guided legally by the 1868 clarification of the 1857 Obscene Publications Act, which defined obscenity as that which had a 'tendency to corrupt and deprave', a definition given statutory authority by the 1959 Obscene Publications Act. In the days when jury service was required only of a restricted strata of the population jurors might conclude that the lesser orders were indeed open to corruptible tendencies, but now jury service is virtually universal it is almost impossible to find jurors prepared to admit the possibility of corruptibility. Furthermore, the Act specifically exempted works of artistic merit or those which served the public good, and peripatetic posses of self-styled experts were recruited to appear in court to identify artistic merit for the benefit of the less enlightened and to argue the case for explicit presentations whose very public performance might allay the uneasiness of persons involved in dubious practices the pursuit of which troubled them with an unwholesome level of guilt. Prosecutions failed with such regularity that they are now seldom even initiated.

Those charged with censorship responsibilities find little guidance in the law, and their duties have been exercised more under the influence of what the public find — or is believed to find — acceptable, rather than what authority deems proper. The public are not of one mind. In the late eighteenth and early nineteenth centuries the censors were more often upbraided for laxity than for severity, and in the late nineteenth century the only pressure for the abolition of censorship came from those averring that it was unnecessary, since public taste would not condone public indelicacy.

In the twentieth century appetites, or at least the public expression of them, have totally changed. Scenes of explicit sex and violence are now big box office, and the censors have responded with a progressive relaxation of control. The evolution has been rapid — *Reservoir Dogs* for instance, considered in 1993 too violent for home viewing, had been recategorized within two years. The main criterion appears to be whether the public are 'yet ready', which assumes a perpetual one-way evolution of public taste.

There is no doubt at all that periods in which entertainment exploits the sensationalism of casual sex and callous violence are also periods when violent crime and a breakdown in 'family values' are prevalent. But which is the chicken and which the egg is another matter. There is experimental evidence among children of a correlation between violent conduct and the viewing of violent material — but that may be because those predisposed to violence choose violent entertainment. It is significant that Martin Scorsese defended his *Cape Fear* (an orgy of murder) by remarking that it was 'a lot of fun', the very phrase used by another Martin, Martin Bryant, as he shot 35 people to death in Port Arthur in 1996. My own view is that once conduct is advertised, particularly on film which is so universal a medium, the very fact that professional people have gone to the trouble to enact and record it validates its acceptability. The argument that the more skilfully it is done the more immune it should be from moral criticism strikes me as lunatic; there are talented psychopaths working out their tensions in film studios and viewers cannot be guaranteed immunity from the contagious drip of their enjoyments.

One lesson is clear. If you are confronted with material which you consider depraved — say so. Your opinion is as valuable as anyone else's. Don't be deterred by the 'there's always an off switch' argument, you pay your licence fee and have as much right to enjoy what is on offer as anyone else.

Should we go further and say that some material is so depraved it should be entirely banned? In fact we do operate such a ban — the sort of paedophilic material mentioned above has not been transmitted on TV. But it exists on the Internet and is virtually uncontrollable. Do we then throw our hands in and admit censorship has had its day?

Yes, if 'there is no such thing as society'. If 'society' means anything, it means an assembly of people who feel some responsibility for one another, that there is more that binds them together than separates them. Moral norms publicly upheld by society may indeed not control the Internet, but they mark a shared recognition of the boundaries of decency. Where religion is a binding force (oddly enough, that is exactly what the Latin verb *religo* means, to bind), communities have the inner self-confidence to assert their values. Compare the response to the (inadvertent) offence given when verses from the Koran were used to decorate an *haute couture* dress, world-wide boycotts of the offending fashion house being threatened, with the total absence of response when the Lord's Prayer was similarly commercialized. We know where the strength of Islamic principles can lead — the street violence, book-burning, death threats, even murder, that we saw in the Salman Rushdie case. As a result British publishers, whatever their protestations in favour of free speech, are not now in the forefront of those publishing works critical of Islam.

We do not want such extremes of censorship. But it is a sobering reflection that the successor civilizations to all those which have disintegrated in lawlessness have been mercilessly authoritarian. If we want to avoid such a fate we have to find ways of re-establishing restraint and self-discipline, not only in the self-indulgent world of uninhibited artistic expression, but in every other aspect of life today. As Edmund Burke said at the time of the French Revolution: 'Men are qualified for civil liberty in exact proportion to their disposition to put moral chains upon their own appetites.'

In the absence of a shared sense of religious commitment previous generations have failed the test. At present I see no sign that we are going to prove an exception.

Roger Deakin

Stupidity

In 1976 Dr Feelgood launched an album, recorded live at the now derelict Kursaal dance hall in Southend, which went straight to number one and stayed there for weeks on end. It was called *Stupidity*. It was far more successful than the Canvey Islanders could ever have dreamed and remains one of my own favourites, but the image of thousands of people going out and spending hard-earned cash on something called *Stupidity* somehow prefigures the story of the National Lottery nearly twenty years later.

When it was launched in 1994, nobody — not even Camelot — realized quite how successful the Lottery would be, and everyone has been falling over themselves to chase the silly money it generates ever since by buying tickets or applying for grants. A total of £15.78 billion was gambled from the Lottery's beginning in 1994 to the end of January 1998. The 'good causes' it was meant to benefit are still being breathlessly redefined as I write: the term 'Instants' has been coined to describe the allegedly addictive Lottery 'scratch cards', but many of the policies and Lottery funding schemes — such as the Arts Council's Arts for Everyone — have been 'instants' too. Invented on the hoof, and created to give an impression that the Lottery funds are used for the benefit of 'the people' (especially those 62% of households who play the Saturday draw every week), the moving target of the Lottery funding policies of the Arts Council, Heritage Lottery Fund and the rest continue to raise interesting questions, moral and cultural.

We are dealing, of course, with a massive industry that sprang up like a giant toadstool one night in 1994. We woke up one morning and there it was on the lawn, far bigger than we

had been led to expect and *still growing*. A third of households
in this country now 'play' the 'game' twice a week, spending
on average what the National Lottery Commission calls a
'modest' £5.37 on tickets. 'Play' and 'game' are typical of Lottery hype, given the minuscule chance of winning the jack-
pot — one in 14 million. This is the first and most obvious way
the lottery dumbs down our language and the lives of, in particular, poorer sections of society. It is C2 households (skilled
manual workers) who 'play' the most, while AB households
(professionals/senior and middle managers) are less interested. The Lottery Commission's recent research confirms
that those who have gone on to higher education are least
likely to participate.

Every week, the Lottery invites us all to indulge in the
nation's prime emotion: envy. Eleven million viewers regularly watch the television draw. In his book about the lives of
lottery-winners, *Living on the Lottery*, Hunter Davies endorses
this new 'Lottery culture' as an inspiring influence, stirring
the hearts of the nation to a new Dunkirk spirit in the face of
near-certain failure:

> Far from deadening the spirit, dampening and
> demeaning individuals, as an opiate might, the
> enormous popularity of the Weekly Lottery is based
> on the fact that people are engaged in shared fanta-
> sies and daydreams. You hear it discussed every-
> where, what each person would do if they won,
> most of them saying, 'You won't see me for dust.'
> Each Saturday evening there is a communal
> involvement. Families, of all sorts, all classes, do
> wait for the results, either on television or else-
> where, and then swap thoughts about what hap-
> pened, or what nearly happened. Families talk to
> each other, which we have been told hardly happens
> these days, not since we started sitting in our iso-
> lated corners of the electric village. The Lottery is
> reactive. People are involved, not passive. They
> don't expect to win — yet they look forward to next
> Saturday, to not winning again, knowing they can
> enjoy and share their daydreams with the rest of the
> nation for another week.

This vision of a nation of Walter Mittys in mass denial, conversing like the characters in Pinter's *The Caretaker* about what they would have done 'if only', is hardly inspiring. What would George Orwell have made of it? In his essay on 'The Art of Donald McGill', Orwell applauds the vulgarity of seaside postcard art and adds 'the slightest hint of higher influences would ruin it utterly'. In other words, popular culture is either the real thing, growing spontaneously from the roots up, or it is nothing. You cannot cultivate it, control it from on high, 'encourage' it; least of all patronize it. So when the Lottery funded the new National Foundation for Youth Music in Sheffield with £30 million, under the headline 'Prime Minister Wants More Beatles', it was more likely to be a draught of poison than a tonic to Britain's status as number-one exporter of 'youth culture'. When Tony Blair said, as he opened its architect-designed doors, 'Britain will now rock the world', he should have known better. Rock music is essentially subversive, and a Lottery-funded institution is about the last place on earth likely to nurture more Beatles. The damp brickwork of the primeval Liverpool cave, the appropriately-named 'Cavern', was a far better breeding ground.

The thinking behind the allocation of Lottery funds often seems to miss the point. The muddle-headed Dome in Greenwich appears likely to become another in a line of spectacular own-goals that began with the Royal Opera House exposing its Lottery-inspired chaos to the nation in Channel Four's documentary series *The House*. The Dome focuses attention on the emptiness and moral confusion that characterize our age, with its well-publicized bankruptcy of ideas expressed in the bizarre 'Spirit Zone', 'Play Zone' and 'Body Zone', each sponsored by the highest corporate bidder, and with the acrimonious comings and goings of the likes of Stephen Bailey and Peter Mandelson. No wonder the organizers kept falling out with each other: people often do when they panic.

Unlike St Paul's and every cathedral and church in the land, the Dome was built with no particular internal purpose in mind. Earlier state lotteries have funded more straightforwardly practical projects. Westminster Bridge and the British Museum are two examples. In any earlier century than this, the natural construction to celebrate a millennium would have been a cathedral – or in yet earlier days, perhaps, a great stone circle. Function has a way of enhancing form. When Mies van der Rohe first visited England he went straight to the building he considered its finest: the Great Coxhill Barn, not far from Kelmscott on the Thames where William Morris lived. He too considered it 'as dignified and beautiful as a cathedral'. The building was raised to the greater glory of the harvest gods and for the storage of grain: two simple enough purposes that would have required no spin doctors or copywriters to explain. The barns, churches, stone circles, wood-henges and cathedrals of our land were all built with a commonly understood function in mind, on the foundation of a common faith. Strung somewhere between God and Mammon, the Dome is a building agonizing over its content. It looks clear and confident enough from the outside and makes references to what has gone before. But inside, it is a dumbed-down Tower of Babel.

If the tented steelhenge on Bugsby's Marshes is designed in the image of St Paul's, the comparison is instructive.[1] Dome for dome, you can read the effect of the Lottery's £450 million contribution to the Millenium Experience's £758 million budget as filling a vacuum where religion used to be as a means of social control, keeping the poor poor and the rich rich. The poor could temporarily content themselves with their lot on earth, so the argument used to go, because soon it would be their turn to step into heaven. Today, the lottery win is a passport to a supposed heaven which, in reality, more often consigns the 'winner' straight to the hell of an unaccustomed social milieu, forsaking their roots, neighbours and friends for a life of social exile where nobody, except the besieging spongers, wants to know them. As we were all once the children of God, and equal in His sight, now we are all punters, with an equal (if remote) chance of a win. Those winners pictured lovingly in the *Sun* as redeemed souls entering the pearly gates may, ironically, be heading elsewhere.

A preoccupation with outward appearances has so far characterized so much of the Lottery's funding of our arts, envi-

---

[1] 'This awesome structure dwarfs the famous domes of history', said one of the many promotional blurbs of the New Millenium Experience Company quoted to disturbing effect by Iain Sinclair in his sceptical *Sorry Meniscus: Excursions to the Millennium Dome*.

ronment and culture. The Tory Government's bias towards capital funding of buildings – rather than revenue funding of people – led to a series of spectacular crises by the end of 1997. The Royal Opera House embarked on its £214 million Lottery-funded redevelopment scheme, and all but collapsed altogether. The Cambridge Arts Theatre was awarded a Lottery grant of £6.64 million by the Arts Council towards its £12.14 million refurbishment and renovation project, and ended up insolvent, paying out 25p in the pound to its creditors and only just surviving, thanks to a £574,000 rescue package from the Arts Council, which included the sale of the Festival Theatre and the Arts Cinema.

Both of these Lottery projects had been heralded as great benefactors of the people when they were announced. Both resulted in wholesale misery, dismissals of staff and resignations of arts workers, who had found themselves under intolerable strains of one kind or another. Meanwhile, also in Cambridge, the Lottery-funded rebuilding of the swimming pool at Parker's Piece has resulted in the demise of the City's swimming club, a central part of the city's culture going back well into the 1920s, which used to meet and train in the pool one evening a week. The terms of Lottery funding dictate that the pool must now be open to the general public at all times. The policy is helping to ensure that excellence in swimming, and the nurturing of talented young swimmers, as well as the camaraderie of well-established swimming clubs, is now effectively discouraged anywhere that is 'benefited' by the Lottery. At the same time, the Prime Minister announced in July 1999 that the Lottery is to fund 600 school sports co-ordinators to the tune of £60 million 'to revive the playing of competitive sports such as swimming, football, hockey and tennis, within and between schools' – a tradition which, according to the Secondary Heads Association, fell by 70% between 1987 and 1994. No wonder, when the last wave of political involvement in sport – politically correct disapproval of 'competitive sports' – encouraged councils to sell off swimming pools and playing fields for development all over the country.

A good deal of the Lottery's grant-making policy seems informed by a desire to effect a version of social engineering, to be determined behind the closed doors of the various Arts

Council or Heritage Lottery Fund selection committees. Most of it is revealed as mere tinkering at the margins when you set, say, the funding of new village and 'community' halls against a background of the simultaneous wholesale closure of public libraries, in spite of the protests of real local people. Village halls are a popular subject for Heritage Lottery Fund applications, yet it is by no means clear how wanted or needed some of them actually are. Many of these schemes involve the demolition or incorporation of simple, vernacular buildings of considerable value, often predominantly wood or stone, in favour of far less attractive new halls, hastily designed by committee to meet the application date. The result can all too often be the loss, or alteration beyond recognition, of an older village hall that was a vital ingredient of the local distinctiveness of a place and a living embodiment of its social history. In the case of a village hall, small is often beautiful, because a packed hall, for a meeting, dance, vegetable show or pantomime, generates so much more atmosphere and sense of community than a thinly-populated un-fugged new hangar with space to spare. As with the Dome, the glamorous idea of an expensive new building too often precludes much serious thinking about its actual content.

Questions about content certainly arise in relation to some of the Millennium Festival Lottery grants. Haverhill Town Council has been awarded £25,378 for a project entitled 'Haverhill — The Face of 2000'. During the year 2000, so the idea goes, 2000 townspeople will photograph each other and , using computers, will 'morph' their faces to produce 'The Face of Haverhill'. Will the resulting Identikit picture really make a fitting memorial to the Millennial year? Will the Haverhillians consider it a worthwhile return on their investments at the local newsagents' each week?

Many of these Millennium Festival grants — all in the region of £15–30,000 — seem, on paper, at best vague. In Norwich, Cinema City plans to spend £29,255 'to collaborate with cinema-going communities throughout the Eastern Region to choose the film, the venue and the decade that best combine to represent local identity and experience'. As with the Dome, one senses the glossy shell of a promise without inner substance. Reading the endless torrent of words, words, words, mostly the product of a new breed of arts copywriters hired by the Arts Boards and the various Lottery departments, it is hard not to wilt under Lottery hype fatigue.

The other variant of 'Lottery fatigue' is the one experienced by countless small arts organizations in the disproportionate extra work-load involved in applying for Lottery grants and raising matching funding. It is not an exaggeration to say that the Lottery has tyrannized a great many of the organizations that should be working productively for the arts, the environment, and other aspects of our culture. Instead of getting on with their traditional tasks of forging links within their communities and enabling activities for which there is actually a demand, they go for the 'big one' because it is there. Their working lives are caught up in the production of proposals, the filling-in of complex applications, and the pursuit of sponsors and matching funding. In the words of Sir John Drummond, ex-head of Radio 3, 'The application forms are beyond the comprehension of even well-educated people, and the stress of business plans and financial forecasting has given a totally new impetus to management consultants, who are getting fat on money that should be spent more wisely.' The Lottery has turned every aspect of our culture into a business.

It has also strongly influenced the aims and direction taken by its supplicants, with its prescriptive lists of favoured aims and criteria. The requirement to match funding from the lottery with funding from the private sector has produced some strange bedfellows. The Suffolk Wildlife Trust's major Lottery grant to restore Redgrave Fen has Anglian Water as a main corporate sponsor — the very company whose over-abstraction of the natural spring-waters from beneath the Fen necessitated the expensive rescue work in the first place. Thus nature conservationists, who should be standing up against the water companies' depredations, are obliged instead by the imperatives of the Lottery to go meekly hand in hand with them.

The National Lottery is now apparently as unstoppable as the new Railroad which Dickens described in *Dombey and Son*: 'From the very core of all this dire disorder it trailed smoothly away, upon its mighty course of civilization and improvement.' The dumbing down of our culture through its universal influence is actually a numbing down, because it is about losing touch with a great many of the simplest, most basic moral values. Everyone who receives Lottery money agrees, in effect, that the nation's arts, its environment, its churches and other historic buildings, and its sports are no more than 'good causes', not central to our culture, our values, our whole way of life. Even the Methodist Church, which abhors gambling as a matter of principle, has joined the jamboree and accepted Lottery funds for the repair of its churches.

The gathering and distribution of Lottery funds is not even-handed. There have been dramatic discrepancies between regions. The Arts Council's Lottery awards, including Arts for Everyone, between March 1995 and March 1998 provided grants per capita of £37.70 in London, £25.48 in the Northern Arts region, £14.23 in the West Midlands, £11.71 in Yorkshire and Humberside, and £5.83 in the Eastern Region.

I enjoy a day at the races as much as anybody, all the more since there is no pretence at a higher purpose. The Lottery is different. It is neither an honest gamble, nor a straightforward tax but a a patronizing wheeze, premised on immoderate greed. It diminishes the citizens by hoodwinking them, raising and distributing money inequitably; confusing and withering the moral basis of the very culture it pretends to nourish. For a supposedly intelligent nation, democratically bent on raising our common outlook through education, isn't it plain stupidity?

Mark Ryan

Turning on the Audience

It is not by chance that the Orchestra has been called the 'people's orchestra', indeed, the audience is at the very centre of our activities.   Serge Dorny[1]

One of the most distinctive features of contemporary culture is the importance assigned to the audience, both as an object of interest in itself and as a factor in the making of a work of art. Museums and galleries now seem embarrassed to have nothing to offer the visitor but inert artefacts or paintings, preferring instead to 'tell stories', a concept which deliberately blurs the distinction between objective presentation and subjective perception. If the old museum was distinguished by the distance it placed between the visitor and the exhibition, that distance is now considered exclusive, off-putting and a sign of the snobbery and elitism which once ruled the art world. Interactivity is now the buzzword. In education, the last ten years has seen the development of 'student-centred learning' and a curriculum geared more towards meeting the specific learning needs of the student rather than holding up to him a body of abstract thought which he has to master as something external to himself. Most symphony orchestras have schemes similar to the London Philharmonic's audience development programme, aimed not just at finding new audiences for its existing repertoire, but at developing a new repertoire in accordance with the assumed tastes of audiences which would not normally attend classical concerts. When the new Globe theatre in London was completed

---

[1] Chief Executive and Artistic Director of the London Philharmonic Orchestra, introducing the 2000 season.

in 1998, a replica of the original theatre in which Shakespeare's King's Players performed, its main selling point was the unusual intimacy it created between the performers and the audience.

Even the content of art has become much more audience-conscious. At the Sensation exhibition in London in 1997, and which went on to stir passion and fury in New York at the end of 1999, it was difficult to escape the suspicion that many of the exhibits were calculated primarily to get a rise out of the audience. From this point of view at least, the exhibition was a spectacular triumph. But perhaps the most extreme case of the audience actually dictating the content of art is the new Dundee Museum of Modern Art. When the gallery took on its first resident artist it did so with a novel set of conditions. Not only would visitors be able to watch the resident working, they would also be encouraged to ask him questions and make suggestions as to how his paintings should be executed.

This is all part of the new age of cultural democracy we are supposedly entering, in which art and culture are no longer for the educated elite but are now for all the people. In reality, however, the turn towards the audience is a threat both to the public's artistic appreciation and to art itself. By shifting the focus from what is being produced onto who is receiving, the new cultural elite degrade art and culture while setting new standards for interference in the life of the public.

The separation of higher thought from its recipient, what in philosophical terms would be called the separation of subject and object, is one of the most important preconditions both for the existence of higher culture and for its dissemination. For as long as man was caught up in the immediacy of existence, in which even religious rituals were an extension and affirmation of the life of the community, the possibility of standing back from life and developing the powers of reflection and judgment were limited, and culture remained at a rudimentary level. It was the separation of culture from day-to-day life that marked the highest achievement of the civilization of ancient Greece. In all the leading branches of knowledge and the arts man discovered for the first time the full range of his higher faculties. In philosophy, Socrates elevated knowledge above the life of the community with its laws and regulations and made of it a distinct object of enquiry. Aeschylus, Sophocles and Euripides developed tragic drama, allowing men to contemplate humanity's eternal struggle with necessity. The great sculptures of Phidias and Praxiteles gave men for the first time the power to reflect on the nature and perfection of the human form itself. Plato (theoretically) and Pericles (practically) began to define some of the essential attributes of the political state. Herodotus discovered history as a category distinct from the lived and forgotten experience of individuals. Demosthenes perfected the art of oratory. The list could go on.

Taken together, the different strands of Greek thought gave to man for the first time the powers of contemplation and reflection, as independent human faculties to be cultivated separately from the day-to-day life of the individual and the community. These powers are perhaps the most important ingredients in the formation and development both of the cultivated individual and of a civilized society.

In order for the individual to develop these powers, a distance must be put between him and the object, whether the object be a work of art or form of knowledge. This critical distance is essential in order to separate the recipient from immediacy and the everyday concerns with which we are all bound up. By entering into a relationship with the object from a point of critical distance, the recipient can begin to form a view that is more than an immediate first impression and is more all-rounded and objective. The more this capacity is exercised, the more balanced becomes the sense of judgment and objectivity.

Critical distance must be established in the first instance by the performer, educator, artist, curator, or whatever. The creator, if you like, must perform the act of exclusion, holding the audience back while he attends to his artistic concerns. Take the example of a performance of a play. It is only by excluding the audience to the highest possible degree and concentrating single-mindedly on the task at hand that the actor can realize to the full his own ability and deepen his understanding of the character he is playing, his role in the play, its overall meaning and so on. Likewise with a museum. An ideal curator, his first duty being to the collection, will quite naturally want to exhibit the collection in a way that will most fully reveal its true qualities.

In these cases, both the actor and the curator perform a mental exclusion attending in the first instance to their respective professional duties. They remove the audience from their minds and put it at a distance until such time as they have resolved their professional tasks. By fulfilling their obligations towards their own profession they can then present to the public a work of integrity which has absorbed their undivided attention. For any artist, looking over his shoulder to see what his putative audience might think of what he is doing would paralyse his concentration.

From the audience's point of view, its absence from the creative process is not a loss but a gain. By virtue of its absence, it has a chance of receiving a work that is faithful to the artistic intention of the creator. Later, the audience might desire and perhaps receive insights into the creative process; this is very different from the audience being there at the time and making nagging demands. Similarly, it might benefit from help in understanding the work; but this is again different from it telling the artist what to do. The separation of the audience from the act of creation establishes the critical distance that makes judgment possible. Because of the distance between the creative act and the viewer, the artifact can become a proper object of contemplation.

Under the slogans of relevance, accessibility and inclusiveness, that critical distance is being whittled away. Relevance whittles down what it is that can be made available in the first place. We are told art should be appropriate to the direct experience of the audience; what is remote, or needs to be worked at, is out of favour. 'Relevant' art is always accessible, since the audience can walk straight into it and feel completely at home. What is not 'relevant' has to be made accessible so that the audience does not feel in any way intimidated. Some people think accessibility has something to do with ticket pricing, but that is not the case. The Royal Opera House in Covent Garden has undergone a £45 million 'accessibility' makeover. The cheapest seats are now more expensive than ever before. No—'accessibility' is about the arbitrary lifting of the barriers which all true art erects around itself, and declaring that from now on the audience will be able to understand what it is seeing or hearing. If accessibility lifts the barriers, inclusiveness shrinks the distance so that the audience does not experience that sense of disorientation and remoteness which great art so often elicits.

The disastrous consequences of this turn towards the audience are most evident in museums throughout the country. Where once the museum was a place of study and reflection, where you stood back and looked, now it is a place where you are activated and drawn in. Video footage, sound effects and interactive units have filled the space that was once taken by silence. In almost all cases, these hi-tech gadgets add nothing to the understanding, are very often obsolete as soon as they are installed, and simply replicate what the visitor is likely to have in the home, the workplace or the school. But above all their effect is to stimulate the senses rather than the mind. They transform the museum from a place of learning into yet another entertainment venue, one more place where you can have 'the ultimate experience'.

The introduction of hi-tech gadgetry is only one aspect of a widespread desire on the part of arts institutions to interfere with and play on the audience. A whole bureaucratic layer has grown in recent years dedicated solely to this function. Where once curators dedicated themselves to the classifying, cataloguing and exhibiting of their artefacts, now they spend a greater part of their time thinking how they can enhance the experience of their visitors. Even at the British Museum, whose director has fought valiantly to maintain the institution as one of the great world centres of culture and scholarship, most of the curators will now have to double up as education officers and helpdesk assistants to follow new DCMS guidelines issued in 1999. While the last 10 to 15 years have seen a steady decline in object-centred curatorship, there has been a quantum leap in the amount of visitor-centred staffing. This see-saw effect can be seen at London's National Gallery. In 1974, the Gallery had one information officer and one education officer. Today it has 66 education officers and 26 Information officers. Then it had seven administrators, now there are 52; the non-warding staff totalled 25, that figure is now 300. The curatorial staff of five comprised a fifth of the total staff; today the nine curators comprise less than a thirtieth.

This change in staffing priorities represents not just a growth of bureaucracy, something which, unless checked, seems to afflict most institutions. Unfortunately, much of the

new generation of audience-centred administrators are zealous officiates of the new culture, eagerly devising new
schemes to interfere with the public. The growth of this new
layer of bureaucracy reflects the belief that art is as much
about the audience as it is about art or, to put it another way,
that the future of art lies in breaking down the rigid distinction
between art and audience.

In a recent contribution to a collection on the future of museums, the former director of the V&A, Dame Elizabeth Esteve
Coll observed that 'it is important that the museum is not just
a passive collection of wonderful objects, but a springboard
into the community'. It may not have occurred to Dame Elizabeth that a museum can only ever be a passive collection of
wonderful objects. The function of a museum is to put before
us objects and artefacts that are inert and passive, so that we
can look at and study them, as objects, in isolation from the
original circumstances of their creation. If a museum does not
do that, or finds the task as disdainful as Dame Elizabeth evidently does, then it might be all sorts of other things, but it will
not be a museum. For a museum to become 'a springboard
into the community', it must necessarily develop a disdainful
approach towards its primary curatorial function. The two
functions are antithetical in every conceivable sense. The singular attention that a collection demands could never be reconciled with an attempt to fulfil the needs of 'a community',
with its confusion of needs, backgrounds and interests. A
director who was thinking about the integrity of the collection, its preservation and expansion, and at the same time
thinking about the needs and concerns of 'the community'
(whatever the V&A's 'community' might be) would be trying
to reconcile two wholly opposed concerns.

Once an institution starts to shift its focus of attention from
the collection to the visitors or, worse still, to the surrounding
community, then there is an inevitable slippage as it starts to
put visitor happiness before the integrity of the collection.
Advocates of the new museology constantly harp on the fact
that, unlike their predecessors, they put people first. But they
are doing no such thing. They are insulting the intelligence of
the visitor by assuming that the only way that he can appreciate what is available is by the museum meddling and interfer-

ing in how he approaches the collection. What they are putting first is their own ideological and manipulative concerns.

The first duty of the museum, as for any institution devoted to the arts, is to attend to its artistic function. Visitors and audiences, while given the necessary labelling or information to assist their understanding, should be left alone to form their own judgments and to appreciate what is offered in a setting which befits a work of art. The more interference there is in that basic egalitarian meeting of art and audience, the more critical distance is debased. Nobody, with the possible exception of the new cultural bureaucracy, has anything to gain from that.

Adam Boulton

Not So Dumb –
In Defence of Soundbites

As this burnt-out era gutters into a new millennium, the twentieth century's most comprehensively rejected British Prime Minister is enjoying a return to fashion. John Major's catchily entitled autobiography, *The Autobiography*, is a genuine best seller; and his words are listened to on the lecture and plugging circuit. Amidst the homilies, and jokes about parentage, there is one sure-fire crowd-pleaser. 'If a problem can be solved by a soundbite...', he confides in his audience (and we all know what glib problem-solver he has in mind)'...then it isn't a problem at all.' Well, tough on Blair and the causes of Blair; the audience sigh with satisfaction, they were never taken in, the business of government, they always knew, is more complicated than stringing together a few slogans with a back-up poster campaign.

This is not a political essay and I certainly have no partisan point to make, so let's respect conventional wisdom that Mr Major is a pleasant man who tried hard in government. Should we however also respect his wisdom — expressed as an aphorism of course — on the soundbite? Could it be that his is the scorn of the soundbiter bit, rather than the fastidiousness of the genuinely profound thinker? That Mr Major was found wanting in a crucial test for the modern politician? I don't mean failing to cast good bites, but rather failing to deliver on solemn pledges to his electorate.

Think of the memorable pledges of the Major years. John Major promised to set the nation 'at ease with itself', to preside over a 'Britain at the heart of Europe'. Instead of which voters got the uneasy sensation that their tax-funded schools, health service and even pensions were unlikely to endure through another Tory term. While Britain was only at the heart of Europe to the extent that the heart-felt disagreements in Tory ranks left continental 'allies' heartily sick of the United Kingdom. Again my point is not whether the sentiments of either voters or continentals were right in any absolute sense, simply that Mr Major had palpably failed by the measure of his own soundbites.

Mr Major had a further failing, along with the resonant soundbites above he also constructed phrases which only did him damage. The Citizen's Charter is an idea that the New Labour Government has kept, but without the bathos of its trumpeted title. Only Mr Major could ever have thought 'the Cones Hotline' was a good way to publicize his worthy efforts to lift the congestion caused by roadworks. (Only an optimist of exceptionally sunny disposition would, in any case, ever risk a memorable phrase on such a Sisyphean task.)

In modern politics the soundbite has become the blood in which a politician makes his covenant to the voters. Its detractors must produce evidence that it has debased the currency of political thought (we are talking about democracy here: mass suffrage choosing a representative government, not the oligarchy of a privileged electoral college). To suggest, as Mr Major does, that a soundbite comes at the end of the process, fraudulently promising the solution to a problem, is to misrepresent it. Rather soundbites make up the contract which the politician is making with his voters.

If elected he promises to make the nation at ease with itself, or to be tough on crime etc. Those who make false promises perish by them. American voters read George Bush's lips on taxes and concluded he was a liar. By contrast the carefully measured equivocations of Bill Clinton's platform were understood and tolerated through two terms.

New Labour has refined the process still further, turning their 1997 platform into a whole prayer book of soundbites. The mantras or verses and responses: 'the future not the past', 'the many not the few'; the Commandments of the Five Early Pledges; the numbered psalms of the 174 manifesto pledges, rehearsed and inspected in the annual reports. At one level this orthodox version is clearly designed to limit the demands of the electorate. They were never promised a rose garden, just that class sizes for the under-sevens would be cut to below 30 by the next election. But at another level it's obvious already that the small print won't save them. Tony Blair himself has too often elided his careful wording into 'better schools, hospitals, clean government etc'. If he is not to be ejected from office, voters must feel that 'things have got better ' for them, especially in these targeted areas. Ministers will have to learn that the mere recital of money spent will not save them if the public cannot feel where it is going.

In Britain, John Major's successors in the Conservative Party have not shared his fastidiousness towards the soundbite. William Hague largely credits his success in the off-year elections to his slogan 'In Europe but not run by Europe', which seems to neatly encapsulate his position. He has now matched Blair's five pledges with 'five guarantees' all encapsulated in a policy platform entitled (in his own meaningless mantra) 'the Commonsense Revolution'.

So is this menu for government (without prices, unless you sup with the Liberal Democrats) simply advertising a nouvelle cuisine of small portions and good-looking but blandly tasteless politics? Well, most of the ideology has been removed from the diet of modern campaigning. Politicians are no longer asking their supporters to share in a dream. But then they are not trying to con them that a belief system holds the answers to their problems. The consequences of the swelling rhetorics of socialism and fascism have been experienced at too much cost in the twentieth century. Racism certainly, nationalism probably, one-upmanship even, have all been banished from the tropes of modern-day speech writing. Instead the task is to orchestrate the much more constrained songs of specific services to be delivered to the voter-as-consumer within a set time. But is a nation any worse served by a would-be government which ties itself to measurable pledges on tax, health, education and crime (along with one or two specific notions each, just to separate one party from another)?

By defining and confining political ambition, soundbites and pledges may be protecting the citizen from the worst excesses of government. In a democracy the electorate can always back out of a deal (in the USA they tore up Newt

Gingrich's contract with America) but the political party can never credibly re-define what it was offering.

As so often in Britain, Margaret Thatcher's Ascendancy was the proving ground for both the politics of left and right which followed. The desire for pithy menus of promises now is in part a reaction to the vagueness of her own manifestos. Notoriously, privatization of nationalized industries, ever-tougher curbs on unions, and the Community Charge (poll tax), never appeared in the headlines of her platforms. Back in the late 1970s her imprecision was favourably contrasted with Labour's massively detailed left-wing manifesto, resolved by activists in seemingly endless caucuses (aka 'the longest suicide note in history', in Gerald Kaufmann's famous soundbite). But when it came time to turn the party-political tables again, it was prudent of voters to be more circumspect about the package they were getting. Tony Blair was equally prudent to keep it short and make sure he got the director's cut.

If Margaret Thatcher was old-fashioned in her avoidance of self-limiting precision, she and her party were also the pioneers of the soundbite. Macmillan never said 'you've never had it so good' but a thousand Tory poster sites and millions of passive TV sets blared the Saatchi's: 'Winter of Discontent' and 'Labour isn't working'. Such pithiness caught the spirit of the age and the Labour Government was duly ejected. However the prototypical use of the soundbite that was evident in the message during the Tory years stayed negative right through to John Major's successful 'tax bombshell' and his hubristic re-election slogan 'don't let Labour ruin it'. Eventually the electorate reacted negatively to the tone as much as to the substance of these messages, an impression reinforced by spontaneous soundbites. 'Moaning minnies', 'the Lady is not for turning', 'no such thing as society' were far more resonant than the disposable present participle slogans denoting positive action which became invisible even while they were still suspended above party conference speakers' heads. A good soundbite strikes a chord and reverberates — it bears repetition. A bad one might never have been uttered at all.

In the present stage of evolution, the New Labour injunction is above all 'to keep it positive'. Straining to stay on message, Tony Blair puts himself through agonizing role-playing. If the Conservatives slip up, don't say 'the Conservatives have slipped up...', do say 'If I had slipped up like this you guys/people would be saying...'. If William Hague's debating points are stinging, make sure you praise him first: 'Good jokes but ....'. Does this make Blair shallow and manipulative? Or is mimesis the highest compliment a leader can pay to his people?

Let's look at soundbites another way. Whether you think they are a distillation of political wisdom or a dumbing-down of politics to the lowest common denominator of an advertising jingle—why do the politicians do it? Even dummies can get this one. Its because you remember the message. The soundbites take their platform, onto your television, into your headlines, even, irritatingly like the hook-lines of schmaltz rock, into your conversation. Its an intrusion but then look at the cacophony they are trying to overcome: a dozen national newspapers, each (like the man going to market) with a dozen opinionated columnists; a score of radio stations; five terrestrial TV channels; more satellite TV than you can watch; video shops; freesheets; advertisements; and those wretched loose flyers which fall out of every periodical. Welcome to the information marketplace and if your message is good enough to be heard over all that, it's probably good enough—full stop.

Perhaps it's the very accessibility of the contemporary soundbite which so provokes the smugs nodding at John Major. Because until now soundbites were the mark of exclusivity rather that inclusion. That's when they were called tags, or citations, *vulg*. Quotations. Whatever the admonishments surrounding a little learning, attach a smattering of the wisdom of the ancients to your argument and it somehow glowed more. You and I may appreciate the extra dimension but perhaps not everybody would. Today's soundbites speak for themselves, without leaning on outside authority. It doesn't matter that *The Commonsense Revolution* is borrowed from a Canadian provincial politician or that Gordon Brown coined Tony Blair's toughness couplet. In this modern age politicians are more fundamentalist even than the prayer book, back almost to the teaching style of Jesus in the Gospels.

The really dumb people are those whose political analysis ends with a patronizing dismissal of the soundbites. There is now more in-depth political discussion readily available than ever before. Think tanks of left and right may start with the soundbites, but they are constructed and de-constructed in soundbite after soundbite. Much of this material is then recycled and précied in the newspapers (and not just the broadsheets, *The Daily Mail* and *The Sun* will certainly bat an idea around). The current debates about the limits of taxation in a globalized economy, about libertarianism vs. paternalism and about the Third Way, are real and urgent, even if the fastidious reject the jargon. The opportunities to get beyond the soundbite directly are there. It's the Head of News at the BBC, one Tony Hall, who compares his job to (unsuccessfully) 'making the viewer eat greens', it's the commercial satellite channels which carry the debates and the speeches live.

However, if John Major fans reject the soundbite, what about those who never chose to hear it. The greatest challenge to our democracy today comes from its greatest achievement, choice. Nobody anymore has to watch the Reithian self-improvement programme as dictated by monopolistic or duopolistic broadcasters. If you don't like any TV station at all, you can watch a video or make your own. With each technological advance the opportunities are multiplying to feed into this Babel or entropic environment (you can have your metaphors biblical or scientific too). As a believer in the market place, freedom of expression, and this best of all possible ideas, I believe the best ideas will survive, provided scrutiny is maintained on as many fronts as possible. So don't tune out, tune in. Don't be dumb or deaf (in my English dictionary primary definition of those words). Better communication may really be just better, not worse.

Oliver O'Donovan

Publicity

'Publicity' is a term for our becoming known to one
another; but not every way of becoming known is publicity, but a way which belongs especially to the modern
world. We share intimate thoughts with friends, we explain
our ideas in lecturing and writing, we perform actions before
the eyes of others and are reported on, all without 'publicity'.
Being made known is as old as social life itself, and as diverse;
but this word, a coinage of the late eighteenth century,
expresses an experience of it which is no more than a couple of
centuries old. It is, therefore, one of many possible approaches
to an enquiry about 'modernity'.

As soon as we embark on such an enquiry, we find ourselves
sailing between a Scylla and a Charybdis. Neologisms are the
sparks which fly from the furnace of experience and they
exaggerate discontinuity. Later reflection, however, tends to
attribute the appearance of discontinuity to a trick of perspective. Everybody has always thought that the world began yes-
terday; but a cool look can show us that it didn't. So
neologisms are replaced with older, more durable categories
derived from tradition. There then develops a difference
between unofficial language, fluid and fashion-bound, and
official language, which we assume when we intend to be serious or searching. But official *sang-froid*, no less than neolo-
gism, can conceal as much as it reveals. As innovation inserts
itself into the normal lives of a generation or two of human
beings, the gap between official accounts and common experience may widen, and we may discover that the unofficial
term, invented for throw-away use, has acquired associations
more illuminative of experience than the official one. The

independence of the press is still officially defended in the terms of eighteenth-century libertarianism as the essence of a free society, broadcasting in terms of nineteenth-century philanthropism as a tool of 'education'; but when we speak about them both as *media of publicity,* we have the sense of being more straightforward. At that point we may take up again in a disciplined philosophical manner the question of how our own times differ from others, making use of the categories which have established themselves as expressive of that difference. This supposes, of course, a measure of time and an accumulation of experience. Of computer-generated communications, reassuringly labelled 'information technology', it is still impossible to speak in a philosophically descriptive way. But it is possible to gain a purchase, though tentative and partial, on what *has been* happening in generations that have led up to our own.

The terms 'publicity' and the more recently coined 'media' belong together. Publicity is the *operation* of the media; the media the *institutions* of publicity. To explore the concept of publicity is to explore the question of the media, but to explore it not as a question about *malfunction* and *abuse,* the persistent failure of the media to deliver something commonly understood to be expected of them, but as a question as to *what their function is.* We must set to one side both our criticisms and our defences of the media, resolving not to know in advance what a telling criticism or an effective defence would look like.

We begin by contrasting 'publicity' with some older, more traditional terms which border on it and partially overlap it, to get a view of the particular range of experience to which it points us.

In the first place there is the term *'public'.* This has acquired some philosophical currency in the last generation , especially through a phrase made popular by Hannah Arendt, 'the public realm'. Arendt's exposition of this phrase may create the impression at first that 'public' and 'publicity' are the same; for she relates it to what she describes as the universal desire to 'appear' before the eyes of others. 'Appearing' is the condition of 'action' (as distinct from 'labour' and 'work'). To be deprived of the opportunity to appear is the fate of the infant, the sick and the slave. In her use of the *visual* image of 'appearance' Arendt has certainly given an opening towards the idea of publicity. But her conception of appearing in public is not, in fact, a purely visual one, but includes being talked about; and, more importantly, it has not to do with that intensive *unreciprocated* visibility that we associate with publicity, but with a reciprocal visibility, such as is involved in any sphere of social engagement where we are the master of our actions and perform them before the eyes of our fellows as a matter of common interest. Most 'public' things are done without 'publicity'. A day at the office desk filling in forms and writing reports is the archetypal public existence of our time; the standard mode of appearing is appending one's signature to a document, something the camera rarely, if ever, flashes upon.

We come closer to the sphere of publicity when we consider traditional notions of eminence, and here we may mention two different ones, *glory* and *fame*. To have glory is to be looked at intently and admiringly. In contrast to Arendt's public appearance, it is non-reciprocal. One who acquires glory is the object of universal gaze that he does not return, the cynosure of all men's eyes. Glory may be earned, but is not necessarily so; the dairymaid who is discovered to be a princess acquires glory, just as the victor at the Olympic Games does. It may be enduring or short-lived, depending on the institution in relation to which one has acquired one's position. The princess will be glorious for as long as she reigns. The victor's glory will cease when he leaves Olympia and returns to his plough.

He will, however, continue to enjoy *fame*, which is not a matter of being looked at but of being spoken about, a communication of word, not image. It is always earned: one can be famous only for achievements or capacities that have shaped other people's undertakings and expectations, so that they reap the fruits of one's deeds.[1] Fame may persist after one's death — indeed, with widespread fame that is rather more common than to be famous while alive; but there is still a practical point to it. We want to play Bach's music; we want to read

---

[1] With lesser suggestion of eminence we speak of a 'reputation' which can attract the attention of those who need someone who can do their business well. A reputation need not be widespread; but it must be knowable to those who have practical reason to enquire.

Shelley's poetry — or some of us do. These names are invoked as part of our *practical* wisdom.

The Latin word *fama* also stands for *notoriety*, *i.e.* bad fame. To acquire notoriety is to occupy a position in the history of one's society for something one has done that has appalled it. Crime acquires notoriety, always *post eventum*. As with fame, notoriety is earned, and is communicated by report, attaching to the name, rather than the person, so that a notorious person may go unrecognized in the street. More fundamentally, *fama* refers to the process of common report itself, the communication of information between one person and another, and one could not speak of *fama* without a sense of the unreliable, distorting features of that communication. *Fama* may be 'rumour', wild, demonic and destructive,

> . . . the swiftest traveller of all the ills on earth,
> Thriving on movement, gathering strength as it
>   goes; at the start
> A small and cowardly thing, it soon puffs itself up,
> And walking upon the ground, buries its head in the
>   cloud-base . . .
> For every eye she has also a tongue, a voice and a
>   pricked ear . . .
> Loud speaker of truth, hoarder of mischievous
>   falsehood equally.
>
> Virgil, *tr.* C. Day Lewis

So to publicity, which, like fame, makes the unknown known and, like glory, makes the obscure visible. By contrast with fame, it selects its subjects with apparent arbitrariness, irrespective of what they have achieved. By contrast with glory, it selects them without reference to institutions in which they have shone. The visibility it affords, one might say, is neither the radiance given out by significant accomplishment, nor the floodlighting that illumines a major social institution, but a roaming spotlight, catching people unpredictably in its beam. This, of course, is an extreme view of the matter. In fact there are active roles in public life, and there are kinds of activity, which are disposed to attract publicity. A Head of Government who attracted none would be a curious and perhaps short-lived phenomenon. Yet modern publicity, once attracted to its object by what is done in the public realm, is surprisingly indifferent to human action and the institutions which support it. It does not accrue to projects, planning, virtues of performance, teamwork, accomplished execution, durable results. On the contrary, the moments which excite publicity are those over which the publicized agent seems to have no control. Like ancient tragedy, publicity portrays its great ones embattled and its virtuous ones at the moment of their major errors. If it interests itself in some public idol's ambitions, it is the *pathos* of ambition that attracts its attention, the way in which it makes the subject vulnerable, or—to use a word which has come to be essentially a synonym in this context— 'human'. For it is interested not in action but in passion, and in what the ancient world thought of as 'fate' or 'doom'.

Publicity assigns to names and faces the potential for recognition; but unlike fame and reputation, it does so not for the benefit of those who have *practical* business with those names and faces, but for the benefit of a public essentially indifferent to them. It evokes recognition from those who have no apparent interest in recognizing. This betrays its role as a device for *creating* common interests, a structuring device of society itself, like glory and notoriety. One might say that publicity imposes recognition as a kind of civic discipline. To know the names of those in the public eye is a proof of social competence, and to deploy those names without explanation is a test of others' social competence. So somebody may refer, in the course of a conversation that is not about tennis, to 'Sampras and Agassee' —*not* to 'the Wimbledon men's doubles' final', showing that he is *au fait*, and testing whether his conversation partner is. Bishops have boasted to the press that they know the names of all the Spice Girls, thereby hoping to free themselves from the suspicion of social incompetence which surrounds their office.

Publicity is never neutral; it is always 'good' or 'bad' publicity. That is to say, the recognitions which publicity evokes comprise a system of social judgments. With the evolution of publicity, the judgmental element has become ever more overt. The once-professed ideal of journalism to 'tell it the way it is' has been overtaken by a professional ambition to expose and denounce. Publicity is the means by which society communicates favourable and unfavourable verdicts, eliciting assent to them. It does so in a manner characteristic of a liberal society — for only *liberal* societies have generated publicity — at once relaxed and unyieldingly insistent. Because liberal society sets a value on dissent, there are certain publicly recognized matters on which dissent is accorded its own dignity — communists used to enjoy this respected role; today I rather think that gays have taken it over. The price to be paid for it, however, is an extraordinarily wide cultural field beyond those privileged matters in which assent is constantly looked for as a proof of good will. One who refuses it is not thrown into jail; he or she is simply viewed in a peculiar light, as untrustworthy for certain purposes. Liberal society is humane; yet the demand for acquiescence is so encompassing and penetrating that it may sometimes seem to achieve by constant repetition something like the oppressiveness which other societies have achieved by severity.

In singling out objects for negative and positive recognition, publicity presents them selectively and interpretatively. They are assigned symbolic roles, standing for something that society currently sees itself, complacently or anxiously, as containing. They become an element in its self-imaging. Publicity thus homogenizes events. Throughout the republic of publicity the platitude and the cliché hold sway, creating and reinforcing stereotypical forms that can be easily recognized. Its concern is not with individual agents at all, but with typical characterizations, their individual distinctivenesses ironed out for the purposes of public representation. If one appears in the public eye, one appears *as* something, and that something is not what one has oneself determined to be, but one of a limited number of fixed roles that society feels the need to have represented to it. The gratification of being the object of attention is the bait with which society allures powerful individuals into accepting prescribed and predictable roles. The project is, one might say, that of overcoming the unknown, closing off the genuinely open, taming the threat of untold and unrealized purposes by associating each new name with a pathos that is familiar, predictable and 'human'. For this reason publicity can be a serious barrier to effective accomplishment, and to the operation of the public realm itself. There is, it is commonly supposed, a wisdom in avoiding publicity, a wisdom not confined to the criminal or conspirator, but to anyone who has serious plans of action. Publicized, one is not the master of one's own appearing. To acquire publicity too soon is to be frozen into an assigned role, denied the open attentiveness which is the condition of freedom.

Nobody directs the roaming spotlight of publicity. The all-powerful press baron, like the all-powerful President, is one of the reifications of our age — paradoxically, a creation of the process which he is supposed to control, the arbitrariness of publicity itself projected back upon a representative type of person. Which is not to say that professionals who work in the media are purely passive and have no sphere of moral decision and influence. Like all who deal with a natural force, they are not only driven by it, but constantly strive to exercise control over it. Journalists are at once the servants and the masters of publicity, as fishermen are servants and masters of the tides. But they are not the only ones: politicians, too, have an interest in the matter. Public judgment is the essential business of politics; and insofar as publicity mediates the unreflective judgments of society, rulers must exercise corrective influence upon it.[2]

Up to this point we have spoken as though publicity were a function entirely of the communication of news. But one of the most fascinating aspects of it is that it embraces at least three different, and professedly quite separate, undertakings, all of which have had a formative role in the shaping of the communications media: news, advertising and entertainment. Whereas news is the strand of the threefold chord which bears the weight of justification for the whole, in promising to produce an 'informed public', the actual bulk of news reporting, in the broadcasting media at least, is comparatively small. Publicity is the unifying factor: each imposes recognitions.

Advertising is a form of communication entirely created within the sphere of modern publicity; and we can see it as a protected enclave in which the rule that nobody directs communications is suspended. It expresses a limit-possibility, at once the goal and the sublimation of publicity, desired and feared in equal measure: that some human beings should con-

---

[2] We may note in passing that the *'spin doctor'*, who has acquired notoriety in recent years, does, after all, pose as a kind of *healer*; it takes a malady to produce even a quack!

trol what others communicate. The nuclear core of direct control is ceremoniously protected from seepage by being defined within the boundaries of a purely commercial transaction. Yet the curious thing is that seepage constantly occurs, so that commercial advertising takes on the form of news and news takes on some of the controlled aspects of advertising. It has never been clear, anyway, that a strictly *commercial* rationale for advertising exists. The necessity for advertising is less a commercial and more a sociological one: commerce is so close to the heart of what we take society to be that it must be represented in our communications. Business wears advertising as Peers wear ermine, not to accomplish anything but to maintain its dignity.

The third strand in the chord is entertainment, and here the situation is quite different. The media have digested forms of communication traditionally sustained elsewhere: on the stage, in concert halls, in drawing rooms and on sports fields. Their value to the modern project is their morally communicative function. Seepage between news and entertainment is continual and hardly resisted. Indeed, anything that happens in a sufficiently prominent sport or soap opera *is* news. These older forms of communication do not remain unchanged by their absorption into the media. Drama, which is of particular importance as morality, has been reinforced in the visual media by making the images of actors and actresses permanent. Many actors have been Hamlet on the stage, but only Dirk Bogarde is Gustav von Aschenbach on the screen. Visconti will do more than Shakespeare to shape the moral recognitions of our age.

Publicity has had its historical phases, corresponding to the technological means which have been its instruments: the printed word, sound reproduction and visual image. Technology develops as an expression of the logic of society's self-understanding, so that the essence of a social era can be traced in the progress of the technologies it generates. In television we see the most elaborate disclosure yet of the communications to which publicity has implicitly aspired.[3] The

---

[3] Of information technology, as I have said, it is too early to speak in other than a speculative manner. It may prove to be another step in the same direction, or it may prove to be a radical turn.

moving two-dimensional image achieves the optimum balance of concreteness and abstractness. More concreteness, as in a genuinely three-dimensional projection, one you could walk around, would sacrifice the necessarily abstract and typical character of the projection; less would sacrifice its immediacy and force.

II

The essence of what it is to be a community is communication. *Koinônia* is a verbal noun, denoting the sharing of some matter between one and another; and communication *in truth* is one of the elementary forms of communication that are indispensible to any society. It is the paradigm form, according to some accounts, for a word is the model of what is essentially shared, indivisible into private lots, enjoyable only in the practice of communication, and so indispensible to the sharing of any other material or spiritual thing.

In communicating the truth of the world to itself, a society communicates to itself the truth of itself *in* the world. Society's shared knowledge includes self-knowledge; those who share a common truth share also a truth of their own community *in* the truth. But this self-knowledge is achieved by symbolic representation, singling out from the whole an element that will stand concretely for the whole. It is a visual device, presenting to our sight a subject who stands for the whole that we cannot see but can only talk about. The relation of society to its representative is a quasi-erotic relation, the love of self in difference; and the imaging of society's qualities and relations within the individual is an erotic imaging.

This function of self-representation culminates in a special case, which is political representation. In the political representative, society focuses its capacity to act together as a whole. The personal form of the representation is the ground of the monarchical principle in government. Monarchy can never be explained in terms of the practical activities of government, for government is never in fact conducted by one person alone; it is always, even in the most simplified societies, a coordinated activity conducted by an elite class; but the legitimation of that class requires popular self-representation

in a single ruling figure.[4] Such political representation, however, depends intricately upon a system of social self-
representations. For in the anointing of a political representative he is invested with a range of symbols which represent the
various strands in the society. This, rather than some kind of a
public debate on policy, is the true function of the electoral
campaign in modern democracy. A wide range of symbols is
made to flow towards this one symbolic representative, legiti-
mating him for the tasks of justice that he must perform.

From one point of view publicity is simply the way in which
these sociological universals are manifest in contemporary
society: communication in word, the representation of society
and the investment of its leaders with representative legitimacy. Nothing is happening that does not have precedents
and forms in premodern social patterns. How, then, is the
modern manifestation of the sociological universal *different*? A
simple answer might be that communication has assumed a
fevered pace: the word trasmitted throughout society with an
intense and all-penetrating insistence, and the generation of
social symbols gone into overdrive. Much may be as it was:
the politician who seeks legitimacy by being seen to support
his side on sporting occasions is doing just as the Emperor Jus-
tinian did. Yet there is now an apparent surplus, an overflow
of symbolic identifications — too great an excess to be
explained in terms of the process of political representation — and they change too quickly to be effective stabilizers
and legitimators. Where symbolic representations of society
used to enjoy some permanence, publicity now constructs
them and reconstructs them at a furious rate.

Here it is worth recalling a feature of our modern communications that is wholly distinctive, its astonishing dependence
on erotic imaging, the dominance of the naked human form in
all possible shapes, textures and motions and combinations. It
is often said that the sexual *mores* of our civilization are
unprecedented; and this may or may not be true. What is
clearly unprecedented is the extent of its deployment of erotic

---

[4] The monarchical principle is as prominent in modern democracy as ever: it
is not for nothing that the President of the United States is constantly
referred to, and without a trace of irony, as 'the most powerful man in the
world'!

images; and whereas this is often taken as a mere aspect of the problem of sexual *mores* ('pornography'), I find it difficult not to think that it relates also, and perhaps more immediately, to the peculiar form of our communications as such. Inescapably symbolic, the erotic image is capable of immediate and irresistible engagement of the viewer's interest as nothing else is. That is precisely what the goal of publicity must be: to locate the viewer unarguably *vis à vis* a typical scene with typical actors. The erotic is, as it were, the stamp of authority by which it commands us to recognize and to take sides.

Behind the intensity and the hectic pace of publicity, we detect a kind of numbness, an incapacity to receive and respond, that seems to demand publicity as its antidote. What is its nature and what are its causes? The kind of explanation to which such a development is susceptible is not a simple one. Many causes can be adduced for the modern condition, but it is never clear which is cause and which effect. What can be ventured, however, is a correlation of this phenomenon with others. Late-modern society has a philosophical and political coherence, within which this phenomenon begins to be comprehensible.

In the first place, it has carried to extraordinary lengths the specialization of social functions, so that the difficulty of social map-drawing has become acute. Coordination is threatened by a degree of diversification that makes each part unintelligible to the others. Space for action in the public realm is found, as it were, only on narrow ledges; and discerning the total terrain of society from the sum of such nooks and crannies is impossible. The intense reinforcement of simple stereotypes can be seen as a response to a crisis of social representation.

Secondly, there is the philosophical conviction that the identity of any thing lies in change, 'historicism' as it is often called. The rejection of fixed essences has as its corollary that knowledge must be kept up to date. Society cannot be known as it is, only as it is becoming, each day's communications making the previous day's obsolete. Publicity mediates change, by putting the work of symbolic representation in a narrative form. Here lies the special nuance in the term 'information', which, unlike 'knowledge', supersedes itself continually. It excludes philosophical utterances, and it substitutes for history in a society which understands itself as constructing its own history.

Here we reflect also on the transformation of *morality* in a society which has abandoned a realist conception of moral relations. We have commented on the 'moralism' of publicity, *i.e.* its reinforcement of negative and positive stereotypes. It performs tasks traditionally associated with moral and religious education, replacing the stable categories and laws appropriate to that task with a sequence of normative exempla, which are, however, no longer exemplify anything, but simply stand on their own as a narrative norm.

Fourthly, we may connect publicity with the evolution of democratic political forms and populist ideologies. Office-holders do not remain in office for long, and are not selected by a fixed rule. So the task of ensuring representative legitimacy for office-holders in government has become much greater. In effect, it has become the primary task of politics; elections and electoral campaigning have become the matrix of all political activity. The means, representation, has overshadowed the end, the enactment of justice. Our political organs are like giant pandas, which eat continually to keep alive. All they can do is eat, and the difference between acquiring and expending energy collapses. The electoral mouth of the body politic is insatiable, which results in the proliferation of communicated symbols. To this we must add the suspicion of political authority itself within modern political philosophy. Enacting justice is no longer felt to justify political difference. Not only the office-holders, but the structure of authority itself seems to need legitimation, and the process of representation has come to be seen as a means to provide this. By reinforcing the identification of the represented with the representatives, it creates the illusion of collapsing political difference into sameness.

Set alongside other aspects of modernity, then, publicity begins to look like an attempt to compensate for the loss of something. Its feverish generation of words and images points to the disappearance of stable and solid points of ideological reference which a pre-modern society could count on, especially the twin realities of secular and sacred government.

III

So far modernity criticism can take us: it can show us how the disturbing and bizarre aspect of our modern culture belongs to a complex of changes which involve the break-up of deep integrities. But the more it undertakes to articulate criticism, the more it must take these old integrities as the norm, and so risk the charge of being nostalgic, of canonizing past and vanished models simply because they are past and vanished. Radical critique needs something more. It needs to attend to the ways in which modernity, in its different forms, replicates standing problems which other forms of society, too, have encountered. Here a theological critique finds its point of departure. For in publicity we have to do with the social communication of words and images, which Jewish and Christian teachers have held to be supremely vulnerable to the dangers of idolatry.

First, we address communication in words. That this is perilous was well understood by classical civilization. We have quoted Virgil's commentary on rumour; for another, no less searching exploration of the waywardness of social truth we may refer to Herodotus's quizzical comparisons of the beliefs and practices of different societies. But what were the options for defending communication against collective self-deception? The ancient world tried to solve the problem by socio-epistemic discipline: the location of responsibility for communication within a distinct social role with distinct rules of practice. The 'wise man' of the ancient Near East was a determinative figure, the original 'elite', whose role it was to correct the popular vision. He stood critically above the passions and misconceptions which dominated ordinary social intercourse. He was a standing resource for the prudent and ambitious, offering instruction in elementary criticism based on organized observation; and he was found especially close to the monarch's throne, for the connection between wisdom and the task of justice, as we find it in the Biblical character of Solomon, was centrally important. But with the complexification of society the ancient world developed a second principle, that of socio-epistemic differentiation. Different forms of socially-disciplined wisdom were to be called upon for different purposes: priestly, artistic, philosophical, legal, and so on.

A striking feature of this arrangement was the absence of anything that we would recognize as 'news', *i.e.* a universal diffusion of information about universal happenings. Information, too, belonged within a specialist sphere, the sphere of government. It was the ruler's task to interest himself in what was going on beyond the local horizon, and messenger services were, not accidentally, the creation of empires. 'As the eye is in the body, so is the king in the world.... It brings distinction to the imperial power to have a comprehensive surveillance of its own, or to draw upon others', unashamedly acquiring knowledge and putting it to service promptly' (Agapetos). Ordinary people did not need 'news', just as they did not need a knowledge of religious ritual. Spheres of knowledge went hand in hand with spheres of responsibility; disciplined communication was ensured by disciplined social roles and responsibilities.

The general anxiety about the communication of truth was, if anything, even more strongly felt in ancient Israel. It gripped the prophetic movement of late seventh-century Judah and those whom it influenced, the royal administrators responsible for the great reform attempted in the Book of Deuteronomy. Anxiously aware of the inconsistencies and eclecticism of law and practice in the Israel of their day, disturbed by the threat it posed in the face of external pressures, they came to understand the process of oral tradition itself as a problem. Jeremiah dared to envisage a day when there would be no more oral tradition, when 'no longer shall each man teach his neighbour and each his brother, saying "Know the Lord", for they shall all know me' (*Jer.* 31:34). The Deuteronomists sought to discipline the process by determining it with a single authoritative and regulatory law-text, given in revelation and sustained in place by the watchful protection of a central sanctuary and a monarch. The authoritative text, however, allowed Jews and, later, Christians to hang more loosely to socio-epistemic differentiation. The Deuteronomists could tell Israel that the authoritative word, which regulated and made possible all words, was very near them, in their mouths and in their hearts, needing no seer to receive a new disclosure from heaven, no foreign emissary to produce the latest report.

Following the logic of this, early Christianity took a radically egalitarian turn, cultivating a community in which all participated freely of the Spirit of God and had equal access to revelation through faith. 'The Word was in the beginning with God...' Recognize *that* word on its coming into the world, and there can be no significant distinctions; for 'to all who received him, who believed in his name, he gave power to become the children of God'. (John 1:2, 12) There was in the early church, of course, a role for a presbyteral priesthood in safeguarding the integrity of the Gospel word against corrupt imaginations; and this was later to prove of decisive significance in providing a learned class to reconstruct the culture of Western Europe after the withdrawal of the Roman Empire. Yet the striking feature of Christian culture in the Western middle ages remained its homogeneity—that is to say, the interpenetration of the various branches of sacred and secular learning within an all-encompassing word. That this did not have to be the case the rather different culture of Byzantium demonstrates. Only with the birth of modernity did the classical idea of differentiated learning revive itself vigorously in the West within the universities, giving its characteristic shape to academic life as we now know it.

Publicity, however, stands in sharp contrast to this differentiated academic ideal. It reasserts *homogeneous* culture; that is to say one which differentiates neither the matter communicated nor the recipients. Mass man, negatively defined by the lack of special calling and spiritual vocation, transmits a confused mix of news, advertising and entertainment, a populism that may be seen as a late fruit of the Pentecostal inspiration in Christianity. But that poses the question: what prospect can there be for a Pentecostal discourse which depends on no Holy Spirit and acknowledges no Gospel? Is this not another instance of theological hope recast in a secular mould which cannot sustain it? What can stand between this communication and the self-destructive dominion of rumour? The air of unreality surrounding the 'Diana phenomenon' illustrates the extent to which reality and projection become indistinguishable to a media-formed society.

'In the beginning was the Word...' says the Prologue of St John's Gospel, establishing, in a world where there are words a-plenty, that there is such a thing as *the* Word, the normative word, which was in the beginning with God. But when 'the Word became flesh...and we beheld his glory', we have also to recognize a visual image. This image is not autonomous and self-replicating. It is the *particular* image brought to being by the Word in becoming flesh.

The attitude of YHWH, the God of Israel, to images of the divine is well known. God is to be known by word alone, not by visual representation, since depiction can only project onto the divine the self-replication of creaturely artifice. The word is not artifice, but is the element, abysmal and self-sustaining, into which the creature is called by his Creator. This refusal of the image is reproduced in the political theology of Israel, resistant as it was even to the idea of monarchy. The right of government belonged to God, and YHWH would be his people's only king. If, nevertheless, the throne of David could be understood as a condescension to the people's weakness, the throne of Jeroboam quite definitely could not. For the tribes of Jacob had chosen Jeroboam for themselves and this was to place an image in the seat of God. The crimes of rebellion and idolatry seemed to Israel to be one and the same. The early church still regarded political representation as essentially rebellious. The angels, principalities and powers which embodied the governments of the nations had to be disarmed, humbled and overthrown by the cross of Christ. To this view corresponds Saint Paul's famous passage on the role of government in *Romans* 13, in which the whole question of the representative status of government is passed by in silence and its rationale is found exclusively in the tasks of justice. Government is to enact God's word of judgment; that and nothing else. The desire to have a government in one's image is like the desire to have God in one's image. John of the Apocalypse, finally, renews the conception that false government is idolatrous. His anti-Christ sets up an image which his 'false prophet' (the Third Person of his diabolical anti-Trinity) commands people to worship. The word in the service of an image is an upturning of all true relations.

The implications of this were argued out in early Christian history in the course of its least-remembered heresy struggle, the iconoclastic controversy. The *prima facie* strength of the iconoclastic position was undeniable; but those who resisted it were not wrong to recall the prologue to St John's Gospel and the apostolic claim to have *beheld* the glory of the incarnate word. The abolition of images would take us back behind that decisive moment. What was required, rather, was to *situate* images correctly in the service of salvation as ministering to the word. 'We depict Christ as king and lord without stripping him of his array', said John of Damascus. The array was the visibility of his rule. Yet while this licensed artistic depictions of Christ, it also kept them in a subordinate place. For the actual image, the face and form that the apostles saw, will become visible to us only at the *parousia* and resurrection. We may make 'memorials' of it, but we cannot reproduce it. Our images, therefore, though free, are humble. They are objects of respect, not of worship, the creatures and servants of the apostolic word.

Even anti-iconoclastic orthodoxy, then, guarded itself against the autonomy of the image. In its political form it was doubly on guard, for it was precisely the false pretence of imaging Christ, it thought, that seduced the iconoclastic emperors. In trying to abolish the pictorial images of Christ the King, they had tried to seize that image for themselves, overruling the apostles and teachers of the church. The question about the form of communication by way of image turns out, once again, to conceal the question of a realized Utopia, a Kingdom of Heaven laid claim to on earth.

IV

In conclusion, I want to pursue this political aspect of representation a little further, showing how the critique of representation belongs within a programme which I have advocated for political theology, that of recovering the notion of authority.

Political theology of the twentieth century shadowed the wider preoccupation of the century with the dangers of authoritarian regimes and the role of political ideology as a tool of oppression. In doing so it called, with good reason, on the New Testament testimonies to which I have alluded, *i.e.* the passages about the defeat of the principalities and powers and the critique of ideological empire in the Apocalypse. Yet it failed to notice that it is *political representation* against which the critique of these texts is directed. It conceived the problem of political authority entirely quantitatively, supposing that authoritarianism was excess of authority and the cure must either be an Aristotelian moderation or a liberal minimalism. This led it mistakenly to throw in its lot with populist suspicion of authority and so it fell into a trap; for this proceeds, as we have seen, precisely by *enhancing* the importance of representation within government.

But authoritarianism, especially of the ideological kind, springs not from excess of authority, but from a perversion of it, which fails to receive it from its source in the true word of judgment, from outside and prior to all existing society, and attempts to construct it instead upon the self-projection of society. The critique of authoritarianism ought to extend not into a critique of authority but into a critique of social self-projection. It is, in fact, precisely as governments conceive themselves as an image, expressing a soul, or personality, or ideals of a people, that they overreach themselves and depart from the terms of their mandate for justice. The sociological thrust to self-imaging, then, is the root problem, whether expressed in authoritarian forms or, as in late-modern liberal society, in intensified forms of communication. For theology in liberal society simply to join the liberal hue and cry against conspiracies of power-holders is to evade the real critique by displacing it. The media are not the product of a conspiracy. They are the sign of the universal corruptibility of man's communications, of which theology has always known.

'The lie is the specific evil which man has introduced into nature', wrote Martin Buber. A Christian critique of the lie must involve the learning and cultivation of forms of communication which do not resemble those shaped by publicity.

Acknowledgements

An earlier version of this paper was presented at the Society for the Study of Christian Ethics, Wycliffe Hall, Oxford, September 1999, and was first published in *Studies in Christian Ethics* , **13**, No.1 (special issue on 'Media Ethics').

Laura Gascoigne

Mumbo-Dumbo:
Cleverness and Stupidity in
Conceptual Art

Now that the demarcation lines between art and popular culture, art and advertising, art and lifestyle have been breached (allegedly), we are all discerning consumers of art and our new museums are culture's answer to the shopping mall — sleek, desirable and eminently forgettable.

Gilane Tawadros, Director, INIVA, April 1999

When the director of a publicly-funded organization such as the Institute of International Visual Arts introduces the year's artistic programme with a statement of this jaundiced complexion, it may be time to sit up and take notice. It is almost unknown for arts administrators to raise their voices against the current trend towards so-called 'popularization' in the visual arts. For the past decade a conspiracy of silence has reigned over the increasingly sensationalist programming of contemporary exhibitions to appeal to the perceived tastes of a mass market and the preponderance of work in those exhibitions whose justification is conceptual rather than aesthetic.

The consensus in the art establishment appears to be that this is 'a good thing': it generates media interest and audiences and gives Britain a new 'modern' image abroad. But while these objectives may be good in themselves, are they being achieved at a cost to art? Is the work of the neo-conceptualists, which dominates contemporary art programming, really representative of the best work being produced in the visual arts, or are we giving it more space than it deserves? To put it bluntly, is it any good?

This is a question we are not supposed to ask, for historic reasons. The original theory of conceptual art, as developed by the 1960s avant-garde on foundations laid by the Dadaists and Duchamp, is based on the premise that its products are of no inherent value and, as such, immune to aesthetic value judgments. By taking a position that was 'anti-art', the pioneers of the conceptual art of the 1960s, such as Joseph Kosuth and Sol LeWitt, placed themselves beyond conventional criticism. Their aim was to destroy the established hierarchy of the art world, beginning with the perception of the artist as genius and of his work as perfect and unique. In the process they hoped to bring down the capitalist system by which art was traded in commercial galleries for the idle decoration of bourgeois homes or exhibited in public museums for the benefit of a bourgeois elite.

The driving force behind this art was political. It stemmed from a reaction against war — in Dada's case, against the First World War, and in the 1960s, against the war in Vietnam. The artists who practised it put their careers on the line and operated outside the system. They didn't expect to become famous or make money; their art wore its imperfections on its sleeve. The only test of whether it was successful was whether it upset the status quo. As Kosuth wrote in 1969, 'the value of particular artists after Duchamp could be weighed according to how much they questioned the nature of art; which is another way of saying "what they added to the conception of art".'

Art movements are essentially of their time and revivals never replicate them precisely. The first conceptual artists were idealistic: they believed in the possibility of change and trusted that their work would contribute to it. For a post-Cold War generation that has seen the collapse of Communism and the passing of political power to the big multi-national corporations, such simple optimism is impossible. The neo-conceptualists of the late twentieth century have taken everything from their predecessors but their idealism, and in its place have put postmodern irony.

A basic definition of conceptual art is as an artform in which the idea matters more than the object, irrespective of the form the object takes or the medium used to realize it. As Sol LeWitt, the inventor of the term, expressed it in 1967 in his essay 'Paragraphs in Conceptual Art': 'The idea becomes a machine that makes the art.' According to this definition the new generation of British artists promoted under the brand name yBa are conceptual artists. They work on the same premise and attack the same targets: the elitism of the art establishment; the tradition of the artist genius; the celebration of the unique object and the dismissal of the everyday as a subject for art.

The difference is that the situation has changed. Thanks partly to the efforts of their predecessors, art is no longer the sacred cow it was: the art world has opened up to new forms of practice, and the everyday has a place beside the sublime. With these developments have come further changes. Acceptance of conceptual art into the mainstream has subverted the worthlessness of the object and with it the anonymity of the artist as mere source of the idea behind the work. Neo-conceptualists may pay lip-service to a belief in the death of the author and the disposability of the object, but they themselves are lionized by the artworld and their temporary works laboriously preserved in museums. What remains of the early conceptualists' radical spirit is a self-referential concern with the nature of art, a rejection of art history in favour of theory, and a basic feeling that art should be democratic — interpreted by most contemporary practitioners as meaning that it should address the issues and adopt the language of popular culture.

But we must beware of falling into the age-old trap of seeing every new trend as a 'dumbing down'. In an expanded art world growing fat on Lottery money, with new arts centres opening monthly across the country, there ought to be room for more than one sort of art. The traditional artforms are still flourishing — despite repeated announcement of the death of painting, in a London Arts Board survey of 1998 the majority of respondents (44%) were still painters. If neo-conceptualism is but the latest arrival in a vibrant, thriving, multi-faceted art scene, what harm is there in giving it gallery space?

Left to itself there would be very little. Painting and sculpture flourished alongside (and learned from) the conceptual avant-gardes of the 1910s and 1960s, and there is no reason in theory why they should not do so today. But in practice the present system is rearing a cuckoo that threatens to push other artforms out of the nest. The fault lies not with conceptual art itself, but with an artworld in which patronage depends on the media: museum-funding follows audiences, and audiences follow the media lead. Such is modern life, you sigh: what is the problem? The problem is that the media love the conceptual, for the simple reason that it makes a better story.

It is always hard to write about painting or sculpture, because you need a developed visual language; to write about them in a way that grips the public is almost impossible. But conceptual art is essentially verbal, consisting in ideas which can be explained. Ideas are a gift to any journalist regardless of a background in arts writing, and the more outrageous they are, the better: hence the column inches given over to conceptual art at the expense of serious coverage of traditional media. This imbalance is reflected in public funding and the programming of public exhibitions, and compounded by a system of public investment in which works of art are purchased by committee. Buying a painting or sculpture is a contentious business, involving personal taste and the emotions; it is far easier to reach agreement on a conceptual work, which involves an intellectual decision.

Against this background, it is hard for painters and sculptors to make a name outside the private sphere or to keep track of what their contemporaries are doing. But the worst sufferers are art students in traditional disciplines. Since the subsumption of art colleges into universities under Thatcher, art teaching is subject to the same criteria as other more academic disciplines. The result is a new premium on words: to compete for funding, art departments must meet targets for research and publication regardless of their records for practical excellence. These targets are more likely to be met by teachers of conceptual than traditional art, who can call on semiotics and contextual studies to fill the quota of verbiage required.

It is already hard for students who are 'just' good at practice to succeed in a system which values written work. Moreover, applicants to art college can no longer assume that they will learn the traditional skills of their profession; to be sure of this they must pick their college with care. Equally, there is no guarantee that they will be taught the history of art before the twentieth century by tutors who have themselves dismissed it as invalid or only of sociological interest. As the present generation of students become teachers these difficulties will be exacerbated.

Do you need to know art history to become an artist? There is a feeling abroad among the yBas that breaking with precedent is a necessary preliminary to doing anything new, but the evidence of their work does not support this. Many of their ideas are not new, but reworkings of the ideas of their predecessors. A case in point is Anya Gallacio's 1996 ice installation, anticipated a generation earlier in ice works by Gyula Konkoly, Allan Kaprow, Ian Baxter, Rafael Ferrer and Paul Kos, most of which were more complex and interesting. Are conceptual ideas in limited supply, or don't conceptual artists know the history even of their own movement? It is noticeable how, when they find an idea that works—like Rachel Whiteread's 1993 casting of an empty house (itself the realization of an earlier idea of 1960s American conceptualist Ed Kienholz)—they stick to it. (One commentator has cruelly remarked of Whiteread that the only space she will eventually have left to fill is the one between her ears.) It seems that artists who don't know art history are condemned to repeat themselves.

The best conceptual pieces, like the best traditional works, operate on a variety of levels and do so visually, without need of explanation. When the idea is the art, it must be a good one, and this is all too rarely the case. Conceptual art can of course seek verbal assistance in a way that traditional art forms cannot—explaining a painting doesn't increase its impact, just as explaining a joke doesn't make it funny. But while interpretation may make an idea sound clever—especially when the full intellectual panoply of new art theory is brought into play—it won't turn a bad idea into a good one. Add mumbo to dumbo, and you get mumbo-dumbo.

Bad and good ideas? This smacks of value judgment. Surely conceptual art is immune to this? No longer. It lost its immunity when it came in from the cold to warm itself at the establishment hearth—a move which might find ideological justification in the argument that institutions are best undermined from within, but is tactically a stupid mistake. For official acceptance and the accompanying price tags have removed its precious exemption from the value judgment and made it as vulnerable to criticism as any other art form. When ideas change hands for tens of thousands of pounds, it is a valid question to ask if they are worth it.

At this point, its defenders play their last card and claim that the value of conceptual art lies in something less quantifiable even than an idea: it lies in the questions it raises. But even this special pleading will not protect it. For just as there is such a thing as a bad idea, there is also such a thing as a stupid question.

David Lee

What Contemporary Art Means to Me

followed by a conversation with *Ivo Mosley*

What does 'contemporary art' mean to me, as distinct from plain old 'art'?

First of all, it means an income. Not a very good one, but editing a magazine like *Art Review* beats working for a living, especially if the alternative requires kowtowing to a suit with business studies degree from the University of South Bacup.

It means having to look at and read about a huge quantity of fashionable art whose qualities, when judged against any known criteria, are conspicuously absent. Qualities claimed for the work have to be taken on trust, there being no method of objective assessment. Criteria proposed for evaluating the work are arbitrary, and made up as the arbiter goes along. In order to enjoy most fashionable art it is necessary to have endless patience and the blind faith of a religious convert.

It means the tyranny of the young and therefore, very probably, the tyranny of the badly educated — those who have no awareness of their own derisory pretentiousness.

It means that in figurative painting one is expected to overlook bad drawing and inept composition and pretend it doesn't matter, because the artist is allegedly attempting something else 'challengingly' beyond the range of the normal. In any other discipline — music or literature, say — the equivalent 'experiments', with their demonstrable incompetence, would be laughed at.

It means graduating students pursuing a reputation as fast as possible and at all costs. The belief seems to be that there's no virtue in obscurity, however brilliant you may be. Thus there is a frenetic rush by youngsters to provoke column inches and air minutes of news for their activities, because this personal visibility will be the yardstick by which their artistic success is judged. When notoriety is all, the work becomes an impertinence, a mere epiphenomenon of the reputation.

It means the establishing of an instantly recognisable brand image. In a competitive market, branding and distinctiveness is the ticket. It is all that counds.

It means unreadable, lazily-edited art magazines of predictable content.

It means institutionalized corruption, prejudice and censorship, and the self-perpetuation of governing oligarchies so narrow-sighted that they are effectively blind. The Arts Council springs to mind as an organization which has done nothing to suggest that public funding of the visual arts should be continued. Indeed, their antics over the last decade might be looked upon in the future, when we get around to deciding a better structure for arts funding, as a way of how not to do it.

It means, through public funding, the institutionalization of mediocrity, the creation of a layer of artists who previously did not exist but which exists only because public funding is there to pay for it.

It means young artists bleating incessantly about how little they earn, as if the world owes them a living regardless of whether they produce something anyone wants to buy.

It means self-pitying artists thinking their work is not appreciated because viewers and collectors are blind, ignorant, ill-educated *etc. etc.* It never occurs to these artists that the reason they are ignored might be because they are no good.

It means an art-funding apparatus in which crucial decisions are made by administrators, and not by those known for any judgment in art matters. And it means, therefore, the accession to authority of the art-historically ignorant. Many of today's art bureaucrats give every indication of having an encyclopaedic knowledge of what happened a week ago last Monday, but know bugger all about what happened at almost any other period before that.

It means an Arts Council which discriminates against *anything* historical or traditional, and which routinely contravenes the principles of its charter, which states that the best is to be taken to the majority.

It means stunts, diversions and pseudo-entertainments dropped on our streets and in our countryside which the perpetrators have the effrontery to call 'public art', a misnomer on two counts as it is rarely art and the public couldn't give a toss.

It means good artists are *not* exhibited because they are old or unfashionable, and fail to come within the brackets of 'young', 'contemporary' and 'innovative'. They may excel at their style, medium, technique, or whatever, but their efforts are censored by a prejudiced state apparatus. In short they are the wrong kinds of artists.

It means a great many artists working honestly, modestly and quietly in obscurity, struggling with poverty and a lack of recognition; resigned perhaps to these, but bitter at the manipulation of art by a very few powerful people and galleries.

It means that, because conceptual art monopolizes art publicity, all contemporary art is perceived by most people as a monumental confidence trick.

It means that art, as an activity whose purpose is to give pleasure and profound experience to the viewer and to arouse and educate dormant imagination has been exterminated by a deadly cocktail of polytechnic theorists, lazy educators, political manipulators and gender bores.

But, most of all, it means an income. When I retire, for all I care 'contemporary art' can vanish even further up its own arse.

* * *

IM: It would seem you have nothing good to say about contemporary art. How do you see your role as editor of Art Review?
Well, for a start I have always maintained that we should be acknowledging good aspects of *all* the different types of art that are going on, instead of establishing a monopoly for one type of work.

IM: How has this monopoly been established?
It is very difficult to say. But if you institutionalize a culture — and that inevitably had to happen once the Art's Council was founded in 1946 — then you create bodies in museums, art institutions, regional art schools, which are self-perpetuating cliques. Very often, the personnel who organize one strand have a foot in the other strands as well. So you get certain very influential people sitting on various apparently

unrelated committees for decision-making in the visual arts, and the result is a monopoly of taste. Now, that monopoly was going unchallenged. It seemed to me when I came here as editor, that we ought to make an attempt to challenge it, however ham-fisted. We've started, but we've not made a good job of it, often resorting to hectoring, satire and scurrility instead of close argument.

IM: As an editor, you make judgments of what is good and bad. On what basis do you judge?
I haven't any rigid answers. There aren't any. I will openly admit that I am just as much at sea as everybody else. But I would like to be able to acknowledge any good work of its type, whatever that type is. Now this is precisely what the monopolizing institutions of the visual arts are not prepared to do. The criteria of judgment also seem arbitrary, wayward. One set of almost blank canvases are masterpieces. Another set are no good. I'm mystified by such distinctions.

IM: Where does the corruption you spoke of come in?
When you institutionalize certain types of work, you put behind them the huge apparatus of the state and its undeniably impressive PR machines. They're brilliant at the Tate Gallery and at the Arts Council which, contrary to the moaning minnies of the Melvyn & Joan Club have money absolutely thrown at them. They are always pleading poverty, but have always got millions to be building this and buying that.

The monoliths have created a false market. There is a relationship between that state apparatus and half a dozen galleries in the West End of London, who are extremely wealthy and who promote the kind of artists who get nominated for the Turner Prizes, NatWest prizes, Venice Biennale's, and so forth, which is questionable. I wouldn't be at all surprised if, in fifty years, books weren't published identifying very dubious connections between the Establishment and the way its facilities have been exploited by commercial dealerships. There is a great deal of money at stake when the state is used by commercial dealers to endorse the reputations of their artists.

For instance, take the Turner Prize. They give it a patination of democracy by soliciting nominations from the public, then they completely ignore them. When a newspaper follows up on what the public would like to see winning the Turner Prize, they are completely different to what actually gets nominated. The reason why the Turner Prize appears to be given to the same kinds of 'cutting edge' artists every year, often friends of friends of friends of friends, is because the person who selects the judges dictates what kind of a shortlist the prize is going to be. Therefore, nobody is ever nominated to be a Turner Prize judge unless they are reliably subservient to the cause. Don't forget that the Turner Prize has been won on nine out of fourteen occasions by artists from only two commercial galleries.

IM: So the state and private interests are in league together?
I'm not being a conspiracy theorist but I am sure there is an overlap between the aims, ambitions, motives of certain private collectors and certain private dealers and the way in which the visual arts have been organized by the state.

IM: Is a recovery possible?
I don't think that there is any recovery possible, simply because the present apparatus is so firmly entrenched. They are so all-powerful, untouchable. They are impregnable, they can just sit there and people can throw brickbats at them for as long as they like, and they're still there at the end. It's like Saddam Hussein — he can be wrong, you can keep challenging him, but in the end he just says, 'I won, because I'm still here.' It's a very similar situation with the paladins who run visual art. It is, however, inevitable that publicly-funded galleries, especially those run by the Arts Council, will have to widen their selection procedure so that they not only acknowledge history but also show work by the best representational painters of all ages, rather than just 'innovative' work by the young.

IM: So do you think that all state involvement in funding and subsidy should be withdrawn from contemporary art?
I think we should re-think how state subsidy operates in relation to the visual arts. I've recently come to the view that we ought to suspend all funding of visual arts until a better way of disbursing money is identified.

IM: It seems to me peculiar, that a state run by the liberal bourgeoisie is promoting art that is supposedly for permanent revolution. I

always thought the bourgeoisie stood for stability and moral values.
Well, that's the inversion that has taken place. Let's date the
beginning of the avant-garde to the mid-1850s, when Courbet
decided that he would confront the art establishment. He put
on his own exhibition, and was followed in that process by
Manet and organized the first Impressionist exhibition in
1874. So between 1854 and 1874 the avant-garde began, in
opposition to the 'bourgeois state' as represented by the *salon*.

Well, now the situation is completely reversed. We have
institutionalized the avant-garde so that it is emasculated. The
people who are supposedly on the 'cutting edge' are the ones
who are receiving state sponsorship. The people actually
going against the grain are those who continue working traditionally! Their work is vilified or ignored.

When the Turner Prize was awarded a few years ago, that
ridiculous berk Peter Palumbo talked about how these poor
artists nominated for the Turner Prize are the inheritors of the
mantle of Van Gogh. Well, there isn't any comparison. Van
Gogh really was an avant-garde artist. These people, about
whom he was talking, were full of the best wine and food that
money can buy and exhibit in the most prestigious contemporary art space around the world. Van Gogh actually starved!

*IM: You've expressed disappointment that art is so withdrawn
from what's actually happened in the times we've lived through. Do
you come across artists who have tried to come to terms with that?*
There are contemporary painters who are dealing with serious
social issues. Not agit-prop, I'm not interested in that—we
had enough of that in the sixties and seventies, it was bilge
and it has ended up in the basements of museums never to be
seen again, and that is where it deserves to be until finally
someone passes an Act of Parliament so that they can pile it up
in the courtyard and set it on fire. But there are artists, who
through the themes of their work have looked at life in Glasgow, or wherever, and tried to produce something which is a
modern history picture.

The artists doing that don't get much acknowledgement.
Take a painter like Mark Lanson, he's a very young artist and
he's doing something serious. He's looking at people with the
same intensity, fears, emotions, sensitivities and sensibilities
as Rembrandt was looking at himself. Paul Reed is another—

very young, a Scottish artist—who deals with them in a different way. But you can't write a news story about somebody like that, because they are just artists. Whereas someone exhibits a bed covered with semen and it's a news story, an 'issue'. So that makes it art? It's madness! We don't treat any other discipline in the way we treat art.

IM: It seems you get a lot of people coming to you because they see you as a voice crying in the wilderness.
I don't think so; if they did it would be reflected in the circulation of the magazine and it would mean I'd get paid more! The circulation of the magazine goes up painfully slowly, drip by drip. I just want to establish that there is another way of looking at things. There are other things happening, but they require concentration and can't be reduced to sight-bites. I don't know—maybe in fifty years time I'll look back and think, 'Christ, why couldn't I see that Gary Hume's so good, why couldn't I see that Damien Hirst's spot pictures are wonderful?' But I don't think I will, because I am 99.9% sure that there is nothing there, just trademarks. The rest of the '90s will eventually be seen as opportunism or perhaps careerism.

IM: Is it difficult to find things to celebrate nowadays? Looking at nature, it has been so polluted and dominated by man...
Well, you can convey all that in landscape painting. An artist can do great work about any subject. It doesn't matter how humble it is or how small, there are great paintings of paving stones, just as there are great paintings of great historical events. I just love looking at great things. I don't want to waste my time with shite, in the same way that I want to read great books instead of wasting my time reading about modern art, 99.9% of which is pretentious gibberish. I want to read *Birthday Letters* by Ted Hughes, which is what I am doing at the moment. I can't wait to go home tonight so I can get going again. It is wonderful. I thought that with the death of Larkin we had lost the ability to produce poets who could produce verse as rich and multi-layered as that.

IM: So you don't see the dire state of the fashionable art world as symptomatic of a decline in Western civilization, or anything as grand or alarming as that?

No, not really. I can't think in those kind of terms, because in the end art is of minor significance. It doesn't matter. When perople are starving or living in snow-covered tents because a fat and greedy West is too complacent to do something about it. My family was recently in the middle of a very bad earthquake in Turkey. For several minutes of great intensity I thought I was going to die. That kind of experience puts art in its true insignificant light.

IM: You think it is a temporary blip and things will clear......
I think we will come round. There are cycles in taste. We will have to get to grips soon. I think in the end, art education will have to be re-thought in much the way in which people are beginning to think it ought to be. The way to get people involved with art is to get them when they are young. If you don't, half the population will be lost to art for ever, as current statistics demonstrate. At the moment for most people the Elgin Marbles can't compete with *Eastenders*. We will have to rethink public funding of the arts, because once people become aware of how much is being spent in their name they are going to be more critical, vociferous and demanding.

IM: But do most voters care?
Well no, they don't at the moment, because when you go in a cubicle to cast your vote in an election you do it based on whether you have got a job, enough to eat, whether the kids are adequately clothed and educated or whatever. You don't think, 'Ah! That piece of public art on the pavement is shite, and we shouldn't spend 60,000 quid on it. Therefore I'm voting for...' But eventually, I think we will demand greater accountability for art, and not allow a small number of people to dictate everything that is going on.

IM: There is a certain kind of complaining which is just part of the general game, and which the Establishment feels quite comfortable with. But I think that your more aggressive and insulting way really gets up their noses.
I want to be insulting. I want to be malicious. I am angry that so few people have been allowed to monopolize a system for so long, and that there has been so little criticism of them for doing so. It's an affront, an affront to the vast majority of artists.

Peter Randall-Page

Form, Transformation and a Common Humanity

We inhabit a world of forms which includes our own bodies, and the universe is animated by ceaseless change and transformation which articulates time itself; our universe is form in constant transformation.

The aspect of transformation which particularly interests me is that which takes place when we make things. The products of the human imagination tell us about our fundamental nature and our relationship to the rest of the universe. These insights may be into the culture to which someone belongs; they may be more personal and psychological; and, I would argue, they also inform us of our common humanity.

In cultural terms, human artifacts can reveal an enormous amount about societies from the distant past. The Egyptologist gleans a great deal about the hierarchies, beliefs and the everyday life of ancient Egypt by the study of the artifacts of that civilization. This way of understanding cultures focuses on differences rather than similarities. The ways in which cultures are similar are less apparent, because we expect them as the norm, the background against which the differences stand out.

It is hardly surprising that there are huge areas in common between diverse cultures even when there is no history of contact, because as human beings we share so much in common: our physiology, our physical needs, our very nature. The way these basic human concerns are evoked or depicted are like dialects within one single language.

It is true, of course, that things change their meaning radically in different contexts. A tribal mask in a museum case becomes a very different object from the animated embodiment of an animal spirit for which it might have been intended. The religious belief systems to which an object refers can only be fully understood in the context of the whole culture. On the other hand, I have always been struck by how sculptures made in cultures as diverse as ancient Egypt, India, pre-Colombian South America and sub-Saharan Africa can communicate to me intensely and eloquently, and on a fundamental level, despite the differences in centuries and geography between myself and their makers. I am no expert in any of these civilizations but nevertheless their artifacts speak to me of the human condition, by virtue of my common humanity with that of their authors.

Certain universally-shared human preoccupations and concerns are apparent in subject matter. Fertility symbols and the depiction of the child at the mother's breast, for example, can be found in virtually all cultures. Myths, legends, traditional stories and religious texts often concern archetypal characters and events which have obvious equivalents in other cultures. The common factors have little to do with naturalism, or verisimilitude — which has in any case been an occasional aberration in the history of art, rather than the cultural norm. In sculptural terms, it seems more to do with a common understanding of form; what can best be described as a sense of 'rightness' which somehow animates an object giving it human meaning. This is not the kind of narrative or symbolic meaning that can be put into words, but a sense of recognition, the apprehension of a consciousness and intelligence like our own behind the object itself. This sense of what constitutes a form which has 'rightness' is so pervasive it seems to happen almost despite ourselves, as an unselfconscious by-product of making things, quite independent of the symbolic, illustrative or narrative intention of the work.

It is as if while the conscious mind is busy with a complex task like painting or carving, the unconscious mind is liberated to make its contribution directly to the hand.

This process is particularly intense and highly developed in art we call 'traditional'. Both symbolic and formal archetypes emerge there through what can be seen as a kind of cultural natural selection: images become refined and honed over many generations, working within certain clearly-defined iconographic and formal traditions. In sculptural terms, this often results in a stylization and abstraction. Rhythms, proportions and patterns take on a language of their own, using a vocabulary which seems to derive more from underlying principals of the way the universe is. In many cases, the formalized aspects of the objects depart completely from representation and become abstract, seeming to embody spirit rather than to illustrate appearance.

What is more, it is on this level of abstract stylization that a common language of proportion, rhythm and pattern seems to exist between disparate cultures. This phenomenon is quite different from the more obvious common preoccupations with such things as fertility, kinship and power.

Why should this abstract language of form be shared by so many disparate cultures?

A concept common to many societies is that the artist is a kind of conduit or medium through which the image becomes manifest. The artist's work seems to aspire to a truth beyond mere appearance — perhaps to an inner model in human nature itself.

In his 1934 book, *The Transformation of Nature in Art*, Ananda K. Coomaraswamy analyses a community of theory behind pre-Renaissance European and Asiatic art, and contrasts this with post-Renaissance European art. He reveals a basic philosophic orientation on the part of the Mediaeval European and Asiatic artist, in which art and religion are the same, not merely related, and I suspect that this idea could be equally well extrapolated to encompass 'traditional' cultures throughout the world.

He states in this context, 'Naturalism is antipathetic to religious art of all kinds, to art of any kind.' He describes the process by which the Indian artist approaches the making of an iconic image.

> The maker of an icon, having eliminated the distracting influences of fugitive emotions and creature images, proceeds to visualise the form...The mind 'produces' or 'draws' this form to itself, as though from a great distance.

He goes on to state:

> The principle involved is that true knowledge of an
> object is not obtained by merely empirical observa-
> tion or reflex registration, but only when the knower
> and known, seer and seen, meet in an act transcend-
> ing distinction.

Here Mediaeval European and Asiatic Art meet on common
ground. According to the fourteenth-century German mystic
Meister Eckhart, 'the skilled painter shows his art, but it is not
himself that it reveals to us'; or in the words of Dante, 'Who
paints a figure, if he cannot be it, cannot draw it.'

There are echoes in these ideas of the Platonic concepts of
'ideal' archetypal forms existing somewhere behind the material manifestations of our world.

In our own highly personalized materialist society we
equate 'likeness' in art with verisimilitude, but in the context
of traditional art 'likeness' takes on a quite different meaning.
For example such terms as 'following the movement of the
world' and 'designating the intrinsic nature of the world' are
used by Seami, the greatest author and critic of Japanese Noh
Theatre, to describe how a drama should be performed. He
asserts that the arts of music and dancing consist entirely of
imitation, though Noh theatre is undoubtedly amongst the
most stylized and least naturalistic forms of drama in the
world. This kind of imitation is not to be confused with illusion, nor with an idealized image of things in the sense of
'nearer to the heart's desire'. Rather Asiatic art is ideal in the
mathematical sense—like nature not in appearance but in
operation. The essential prerequisite of this approach is that
subjective and objective need not be mutually exclusive, irreconcilable categories, one of which must be regarded as real at
the expense of the other. Reality, in this view, is where the
intelligible and sensible meet in a common unity of being as
knowledge or vision.

Once again, the same concept can be found in Mediaeval
Europe, this time in the works of St Thomas Aquinas. 'Knowledge comes about insofar as the object known is within the
knower.'

Bearing these traditions in mind, the post-Renaissance
Western obsession with literal verisimilitude appears a

strange phenomenon, an aberration. So what is the nature of these underlying models, or platonic archetypes, of form? As an agnostic myself, I find it difficult to accept mystical or religious interpretations. Similarly, my rational mind is suspicious of concepts such as intuition.

Taking a cue from science, however, we may move on to explore what might lie behind this, helped in particular by the scientifically reputable concept 'instinct'. It is sometimes easy to forget that art and science both stem from the same human combination of intellectual curiosity and satisfaction in discovering meaning, pattern and order in the universe. The importance of pattern recognition in particular can hardly be over-estimated, both in the evolution of human consciousness and in the development of science and art. The ability to recognize patterns makes it possible to predict future events; night follows day, the moon waxes and wanes, the seasons' inevitable 'procession' can be used to predict such things as the migration of game animals and the appropriate moment to sow seeds and harvest crops. The recognition of patterns liberates human beings from a perpetual present. Mathematics itself, fundamental to all systematic scientific study, can best be described as a study of patterns.

The gulf which has grown between science and art belies this common ancestry. Science now aspires to an impersonal and objective account of the world, deliberately devoid of 'meaning', revealing its workings but nothing of it as experienced, its joys and sorrows. Art, on the other hand, has become the antithesis — 'an untrammelled celebration of that human subjectivity that divides us from the beasts'.

In his 1995 book *The Artful Universe* John Barrow explored 'the ways in which our common experience of living in the universe rubs off on us'. He writes:

> It has become fashionable since the 1960s to regard all interesting human attributes as things that are learned from our contacts with individuals and society — as the result of nurture not nature — and to ignore the universalities of human thinking. Recently, this prejudice has been seriously undermined. Things are far more complicated. The complexities of our minds and bodies bear witness to a

long history of subtle adaptations. Human beings,
with all their likes and dislikes, their senses and sensibilities, did not fall ready made from the sky; nor
were they born with minds and bodies that bear no
imprint of the history of their species. Many of our
abilities and susceptibilities are specific adaptations
to ancient environmental problems, rather than separate manifestations of a general intelligence from
all seasons.

We have evolved in this universe and it has evolved in us, so
it is hardly surprising if some of these environmental univer-
salities reflect the regulations of the solar system, galaxies, the
whole universe. What we call intuition, Professor Barrow suggests, is better described as instinct, hard wired into our very
being.

The separation of science from the creative arts in Western
philosophy really only began with Descartes. It was he who
emphasized a clear division between the observer and the
observed, making possible the birth of the idea of dispassionate objective science. The idea of pure objectivity is nevertheless fundamentally flawed. We are part of the universe; can a
part of something objectively analyse that of which it is part as
if it were separate, detached, dispassionate and uninvolved?
Even a concept as fundamental and seemingly unquestion-
able as numbers has origins in an artificial construct — the way
we think of ourselves and others as singular and discrete
entities.

So both science and the creative arts have come to misrepresent themselves. Science is less objective, and the creative arts
less a matter of the free expression of the unique and idiosyncratic response of the individual, than we might suppose.

The innate ability of human beings to acquire language is a
compelling example of predisposition, which can be extrapolated into other areas of human activity such as music and the
visual arts. The American linguist Noam Chomsky explored
and developed his ideas in the face of much opposition from
anthropologists and social scientist in the late 1950s. For
Chomsky, language is a cognitive ability innate to humans.
Our brains contain genetically programmed neural 'wiring'
which predisposes us to the acquisition of language. This pre-

disposition is not for any particular human language, but rather for the building blocks of language. He noticed that we have an innate intuitive feel for the formal structure of language, and that this can flourish in whatever linguistic environment a child finds itself. All human language shares certain fundamental structural characteristics which can be seen as variations on a theme, a theme embedded deep in the genetic make up of the newborn child.

This concept of how we are able to learn something as complex as language at such a young age is now well documented and widely accepted. Less well documented, but I believe equally plausible and compelling, are the arguments that our abilities to create and appreciate music and the visual arts are also innate, laid down in prototype form as grammatical structures which we inherit from our forbears and which originate as by-products of long forgotten adaptive developments in our evolutionary past.

There is not time here to go into these predilections for pattern and structure in music and art in great detail. However, certain musical sequences and rhythmic patterns have been found to underlie music from diverse cultural traditions, and it has been suggested that these may relate to the patterns of language as well as to the internal rhythms of the body. In the visual arts, similarity of pattern and ornament from a wide range of different cultures bears witness to a kind of universal grammar in our visual inventions.

The Grammar of Ornament, by Owen Jones (1856), illustrates strikingly fundamental similarities in the formal solutions to universal design problems. Symmetry is one of the most obvious and universal human predilections. Symmetrical things have been generally of more significance to our survival— what we eat, what eats us and what we mate with are all more-or-less symmetrical. The degree of subtlety of expression which we are capable of perceiving in the broadly symmetrical constellation of the human face shows how keenly attuned we are to symmetry and the slightest divergence from it. We look for pattern and symmetry where none exist; the random damp patch on the wall is more likely to appear to us as a face, body or animal than anything else, a tendency put to use by psychologists in the ink blot test.

I hope it is now becoming apparent that we assume that our conscious mind has far more control over our thoughts and actions, our likes and dislikes, our desires and fears than it actually does. When we are involved in such complex tasks as writing or playing music, drawing or painting, carving or modelling we are engaged in activities which draw on our own experience and fundamental nature in many different ways and on many different levels. The qualities that give a work of art universal meaning result from precisely those unarticulated feelings which slip through the conscious mind unnoticed while it is busy with the task at hand.

As a sculptor working mainly with stone, I am aware of this in my own working practice. It is when thought and action become fused and indivisible in the working process that unarticulated feelings rise to the surface. In this way of work-ing it feels as if the sculpture takes shape despite, rather than as a result of, one's carving. Subjective and objective are no longer in opposition. It is easy to see how this process might feel like a 'drawing-down' of forms from Heaven, as in tradi-tional Indian texts; the mind of the artist 'drawing the form to itself, as from a great distance, through meditation'. Could this 'great distance' be that between our everyday conscious world, structured by its nurture in our own society, and the fundamental predilections of our very nature, evolved in the genetic code of our ancestors?

The universe exists inside us as well as all around us, and we understand it as participants as well as voyeurs, viewing it from the inner surface. In this sense human consciousness can be seen as a mirror in which the universe reflects upon itself; and in this perspective boundaries between biology and psy-chology, science and art, genetics and aesthetics begin to break down in a way that makes nature and culture seem a little less irreconcilable.

Interview: Peter Randall-Page with Ivo Mosley

IM: Your essay is a positive vision of what art can be. With these questions I'd like to extract a few observations from you about what seems to be happening in art today. I wonder if some of the triviality and banality, the self-destructive side of modern art and even its totalitarian feel come from abolishing the idea of the sacred in art?

Well, it's true we've become rather alienated from that, and it's a well-documented process of urban twentieth-century alienation. I think that a lot of the art that is produced now is tremendously nostalgic for a state of grace which we don't feel any more. I think it is difficult now, when the person making the art is so much more self-conscious. If you live in a culture where the stories and the metaphors and the symbolism and iconography seem absolutely real, making an artifact must feel very different.

IM: So is there an answer to the question, 'What's art for?'?
I think it's reconciliation in a way, or it's sort of trying to make things whole. For us in our culture, it's trying to make the inner life reconciled with the world as perceived and lived in outside. In other cultures, where art and life are more at one, it's an expression of making sense of the world, of understanding it. I suppose an example of that would be looking at the stars which are random little points of light and coming up with things like Orion's Belt.

IM: So people didn't believe the story about Orion's Belt in the same way we believe for instance that two-plus-two is four. They felt it because it drew the universe in to be part of themselves.
Yes. It's not like science, not reductive, analytical. Of course, if you look at it from a scientific perspective, it is a lot of nonsense. But I don't think it is nonsense, because it's a different kind of truth.

IM: The truth of our connection with the outside world expressed in a metaphorical way?
It is very easy to believe that the sum total of our intelligence is a reductive kind of intelligence. I think our intelligence has other potentials which are very apparent, have been very apparent in human history and actually are not very apparent at the moment. That is very distinctive about our culture.

IM: So why has that come to be?
It's because those reductive ways of understanding the world have been so fantastically successful, in such tangible ways. They've given us all the technology we have. We have been kind of awe-struck by it, it's a new magic. But scientific truth

can only fill in the detail, lots and lots and lots of detail, it doesn't answer any of the really big questions.

IM: So it's like the classic story of Moses and Aaron. Moses is up the mountain talking with God, and Aaron builds a great golden statue and all the people start worshipping it. Then people get brought to earth with a jolt.

There's an understanding of these issues in those old stories...the Icarus theme is absolutely classic. But I wouldn't want to knock the scientific method. It is quite specific, and extraordinarily exciting and amazing. I wouldn't want to knock it for one minute. It's a faculty that human consciousness has been able to develop, an extraordinary faculty of reductive, analytical understanding which has uncovered many profound truths about the world we live in, but I don't think it is the whole story.

IM: So there is a power struggle going on between traditional interests and a new technocratic power-base, fighting for the votes of the masses; and the lure of technocracies – the huge, material rewards – makes people think 'it would be stupid not to go along with this'. Meanwhile, everything is getting much more dangerous and alarming as the technocrats are winning.

Yes, I think that is probably true. Although I think everybody has other kinds of feelings which aren't really being properly acknowledged. People are becoming more and more internalized, because you leave so much out of your relations to the rest of the world if you just analyse it and exploit it.

IM: So people are unfulfilled?

Yes, but I think it may equally be because people are alienated in a more obvious way, in that they don't have a shared culture or a shared symbolic order of any kind. The reductive, scientific process has no compassion in it. It is a pretty ruthless idea. I am not at all anti-rational, but I do think there is an imbalance now, that society does not acknowledge what human beings are actually like.

Our legal system, our political system, everything, starts to be judged in a pseudo-scientific way and even art starts to become pseudo-scientific. That is the interesting thing. Art has embraced that analytical, reductive method and has become pseudo-scientific.

IM: How do you mean?
Well, it's become rather literal, so the idea of using a parallel metaphorical language, which isn't like the real world but can talk about the real world, is gone. So for instance, if you want to talk about mortality, you present a dead thing, which seems to me not the most subtle and potent way to talk about the nature of mortality. Or if someone wants to talk about nature, they use leaves and twigs and it seems to me, again, to be incredibly literal. I have a feeling that this somehow ties up with an obsession with empiricism. A lot of things to do with process art and conceptual art depend very heavily on whether it really happened, whether you really went through this process, whether you really covered your body with whatever and the marks you made were really the result of having rolled on the canvas. I think that the scientific attitude, 'Did it really happen?' has become terribly, terribly, pervasive. I have been more moved by things which are a little more oblique.

IM: Is the metaphorical world of art that you talk about like an intermediate world, between one's knowledge of the real world and what you might call divine order or God?
Maybe. I'm not in any way religious and I haven't got a mystical belief that any human can find ultimate truth. It's more to do with the levels of sophistication about how we can understand what we are, and where we fit into things.

IM: It seems to me illogical to be fanatically atheistic. Why do you think there is such a strong impulse to think that the universe and one's consciousness are freak events?
It's easy to stop at some given point in one's thinking as you grow up. You can get fixated on a particular thing, which can limit the growth of your imagination or your consciousness. I think one should try and understand things as best one can with the faculties one's got. I don't know very much and never will know very much, so as I get older I get more and more suspicious of people who are dogmatic about anything. And

I'm more and more interested in people who are quite open about not knowing.

IM: Another essay in this book makes the point that there is a conflict in each of us between the individual and the mass person. Art has now got so individualist that it is difficult to operate in one's identity as part of a community. People who are unhappy competing as individuals are deprived of the world they once had, of surety and security...

And of creativity and all those things. They become vicarious, living through the big names, living through the stars. Maybe before, people lived through the gods; perhaps that's the same in one sense, but when our gods are real individual people — when it's Princess Diana rather than Thor — it becomes a bit prosaic. It's awful, how our heroes are people who can then be caught doing some mischief and brought down, and the desire to bring them down by the Press is so strong.

In the Renaissance, art was commissioned by the Church, and artists were asked to depict particular religious scenes in a certain way. Now, creative people are employed by companies to advertise their products. Advertisements are incredibly clever and sophisticated and a great deal of creativity goes into them. But there is nowhere to go with them. Even if you are a jobbing sculptor making a Madonna and Child, there is the possibility that it can transcend the brief. The terms of the subject are bigger — the relationship between child and mother.

So I think we are in a barren time in many respects. But when I am working I feel optimistic. There are things to be explored about our relationships with each other and the wider world which are intensely potent and real to me. So that's kind of optimistic.

Bill Hare

Glasgow Belongs to Whom? Civic Identity in the Visual Arts in Scotland

The ongoing and seemingly irreconcilable antagonism between high art and low culture (aka art and kitsch) has been a running sore in the body politic of modern British social debate since the days of Matthew Arnold. This critical civil war between those who doggedly support aesthetic quality and lofty cultural standards on the one hand, and those who fiercely champion accessible contemporary art forms and popular entertainment on the other, is probably most exemplified by the critical writings of TS Eliot and George Orwell. In the visual arts of this country this socio-political struggle has been no less vigorously fought—from the Ruskin versus Whistler court case to Lord Clark's *Civilization* set against John Berger's *Ways of Seeing*, the battle lines have been clearly etched on the public's consciousness. Coming right up to the present this division between cultural elitism and mass populism is still a topic of great contention as witnessed by the recent editorial in *Art Review* (October 1999). There David Lee robustly airs all the old issues yet again, with the usual dire warnings of barbarians hammering at the city gates.

> The Culture Minister should not force museums to become amusement arcades in order that he can announce triumphantly to the dinosaur Left that those who previously ignored museums are now coming round. He should encourage hard-line elitism and concern himself with making museums free

while further extending opening hours. The rest is up to the individual. To try to appeal to the uneducated by spoiling the experience of the museum for the rest, with the inevitable result of demeaning the art itself, is unhinged.

The Culture Minister ought to think hard before forcing museums down the populist avenue antipathetic to their real purpose and which trivialises knowledge and learning and discourages scrutiny. The potential for irreparable damage is enormous, the first results already visible.

Such cultural Jeremiahs have been with us for an awfully long time! For this essay I would like to focus on this apparently never-ending debate but within the particular context of the role played by the visual arts in the civic politics of Glasgow over the last two decades.

From the outset we should remember that because of its particular circumstances and development the overall history and character of the visual arts in Scotland is decidedly different from that pertaining to England. The most striking contrast is that within the Scottish context there is little or no public art in any real national or sovereign sense — that may explain, for instance, why there is no discernible sculptural tradition in Scotland. The causes for this are long and complex, but a few salient factors need to be noted here. More than in any other area, public art requires an infrastructure of extended patronage, and this the visual arts has decidedly lacked north of the border. From the Reformation onwards the Church, for example, has been hostile to images, preferring the Word, over which it could have much more control within the social as well as the spiritual life of the Scottish people. Furthermore, in the area of secular patronage the visual arts were also poorly served. When the Stuart royal dynasty moved to London and on to the British throne in 1603 they, and their Scottish nobility, quickly Anglified their image and turned to non-Scottish artists to glorify their self-regarding importance.

Thus the dominant characteristic of art in Scotland is primarily of a private nature, with informal naturalistic portraiture predominating during the Scottish Enlightenment and

this then being replaced in the Victorian period by a preference for deserted romantic landscape or nostalgic genre
scenes from a lost rural idyll. It may be because of this predominantly private and subjective strain in Scottish art that it
was here that there was a much more positive response to
modern art, compared to the suspicion and hostility that it
encountered from most of the public art institutions in
England.

With this Scottish enthusiasm for modern art, Glasgow led
the way — with dealers like Alexander Reid, whose portrait by
Van Gogh now hangs in the Kelvingrove Gallery; with collectors such as William Burrell, who skilfully acquired some of
the finest examples of modern French painting in the country;
and with the internationally acclaimed group of progressive
young painters, The Glasgow Boys. Right at the heart of the
town, as the jewel in the crown of Glasgow's reputation as one
of the leading modern cities, there was Charles Rennie Mackintosh's celebrated building for the Glasgow School of Art.
Mackintosh's masterpiece was opened at the turn of the century, just as Glasgow's role as the second city of the Empire
was beginning to wane with the decline of Britain's imperial
and commercial power. From then on the cultural reputation
of the city increasingly lost out to its popularly-conceived
image as a culturally inhospitable urban waste-land, where
only artists of exceptional social and artistic commitment,
such as Joan Eardley, could produce modern painting of the
highest quality.

By the time Joan Eardley died in the early 1960s, Glasgow
was spinning into a spiral of chronic urban decay. Only drastic
measures seemed the solution to the city's plight, and so the
civic fathers eagerly turned to the utopian culture of modern
architecture and town planning for their salvation. Mass population deportation, the likes of which had not been witnessed
since the Highland clearances, was imposed on Glasgow's
urban working population, who were lured and transported
to the Brave New World of the high-rise housing scheme ghet-
tos dotted around the city perimeter. This then allowed the
historic town centre to be gutted and turned into an eight-lane
motorway. Thus the heart of this great metropolis was ripped
out in the name of progress, or as the cynics thought, political
and economic expediency; and one cannot help thinking that

Eduardo Paolozzi might have had Glasgow in mind when he wrote in black despair, 'Modernism is the acceptance of the concrete landscape and the destruction of the human soul.'

Very rapidly the modernist dream-solution was shown to be a mirage, which quickly turned into a terrifying nightmare with many parts of the sprawling urban mass becoming crime-infested no-go areas. Thus yet again the city fathers were urgently required to find a new way of re-inventing the image of Glasgow but which did not involve further discredited social engineering, or too much cost. To this end the Labour-controlled council reversed its traditional anti-art and culture stance and now looked to support the usually neglected area of cultural amenities by heavily promoting the museums and art galleries of the city.

Throughout the 1980s and early 1990s there were a number of crucial players in the miraculous project of transforming Glasgow from 'No Mean City' into UK Garden City and then triumphantly European City of Culture 1990. Undoubtedly a central figure in all this was the powerful leader of the council, later to become Lord Provost, Pat Lally. It was he who gave full backing to the various ambitious schemes of the English-imported Director of Glasgow Museums, Julian Spalding, by setting aside a separate art purchasing budget of £3,000,000 at the Director's discretion, and supporting Spalding's pet idea to establish a Glasgow Gallery of Modern Art (GOMA). One of the main reasons why such high-profile civic enterprises could be achieved in the 1980s and early 1990s was that under successive Tory Governments Scotland remained loyal to Labour, thus becoming disenfranchised and unable to represent itself politically as a nation. Thus it fell to the Scottish cities, and especially Glasgow, to fill this socio-political vacuum by attempting (not always successfully) to identify with the creative forces within the civic community and encourage a strong sense of distinctive cultural identity.

These creative forces were most spectacularly represented by the young artists emerging from the Glasgow School of Art in the 1980s. The reasons which brought about this phenomenal success are complex, but their achievement in relation to their native city is more easy to discern. The New Glasgow Boys—Steven Campbell, Peter Howson, Ken Currie, Adrian Wiszniewski *et al.*—were part of a world-wide art fashion which returned contemporary art to figurative painting and pictorial narrative. Thus these new boys on the block were uncontaminated by discredited modernism and appeared to speak in a visual language that was immediately accessible to the ordinary citizens of Glasgow.

This was particularly true of Howson and Currie who drew their subjects and inspiration from the street-life and political histories of the working-class community. Furthermore both used a raw aggressive pictorial idiom which seemed to echo west-coast Scottish urban patois. This particularly applied to Howson, who soon became court painter to the New Image Glasgow, his work being eagerly sought out and promoted by Lally and his museum director. Spalding, identifying himself as a man of the people, but with distinctive Thatcherite over-tones, enthusiastically praised Howson on the way his 'paint-ings and drawing celebrated the struggle of *individual* lives' (my italics) and how 'he often depicted the struggle as heroic'. All these eulogies were a clear reference to Howson's most cel-ebrated work *The Heroic Dosser* (1987), which presents a Glas-gow hard-man tramp straining to rise out of the gutter of his ruined life and slum environment. Not surprisingly this macho image became the unofficial icon of the newly regener-ated Glasgow and complemented the ad-men's soft, cuddly Mister Blobby of the *Glasgow's Smiles Better* campaign.

While Howson quickly became the city fathers' favourite artistic son, Currie's art was much more problematic and diffi-cult to accommodate into Glasgow's official publicity image-making schemes. Unlike Howson, Currie was a politically-committed artist and in the 1980s was a member of the Com-munist Party. Thus he was identified and supported by those who were deeply suspicious, if not downright antithetical to the populist art policies of the Labour-controlled city council. At this time Currie's most important patron was Elspeth King, the curator of the People's Palace, which is Glasgow's own local history museum and which was relatively neglected compared to the money being lavished on the Burrell and Kelvingrove Galleries in the more suburban parts of the city. King commissioned Currie to produce an epic mural history of the Scottish Labour movement in the same year as Howson's *Noble Dosser*. Currie's magnum opus was the first major public art work in Scotland to treat seriously such a central aspect of the nation's modern social and historical experience. Needless to say, it created a great deal of controversy, clearly marking the deep divisions between the various left- and right-wing forces attempting to capture the heart of the city and promote the authentic voice of the people of Glasgow. The civic war eventually lead to a show-down between King and Spalding who, with the might of Lally's backing, enforced, like something out of a Greek tragedy, the banishment of the People's Palace champion from the city altogether.

The highly politicized artistic policy of Lally and Spalding achieved its full, if hollow, triumph in 1996 with the much fanfared opening of GOMA. Art critics from all over were bussed, all expenses paid, to witness this important occasion. Spalding's accompanying self-congratulatory publication *Gallery of Modern Art Glasgow* laid out his approach and attitude to art and civic society in an unequivocal manner. He dismissed 'the vacuousness of so much modern art' and triumphantly announced 'Modern art is, I think, over.' For Spalding contemporary art, or at least the stuff he bought for Glasgow, was 'made by people for people'. Unfortunately such unabashed populist sentiments cut little ice with the hard-nosed London critics who were scathing in their attacks on the mediocre quality and undistinguished presentation of Glasgow's contemporary art collection. Furthermore, not being a very popular figure himself with the art community of Glasgow, few rushed to Spalding's defence, and adding further insult to injury the city's own paper, *The Herald*, allowed their critic, Claire Henry, to write a damning piece entitled 'A Sour Taste', which ended by pointing out the seeming falseness of his egalitarian posturing:

> Some gallery directors put the artist first. Inspired directors involve their staff and welcome dealers, middle men, anyone and everyone—but especially the local art community. Spalding has already made sure that GOMA is 'his' museum; and the book 'his' book. Thus the blame for an inappropriate display and exceedingly poor book can be laid at his door too.

Yet in many ways by the time GOMA opened in the mid-1990s it had already become irrelevant to the pressing issues of how contemporary art serves the civic community. Relevant public art was certainly not what was bought on the personal whim of individual publicly-funded patronage and stuck in a local museum. Now if art wished to serve the community it had to find a way to allow artists to engage directly with the lives and urban environment of the city's diverse populus.

As was the norm with most declining post-industrial urban areas, Glasgow had been severely subjected to the most conspicuous aspects of the public art projects in the 1970s and 1980s, with the ubiquitous gable-end mural appearing to be slapped on every run-down housing block in the City. This attempted aestheticizing intervention was however usually resented by many in the local community, as famously exemplified by the graffiti defiantly scrawled across a public mural in the Partick area: 'The artist's work is all in vain, The Tiny Partick strike again.' Such artistic missionary work was clearly failing, equally for the residents and the artists involved. This sense of failure was one of the reasons for the setting up of the Environmental Art Department at Glasgow School of Art in 1986, which took as its guiding principle that 'the context is half the work'. Now young artists keen to practise their work outside the traditional gallery space and in the social civic domain were trained to engage in a long period of preparatory field research. Thus the development and final formation of their site-specific work had to grow out of a sustained dialogue between their own creative intentions and the requirements of the local environment and community which they were to serve.

Over the last two decades young artists in Glasgow have become increasingly independent of controlling institutional support and more involved with collective, self-sustaining action. In fact they have become their own local community within the city, running their own galleries studio spaces and generating and developing their own public art projects in collaboration with facilitating, consultative agencies such as Glasgow Visual Art Projects. Now those seriously involved in public art projects fully realize that neither modernism, in the guise of a generalized, utopian formalist art, nor populism, with its bland folksy insincerity, can be allowed to intervene and impose an all-embracing aesthetic solution to the particu-

lar pressing problems of contemporary urban life. Each public
space is resistant to certain approaches and accommodating to
others. Nothing should be easily taken for granted, and everything involved is 'the contested process of place-making', as
Joanna Spark points out in her *Artists as Researchers*.

   In that essay Spark also raised the contentious question on
which to end; ' Does it matter if people in the community do
not understand the "language" used by artists to articulate
place?' This, in the area of public art, brings us back to the
debate on which we opened — that between the language and
status of contemporary art and popular local culture. However, this apparent gulf in artistic and communal communication can be bridged by responsive artists, especially those
working in the area of text-based art. Two excellent examples
of this practice are the work of Jackie Donachie, a recent grad-
uate of Glasgow School of Art's Environmental Art Department, and the internationally-acclaimed Turner Prize Winner
Douglas Gordon. For instance Donachie, in her *Great Western
Road* project (1990), sensitively adapted and targeted her work
for those working people in the city who are reliant on public
transport, by installing texts on the roofs of bus shelters so that
they could only be read from the upper decks. Her cryptic slogans, although in familiar ad-speak, addressed local issues;
the concerns, dreams and desires of those living, working and
regularly passing through that particular urban environment.

   To date the most successful piece of public art produced for
Glasgow is Douglas Gordon's *Empire* (1999). Although sited in
the heart of the city's thronging shopping precinct this enig-
matic work is again, like that of Donachie, off the beaten track,
tucked away in a narrow alley off Argyll Street. The work
itself is disturbingly yet also intriguingly simple — merely a
piece of neon signage forming the word EMPIRE, but presented in its mirror-image form and attached to reflective
plates on a bare brick wall. It is placed fairly high up and, having to compete with a cluster of pub signs on the other side of
the lane, one can easily miss it altogether. However, once dis-
cerned *Empire* opens up layers of collective and personal associations — from the universal culture of Hollywood cinema, à
la Hitchcock's *Vertigo*, to the avant-garde films of Andy
Warhol, to the imperial history of Glasgow's role as second
city of the Empire, through to the local popular culture of the

famous *Glasgow Empire* music hall. In this very successful contemporary work of public art Gordon subtly negotiates a space and form in which the city can express the multifarious nature of its histories and people.

The official and popular ownership of a city is a complex and highly contested, on-going process. Each political movement, each community and each citizen needs to find a language, a voice, a set of images and texts to represent their place and role within their ever-changing urban environment. No British city has involved itself more in this daunting quest for a revised and relatively contemporary civic identity than Glasgow. The struggle may have been a long and highly contested one, yet it does clearly demonstrate the passion and commitment that Glaswegians have for their beloved city.

Michael Polanyi

The Eclipse of Thought

From a careful study of the history of thought in our own time it is possible to see how freedom of thought destroyed itself when it pursued a self-contradictory conception of its own freedom to its ultimate conclusions.

Modern thought in the widest sense emerged with the emancipation of the human mind from a mythological and magical interpretation of the universe. We know when this first happened, at what place and by what method. We owe this act of liberation to Ionian philosophers who flourished in the sixth century BC and to other philosophers of Greece who continued their work in the succeeding 1,000 years. These ancient thinkers enjoyed much freedom of speculation but never raised decisively the issues of intellectual freedom.

The millennium of ancient philosophy was brought to a close by Saint Augustine. There followed the long rule of Christian theology and the Church of Rome over all departments of thought. The rule of ecclesiastic authority was impaired first in the twelfth century by a number of sporadic intellectual achievements. Then, as the Italian Renaissance blossomed out, the leading artists and thinkers of the time brought religion more and more into neglect. The Italian church itself seemed to yield to the new secular interests. Had the whole of Europe at that time been of the same mind as Italy, Renaissance humanism might have established freedom of thought everywhere, simply by default of opposition. Europe might have returned to—or, if you like, relapsed into—a liberalism resembling that of pre-Christian antiquity. Whatever may have followed after that, our present disasters would not have occurred.

However, there arose instead in a number of European countries—in Germany, Switzerland, Spain—a fervent religious revival, accompanied by a schism of the Christian Church, which was to dominate people's minds for almost two centuries. The Catholic Church sharply reaffirmed its authority over the whole intellectual sphere. The thoughts of men were moved, and politics were shaped, by the struggle between Protestantism and Catholicism, to which all contemporary issues contributed through their alliance with one side or the other.

By the beginning of the present century the wars between Catholics and Protestants had long ceased, yet the formulation of liberal thought still remained largely determined by the reaction of past generations against the old religious wars. Liberalism was motivated, to start with, by a detestation of religious fanaticism. It appealed to reason for a cessation of religious strife. This desire to curb religious violence was the prime motive of liberalism in both Anglo-American and Continental areas; yet from the beginning the reaction against religious fanaticism differed somewhat in these two areas and this difference has since become increasingly accentuated, with the result that liberty has been upheld in the Western area up to this day but has suffered an eclipse in central and eastern Europe.

Anglo-American liberalism was first formulated by Milton and Locke. Their argument for freedom of thought was two-fold. In its first part (for which we may cite the *Areopagitica*) freedom from authority is demanded so that truth may be discovered. The main inspiration for this movement came from the struggle of the rising natural sciences against the authority of Aristotle. Its programme was to let everyone state his beliefs and to allow others to listen and form their own opinions; the ideas which would prevail in a free and open battle of wits would be as close an approximation to the truth as can be humanly achieved. We may call this the anti-authoritarian formula of liberty. Closely related to it is the second half of the argument for liberty, which is based on philosophic doubt. While its origins go back a long way (right to the philosophers of antiquity), this argument was first formulated as a political doctrine by Locke. It says simply that we can never be so sure of the truth in matters of religion as to warrant the imposition of our views on others. These two pleas for freedom of thought were put forward and accepted in England at a time when religious beliefs were unshaken and indeed dominant throughout the nation. The new tolerance aimed preeminently at the reconciliation of different denominations in the service of God. Atheists were refused tolerance by Locke on the ground that they were socially unreliable.

On the Continent the twofold doctrine of free thought — anti-authoritarianism and philosophic doubt — gained ascendance somewhat later than in England and moved straightway to a more extreme position. This position was first effectively formulated in the eighteenth century by the philosophy of Enlightenment, which was primarily an attack on religious authority, particularly that of the Catholic Church. It professed a radical scepticism. The books of Voltaire and the French Encyclopaedists expounding this doctrine were widely read in France, while abroad their ideas spread into Germany and far into eastern Europe. Frederick the Great and Catherine of Russia were among their correspondents and disciples. The type of Voltairean aristocrat, represented by the old Prince Bolkonski in *War and Peace*, was to be found at court and in feudal residences over many parts of Continental Europe at the close of the eighteenth century. The depth to which the *philosophes* had influenced political thought in their own country was to be revealed by the French Revolution.

Accordingly, the mood of the French Enlightenment, though often angry, was always supremely confident. Its followers promised mankind relief from all social ills. One of the central figures of the movement, the Baron d'Holbach, declared in 1770 that man is miserable simply because he is ignorant. His mind is so infected with prejudices that one might think him forever condemned to err. It is error, he held, that has evoked the religious fears which shrivel men up with fright or make them butcher each other for chimeras. 'To errour must be attributed those inveterate hatreds, those barbarous persecutions, those numerous massacres, those dreadful tragedies, of which, under pretext of serving the interests of Heaven, the earth has been but too frequently made the theatre.'

This explanation of human miseries and the remedy promised for them continued to carry conviction with the intelligentsia of Europe long after the French Revolution. It remained an axiom among progressive people on the Continent that to achieve light and liberty you first had to break the power of the clergy and eliminate the influence of religious dogma. Battle after battle was fought in this campaign. Perhaps the fiercest engagement was the Dreyfus Affair at the close of the century, in which clericalism was finally defeated in France and was further weakened throughout Europe. It was at about this time that W.E.H. Lecky wrote: 'All over Europe the priesthood are now associated with a policy of toryism, of reaction, or of obstruction. All over Europe the organs that represent dogmatic interests are in permanent opposition to the progressive tendencies around them, and are rapidly sinking into contempt.'

I remember well this triumphant sentiment. We looked back on earlier times as on a period of darkness, and with Lucretius we cried in horror: *Tantum religio potuit suadere malorum* – what evils religion has inspired! So we rejoiced at the superior knowledge of our age and its assured liberties. The promises of peace and freedom given to the world by the French Enlightenment had indeed been wonderfully fulfilled towards the end of the nineteenth century. You could travel all over Europe and America without a passport and settle down wherever you pleased. With the exception of Russia, you could, throughout Europe, print anything without prior censorship and could sharply oppose any government or creed with impunity. In Germany – much criticized at the time for being authoritarian – biting caricatures of the Emperor were published freely. Even in Russia, whose regime was the most oppressive, Marx's *Kapital* appeared in translation immediately after its first publication and received favourable reviews throughout the press. In the whole of Europe not more than a few hundred people were forced into political exile. Over the entire planet all men of European origins were living in free intellectual and personal communication. It is hardly surprising that the universal establishment of peace and tolerance through the victory of modern enlightenment was confidently expected at the turn of the century by a large majority of educated people on the Continent.

Thus we entered the twentieth century as on an age of infinite promise. Few people realized that we were walking into a minefield, though the mines had all been prepared and carefully laid in open daylight by well-known thinkers of our own time. Today we know how false our expectations were. We have all learned to trace the collapse of freedom in the twentieth century to the writings of certain philosophers, particularly Marx, Nietzsche and their common ancestors Fichte and Hegel. But the story has yet to be told how we came to welcome as liberators the philosophies that were to destroy liberty.

We have said that we consider the collapse of freedom in central and eastern Europe to be the outcome of an internal contradiction in the doctrine of liberty. But why did it destroy freedom in large parts of Continental Europe without producing similar effects, so far, in the Western or Anglo-American area of our civilization? Wherein lies this inconsistency?

The argument of doubt put forward by Locke in favour of tolerance says that we should admit all religions since it is impossible to demonstrate which one is true. This implies that we must not impose beliefs that are not demonstrable. Let us apply this doctrine to ethical principles. It follows that, unless ethical principles can be demonstrated with certainty, we should refrain from imposing them and should tolerate their total denial. But, of course, ethical principles cannot, in a strict sense, be demonstrated: you cannot prove the obligation to tell the truth, to uphold justice and mercy. It would follow therefore that a system of mendacity, lawlessness and cruelty is to be accepted as an alternative to ethical principles and on equal terms. But a society in which unscrupulous propaganda, violence and terror prevail offers no scope for tolerance. Here the inconsistency of a liberalism based on philosophic doubt becomes apparent: freedom of thought is destroyed by the extension of doubt to the field of traditional ideals, which includes the basis for freedom of thought.

The consummation of this destructive process was prevented in the Anglo-American region by an instinctive reluctance to pursue the accepted philosophic premises to their ultimate conclusions. One way of avoiding this was to pretend that ethical principles could actually be scientifically demonstrated. Locke himself started this train of thought by asserting that good and evil can be identified with pleasure and pain and by suggesting that all ideals of good behaviour are merely maxims of prudence.

However, the utilitarian calculus cannot in fact demonstrate our commitment to ideals which demand serious sacrifices of us. A man's sincerity in professing his ideals is to be measured rather by the *lack* of prudence he shows in pursuing them. The utilitarian confirmation of unselfishness is no more than a pretence by which traditional ideals are made acceptable to a philosophically sceptical age. Camouflaged as long-term selfishness or intelligent self-interest, the traditional ideals of man are protected from destruction by scepticism.

It would thus appear that the preservation of Western civilization up to this day within the Anglo-American tradition of liberty was due to this speculative restraint, which amounted to a veritable suspension of logic within British empiricist philosophy. It was enough to pay philosophic lip service to the supremacy of the pleasure principle. Ethical standards were not really replaced by new purposes; still less was there any inclination to abandon these standards in practice. The masses of the people and their leaders in public life could in fact disregard the accepted philosophy, both in deciding their personal conduct and in building up their political institutions. The whole sweeping advance of moral aspirations to which the Age of Reason opened the way — the English Revolution, the American Revolution, the French Revolution, the first liberation of slaves in the British Empire, the Factory Reforms, the founding of the League of Nations, Britain's stand against Hitler, the offering of Lend–Lease, UNRRA, and Marshall Plan aid, the sending of millions of food parcels by individual Americans to unknown beneficiaries in Europe — in all these decisive actions public opinion was swayed by moral forces, by charity, by a desire for justice and a detestation of social evils, despite the fact that these moral forces had no true justification in the prevailing philosophy of the age. Utilitarianism and other allied materialistic formulations of traditional ideals remained merely verbal. Their philosophic rejection of universal moral standards led only to a sham replacement; or, to speak technically, it led to a 'pseudo-substitution' of utilitarian purposes for moral principles.

The speculative and practical restraints which saved liberalism from self-destruction in the Anglo-American area were due in the first place to the distinctly religious character of this liberalism. As long as philosophic doubt was applied only to secure equal rights to all religions and was prohibited from demanding equal rights for irreligion, the same restraint would automatically apply in respect to moral beliefs. A scepticism kept on a short leash for the sake of preserving religious beliefs would hardly become a menace to fundamental moral principles. A second restraint on scepticism, closely related to the first, lay in the establishment of democratic institutions at a time when religious beliefs were still strong. These institutions (for example the American Constitution) gave effect to the moral principles which underlie a free society. The tradition of democracy embodied in these institutions proved strong enough to uphold in practice the moral standards of a free society against any critique that would question their validity.

Both of these protective restraints, however, were absent in those parts of Europe where liberalism was based on the French Enlightenment. This movement, being anti-religious, imposed no restraint on sceptical speculations, nor were the standards of morality embodied there in democratic institutions. When a feudal society, dominated by religious authority, was attacked by a radical scepticism, a liberalism emerged which was protected by neither a religious nor a civic tradition from destruction by the philosophic scepticism to which it owed its origin.

Here, in brief, is what happened. From the middle of the eighteenth century Continental thought faced up seriously to the fact that universal standards of reason could not be philosophically justified in the light of the sceptical attitude which had initiated the rationalist movement. The great philosophic tumult which started in the second half of the eighteenth century on the Continent of Europe and finally led up to the philosophic disasters of our own day represented an incessant preoccupation with the collapse of the philosophic foundations of rationalism. Universal standards of human behaviour having fallen into philosophic disrepute, various substitutes were put forward in their place.

One such substitute standard was derived from the contemplation of individuality. The case for the uniqueness of the individual is set out as follows in the opening words of Rousseau's

Confessions: 'Myself alone.... There is no one who resembles me.... We shall see whether Nature was right in breaking the mould into which she had cast me.' Individuality here challenged the world to judge it, if it could, by universal standards. Creative genius claimed to be the renewer of all values and therefore incommensurable. Extended to whole nations this claim accorded each nation its unique set of values which could not be criticized in the light of universal reason. A nation's only obligation was, like that of the unique individual, to realize its own powers. In following the call of its destiny a nation must allow no other nation to stand in its way.

If you apply this claim for the supremacy of uniqueness — which we may call romanticism — to individual persons, you arrive at a general hostility to society, as exemplified in the anticonventional and almost extraterritorial attitude of the Continental *bohème*. If applied to nations it results, on the contrary, in the conception of a unique national destiny which claims the absolute allegiance of all its citizens. The national leader combines the advantages of both. He can stand entranced in the admiration of his own uniqueness while identifying his personal ambitions with the destiny of the nation lying at his feet.

Romanticism was a literary movement and a change of heart rather than a philosophy. Its counterpart in systematic thought was constructed by the Hegelian dialectic. Hegel took charge of Universal Reason, emaciated to a skeleton by its treatment at the hands of Kant, and clothed it with the warm flesh of history. Declared incompetent to judge historical action, reason was given the comfortable position of being immanent in history. An ideal situation: 'Heads you lose, tails I win.' Identified with the stronger battalions, reason became invincible — but unfortunately also redundant.

The next step was therefore, quite naturally, the complete disestablishment of reason. Marx and Engels decided to turn the Hegelian dialectic right way up. No longer should the tail pretend to wag the dog. The bigger battalions should be recognized as makers of history in their own right, with reason as a mere apologist to justify their conquests.

The story of this last development is well known. Marx reinterpreted history as the outcome of class conflicts, which arise from the need of adjusting 'the relations of production' to 'the forces of production'. Expressed in ordinary language this says that, as new technical equipment becomes available from time to time it is necessary to change the order of property in favour of a new class; this change is invariably achieved by overthrowing the hitherto-favoured class. Socialism, it was said, brings these violent changes to a close by establishing the classless society. From its first formulation in the *Communist Manifesto* this doctrine puts the 'eternal truths, such as Freedom, Justice, etc.' — which it mentions in these terms — in a very doubtful position. Since these ideas are supposed always to have been used only to soothe the conscience of the rulers and to bemuse the suspicions of the exploited, there is no clear place left for them in the classless society. Today it has become apparent that there is indeed nothing in the realm of ideas, from law and religion to poetry and science, from the rules of football to the composition of music, that cannot readily be interpreted by Marxists as a mere product of class interest.

Meanwhile the legacy of romantic nationalism, developing on parallel lines, was also gradually transposed into materialistic terms. Wagner and Walhalla no doubt affected Nazi imagery; Mussolini gloried in recalling imperial Rome. But the really effective idea of Hitler and Mussolini was their classification of nations into haves and have-nots on the model of Marxian class war. The actions of nations were in this view not determined, or capable of being judged, by right or wrong: the haves preached peace and the sacredness of international law, since the law sanctioned their holdings, but this code was unacceptable to virile have-not nations. The latter would rise and overthrow the degenerate capitalistic democracies, which had become the dupes of their own pacific ideology, originally intended only to bemuse the underdogs. So the text of Fascist and National Socialist foreign policy ran on, exactly on the lines of a Marxism applied to class war between nations. Indeed, already by the opening of the twentieth century, influential German writers had fully refashioned the nationalism of Fichte and Hegel on the lines of a power-political interpretation of history. Romanticism had been brutalized and brutally romanticized until the product was as tough as Marx's own historic materialism.

We have here the final outcome of the Continental cycle of thought. The self-destruction of liberalism, which was kept in a state of suspended logic in the Anglo-American field of Western civilization, was here brought to its ultimate conclusion. The process of replacing moral ideals by philosophically less vulnerable objectives was carried out in all seriousness. This is not a mere pseudo-substitution but a *real* substitution of human appetites and human passions for reason and the ideals of man.

This brings us right up to the scene of the revolutions of the twentieth century. We can see now how the philosophies which guided these revolutions—and destroyed liberty wherever they prevailed—were originally justified by the anti-authoritarian and sceptical formulas of liberty. They were indeed anti-authoritarian and sceptical in the extreme. They even set man free from obligations towards truth and justice, reducing reason to its own caricature: to a mere rationalization of positions that were actually predetermined by desire and were held—or secured—by force alone. Such was the final measure of this liberation: man was to be recognized henceforth as maker and master, no longer as servant, of what before had been his ideals.

This liberation, however, destroyed the very foundations of liberty. If thought and reason are nothing in themselves it is meaningless to demand that thought be set free. The boundless hopes which the Enlightenment of the eighteenth century attached to the overthrow of authority and to the pursuit of doubt were hopes attached to the release of reason. Its followers firmly believed—to use Jefferson's majestic vocabulary—in 'truths that are self-evident', which would guard 'life, liberty, and the pursuit of happiness' under governments 'deriving their just powers from the consent of the governed'. They relied on truths, which they trusted to be inscribed in the hearts of man, for establishing peace and freedom among men everywhere. The assumption of universal standards of reason was implicit in the hopes of the Enlightenment, and the philosophies that denied the existence of such standards denied therefore the foundation of all these hopes.

But it is not enough to show how a logical process, starting from an inadequate formulation of liberty, led to philosophic conclusions that contradicted liberty. We have yet to show that this contradiction was actually put into operation, that these conclusions were not merely entertained and believed to be true but were met by people prepared to act upon them. If ideas cause revolutions, they can do so only through people who will act upon them. If this account of the fall of liberty in Europe is to be satisfactory, it must show that there were people who actually transformed philosophic error into destructive human action.

Of such people we have ample documentary evidence among the intelligentsia of central and eastern Europe. They are the nihilists.

There is an interesting ambiguity in the connotations of the word 'nihilism' which at first may seem confusing but actually turns out to be illuminating. As the title of Rauschning's book – *The Revolution of Nihilism* – shows, he interpreted the National Socialist upheaval as a revolution. As against this, reports from central Europe often spoke of widespread nihilism, meaning a lack of public spirit, the apathy of people who believe in nothing. This curious duality of nihilism, which makes it a byword for both complete self-centredness and violent revolutionary action, can be traced to its earliest origins. The word was popularized by Turgenev in his *Fathers and Sons*, written in 1862. His prototype of nihilism, the student Bazarov, is an extreme individualist without any interest in politics. Nor does the next similar figure of Russian literature, Dostoevski's Raskolnikov in *Crime and Punishment* (1865), show any political leanings. What Raskolnikov is trying to find out is why he should not murder an old woman if he wanted her money. Both Bazarov and Raskolnikov are experimenting privately with a life of total disbelief. But within a few years we see the nihilist transformed into a political conspirator. The terrorist organization of the Narodniki, or Populists, had come into being. Dostoevski portrayed the new type in his later novel *The Possessed*. The nihilist now appears as an ice-cold businesslike conspirator, closely prefiguring the ideal Bolshevik as I have seen him represented on the Moscow stage in the didactic plays of the early Stalinist period. Nor is the similarity accidental. The whole code of conspiratorial action – the cells, the secrecy, the discipline and ruthlessness – known today as the Communist method, was taken over by Lenin from the Populists. The proof of this can be found in articles published by him in 1901 and 1902.'

English and American people find it difficult to understand nihilism, for most of the doctrines professed by nihilists have been current among themselves for some time without turning those who held them into nihilists. Great, solid Bentham would not have disagreed with any of the views expounded by Turgenev's prototype of nihilism, the student Bazarov. But while Bentham and other sceptically-minded Englishmen may use such philosophies merely as a mistaken explanation of their own conduct — which in actual fact is determined by their traditional beliefs — the nihilist Bazarov and his kind take such philosophies seriously and try to live by their light.

The nihilist who tries to live without any beliefs, obligations or restrictions stands at the first, the private, stage of nihilism. He is represented in Russia by the earlier type of intellectual described by Turgenev and the younger Dostoevski. In Germany we find nihilists of this kind growing up in large numbers under the influence of Nietzsche and Stirner; and later, between 1910 and 1930, we see emerging in direct line of succession the great German Youth Movement with its radical contempt for all existing social ties.

But the solitary nihilist is unstable. Starved for social responsibility he is liable to be drawn into politics, provided he can find a movement based on nihilistic assumptions. Thus, when he turns to public affairs he adopts a creed of political violence. The cafés of Munich, Berlin, Vienna, Prague and Budapest, where writers, painters, lawyers and doctors had spent so many hours in amusing speculation and gossip, thus became in 1918 the recruiting grounds for the 'armed bohemians', whom Heiden in his book on Hitler describes as the agents of the European revolution. In much the same way, the Bloomsbury of the unbridled '20s unexpectedly turned out numerous disciplined Marxists around 1930.

The conversion of the nihilist from extreme individualism to the service of a fierce and narrow political creed is the turning point of the European revolution. The downfall of liberty in Europe consisted in a series of such individual conversions.

Their mechanism deserves closest attention. Take, first, conversion to Marxism. Historical — or dialectical — materialism had all the attractions of a second Enlightenment; taking off and carrying on from the first, anti-religious, Enlightenment it offered the same intense intellectual satisfaction. Those who accepted its guidance felt suddenly initiated into a knowledge of the real forces actuating men and operating in history, into a grasp of reality that had hitherto been hidden to them — and still remained hidden to the unenlightened — by a veil of deceit and self-deceit. Marx, and the whole materialistic movement of which he formed a part, had turned the world right side up before their eyes, revealing to them the true springs of human behaviour.

Marxism also offered them a future of unbounded promise for humanity. It predicted that historic necessity would destroy an antiquated form of society and replace it by a new one, in which the existing miseries and injustices would be eliminated. Though this prospect was put forward as a purely scientific observation, it endowed those who accepted it with a feeling of overwhelming moral superiority. They acquired a sense of righteousness, and this in a paradoxical manner was fiercely intensified by the mechanical framework in which it was set. Their nihilism had prevented them from demanding justice in the name of justice, or humanity in the name of humanity; these words were banned from their vocabulary and their minds were closed to such concepts. But their moral aspirations, thus silenced and repressed, found an outlet in the scientific prediction of a perfect society. Here was set out a scientific utopia relying for its fulfilment only on violence. Nihilists could accept, and would eagerly embrace, such a prophecy which required from its disciples no other belief than a belief in the force of bodily appetites and yet at the same time satisfied their most extravagant moral hopes. Their sense of righteousness was thus reinforced by a calculated brutality born of scientific self-assurance. There emerged the modern fanatic, armoured with impenetrable scepticism.

The power of Marxism over the mind is based here on a process exactly the inverse of Freudian sublimation. The moral needs of man, denied expression in terms of ideals, are injected into a system of naked power to which they impart the force of blind moral passion. With some qualification the same thing is true of National Socialism's appeal to the mind of German youth. By offering them an interpretation of history in the materialistic terms of international class war, Hitler mobilized their sense of civic obligation which would not respond to humane ideals. It was a mistake to regard the Nazi as an untaught savage. His bestiality was carefully nurtured by speculations closely reflecting Marxian influence. His contempt for humanitarian ideals had a century of philosophic schooling behind it. The Nazi disbelieved in public morality the way we disbelieve in witchcraft. It is not that he had never heard of it; he simply thought he had valid grounds for asserting that such a thing cannot exist. If you told him the contrary, he would think you peculiarly old-fashioned or simply dishonest.

In such men the traditional forms for holding moral ideals had been shattered and their moral passions diverted into the only channels which a strictly mechanistic conception of man and society left open to them. We may describe this as a process of *moral inversion*. The morally inverted person has not merely performed a philosophic substitution of material purposes for moral aims; he is acting with the whole force of his homeless moral passions within a purely materialistic framework of purposes.

It remains only to describe the actual battlefield on which the conflict that led to the downfall of liberty in Europe was fought out. Let us approach the scene from the West. Towards the close of the First World War, Europeans heard from across the Atlantic the voice of Wilson appealing for a new Europe in terms of pure eighteenth-century ideas. 'What we seek,' he summed up in his declaration of the Fourth of July 1918, 'is the reign of law, based upon the consent of the governed and sustained by the organized opinion of mankind.' When, a few months later, Wilson landed in Europe, a tide of boundless hope swept through its lands. They were the old hopes of the eighteenth and nineteenth centuries, only much brighter than ever before.

Wilson's appeal and the response it evoked marked the high tide of the original moral aspirations of the Enlightenment. This event showed how, in spite of the philosophic difficulties which impaired the foundations of overt moral assertions, such assertions could still be vigorously made in the regions of Anglo–American influence.

But the great hopes spreading from the Atlantic seaboard were contemptuously rejected by the nihilistic or morally inverted intelligentsia of central and eastern Europe. To Lenin, Wilson's language was a huge joke; from Mussolini or Goebbels it might have evoked an angry sneer. The political theories which these men and their small circle of followers were mooting at this time were soon to defeat the appeal of Wilson and of democratic ideals in general. They were to establish within roughly 20 years a comprehensive system of totalitarian governments over Europe, with a good prospect of subjecting the whole world to such government.

The sweeping success of Wilson's opponents was due to the greater appeal their ideas had for a considerable section of the populace in the central and eastern European nations. Admittedly their final rise to power was achieved by violence, but not before they had gained sufficient support in every stratum of the population so that they could use violence effectively. Wilson's doctrines were first defeated by the superior convincing power of opposing philosophies, and it is this new and fiercer Enlightenment that has continued ever since to strike relentlessly at every humane and rational principle rooted in the soil of Europe.

The downfall of liberty which in every case followed the success of these attacks demonstrates in hard facts what we said before: that freedom of thought is rendered pointless and must disappear wherever reason and morality are deprived of their status as a force in their own right. When a judge in a court of law can no longer appeal to law and justice; when neither a witness, nor the newspapers, nor even a scientist reporting on his experiments can speak the truth as he knows it; when in public life there is no moral principle commanding respect; when the revelations of religion and of art are denied any substance; then there are no grounds left on which any individual may justly make a stand against the rulers of the day. Such is the simple logic of totalitarianism. A nihilistic regime will have to undertake the day-to-day direction of all activities which are otherwise guided by the intellectual and moral principles that nihilism declares empty and void. Principles must be replaced by the decrees of an all-embracing party line.

This is why modern totalitarianism, based on a purely materialistic conception of man, is of necessity more oppressive than an authoritarianism enforcing a spiritual creed, however rigid. Take the medieval church even at its worst. The authority of certain texts which it imposed remained fixed over long periods of time, and their interpretation was laid down in systems of theology and philosophy developed over more than a millennium, from Saint Paul to Aquinas. A good Catholic was not required to change his convictions and reverse his beliefs at frequent intervals in deference to the secret decisions of a handful of high officials. Moreover, since the authority of the church was spiritual, it recognized other independent principles outside its own. Though it imposed numerous regulations on individual conduct, many parts of life were left untouched, and these were governed by other authorities, rivals of the church such as kings, noblemen, guilds, corporations. What is more, the power of all these was transcended by the growing force of law, and a great deal of speculative and artistic initiative was also allowed to pulsate freely through this many-sided system.

The unprecedented oppressiveness of modern totalitarianism has become widely recognized on the Continent today and has gone some way towards allaying the feud between the champions of liberty and the upholders of religion, which had been going on there since the beginning of the Enlightenment. Anticlericalism is not dead, but many who recognize transcendent obligations and are resolved to preserve a society built on the belief that such obligations are real have now discovered that they stand much closer to believers in the Bible and the Christian revelation than to the nihilist regimes based on radical disbelief. History will perhaps record the Italian elections of April 1946 as the turning point. The defeat inflicted there on the Communists by a large Catholic majority was hailed with immense relief by defenders of liberty throughout the world, many of whom had been brought up under Voltaire's motto 'Ecrasez l'infame!' and had in earlier days voiced all their hopes in that battle cry.

The instability of modern liberalism stands in curious contrast to the peacefully continued existence of intellectual freedom through a thousand years of antiquity. Why did the contradiction between liberty and scepticism never plunge the ancient world into a totalitarian revolution like that of the twentieth century?

We may answer that such a crisis did develop at least once, when a number of brilliant young men, whom Socrates had introduced to the pursuit of unfettered inquiry, blossomed as leaders of the Thirty Tyrants. Men like Charmides and Critias were nihilists, consciously adopting a political philosophy of smash-and-grab which they derived from their Socratic education; and, as a reaction to this, Socrates was impeached and executed.

Yet whatever difficulties of this sort developed in the ancient world, they were never so fierce and far-reaching as the revolutions of the twentieth century. What was lacking in antiquity was the prophetic passion of Christian messianism. The ever-unquenched hunger and thirst after righteousness which our civilization carries in its blood as a heritage of Christianity does not allow us to settle down in the Stoic manner of antiquity. Modern thought is a mixture of Christian beliefs and Greek doubts. Christian beliefs and Greek doubts are logically incompatible; and if the conflict between the two has kept Western thought alive and creative beyond precedent it has also made it unstable. Modern totalitarianism is a consummation of the conflict between religion and scepticism. It solves the conflict by embodying our heritage of moral passions in a framework of modern materialistic purposes. The conditions for such an outcome were not present in antiquity, when Christianity had not yet set alight new and vast moral hopes in the heart of mankind.

Claire Fox

Education: Dumbing Down or Wising Up?

The term 'dumbing down' might seem ludicrous when applied to university education. After all, this is academia and the most prestigious, rigorous and scholarly of all levels of learning; to accuse it of turning into a heartland of dumbness would seem to exaggerate. Yet unease exists and with reason. Everyone senses something is wrong — that standards are slipping and university life is in decline. There is talk of academic drift, degree inflation and the need to retain quality. There are schemes for quality control, quality audit, quality assessment, quality management. But all this quality-babble does not disguise the palpable sense that academia is changing beyond recognition — and for the worse.

The coincidence of the mass expansion of higher education and a decline in quality has led critics to conclude that, in principle, many cannot study at the highest level without a collapse in standards. But the more realistic question is not whether fewer or more people should have access to the ivory towers, but rather what are they gaining access to. The opening up of universities, in the circumstances in which it has occurred, has had a negative impact on what any student can gain from the higher study. There are obvious problems, such as the fact that mass access has not been matched by a mass increase in resources. Staffing ratios have increased from 8.5:1 at the start of the 1980s to 20:1 today. The new universities (former polytechnics) buy less than one book per student per year. But more fundamentally, mass access today is redefining the very idea of what a university education is aiming to achieve.

It would seem that the government dictat that half the population should get a degree or they will be socially excluded, is turning the university sector into yet another arena for social inclusion. Once there, students can expect to find that the whole of university life centres on keeping them happy rather than educating them. The idea of the university is rapidly being transformed into a rather dumb exercise in inclusive self-esteem building.

The government announces that its aim is for 50% of the population to gain a higher-education qualification. It is worth inquiring how this is being achieved and why. Let's consider first how the present expansion has come about. Was it due to a massive improvement in school education that allowed ever more people to make the university grade? No – there are simply more places made available, with financial incentives given to universities to compete for students and more institutions declared as universities. Entrance requirements have been an ever-widening set of goal posts. In September 1998, when Baroness Blackstone announced her changes in A-levels, she claimed that traditional A-levels were too narrow and elitist. Why? Because they prevent too many people from going to university. Her solution has been to change them. Talk of creative accounting – this is creative education! It would seem that the goal of packing more and more people off to universities will be achieved at any educational cost. But why does government want so many people to get a degree?

The expansion does not seem to be driven by an educational desire to produce more critical thinkers, rocket scientists and philosophers, or to expand the field of knowledge. The current proposals for sub-degrees, the ever-expanding range of human activities now merited as arenas for higher study – from golf to curry-making – the decrying of academic subjects as pointless and old-fashioned and the marginalizing of notions of knowledge for its own sake – all this would suggest that mass access is not a matter of creating more and more scholars. In fact, the government is quite clear about its aims. David Blunkett is explicit when he claims that 'widening access to higher education is a key priority and critical to tackling social exclusion'. So the role of higher education is to socially include.

This new educational mantra of social inclusion is one of those New Labour buzz terms that crops up in the plethora of DoEE press releases and green papers. The equation 'education = social inclusion' has a progressive enough ring to it. But if the principal goal of education is to 'include' people, the content of that education and the standards it sets cannot fail to suffer. The passion of government officials and lecturers is not reserved for the quality of ideas in seminars, but for how many students are socially included by gaining the latest spurious degree. When Blunkett states boldly that he 'will remove, one-by-one, the barriers that prevent' young people from achieving their potential, he is not talking, as radicals did in the past, about removing the social barriers denying people access to knowledge and ideas, he is talking about removing the educational 'barriers' which make judgments about ability and attainment. Because universities are being encouraged to act as social includers, many have lost their nerve in the battle for standards. Scared of rejecting potential undergraduates as not being able enough for higher study and so being held responsible for social exclusion, academics constantly cave in to their new role. And if they don't, the university will pay!

The social inclusion approach is being institutionalized through the way HEFC funding is being reorganized. Entrance requirements these days are less a discussion about A-level results and more about social disadvantage. Universities are being given financial incentives to take the socially excluded, regardless of educational achievement. In March last year, the government announced it would pay universities extra for each student recruited from lower socio-economic groups, designated as such through using its own rather perverse geo-demographic studies according to home postcodes. Universities will get 5% extra a year per such students (from a £20 million fund) as part of this 'continuing drive to open universities' doors to students from deprived groups and other under-represented groups'.

This incorporation of social inclusion into higher education has not only been achieved through financial incentives; there are broader penalties if institutions don't cooperate. The government's new performance indicators — so crucial for league table status, and ironically one way quality is judged — now include social inclusion as a measure: 'The access indicators are designed to measure progress in redressing the under-representation of some social groups in higher education.' Now, not only potential students, but universities themselves, are being judged not on educational criteria but on the dubious social criterion of inclusion.

If social inclusion has become the new criterion for student expansion, it is the re-organizing of college life around student empowerment which characterizes what is happening within the mass-access ivory towers. Centring university life around students, rather than the pursuit of knowledge, has its most recent origins in the way that the drive to widen access has seen the university sector aping the market rhetoric of the rest of society.

The shift in government funding to encourage the growth in student numbers in general means that universities are now desperate to recruit ever-larger numbers of new undergraduates. In the past, students had to compete for places at universities, which confidently selected and rejected without apology. Today, with expansion, colleges have to compete with each other for students. Therefore the key task in every faculty is how to make courses attractive to more students. University management meetings are as pre-occupied as any other business enterprise with advertising campaigns, brand loyalty and customer satisfaction. But the consequences when applied to a university mean turning education on its head. Students are no longer supplicants who must demonstrate that they deserve to be accepted as apprentices by the most advanced minds and researchers in the field. Rather students are the masters who must be flattered and cajoled by humble lecturers who are warned that students will take their 'custom' to other educational institutions if they are not satisfied with the marks they receive or the way they are taught. Students who feel they have not got what they were promised in the college's adverts threaten to sue, as if they had bought a dodgy TV.

In the name of funding expansion, the issue of students paying their own fees also accentuates the customer/provider relationship. It is argued that if students are to pay hard cash they will expect to get the product they ordered. This is altering all relationships in universities. Power and authority is increasingly no longer derived from knowledge, specialism or expertise in the field. Instead the academic/student relationship is being equalized through a contract, with an emphasis on what students get as consumers. This will increase the tendency to view degrees as ready-made, saleable commodities. Satisfied customers in University Britain plc demand a worthwhile product.

But while this market-orientation of education sounds like some Thatcherite hangover, it is rapidly being translated into the more politically-correct language of student empowerment, as befitting the New Labour regime. This has been aided by many in academia who are uncomfortable with the language of consumers. By focusing everything on student empowerment, consciences are salved. These days every change in universities is argued for as being in the best interests of students. This is contrasted with what is disdainfully dismissed as an elite system in which academics were the only constituency who were satisfied. Instead New HE is anti-elitist — and proves it by satisfying the alleged demands of students.

How do academics find out what will satisfy their students? They ask them. Accepting student-centredness means adopting a focus-group approach to what happens within universities. One expression of this is the new fad for student satisfaction surveys. These are now routinely used to ascertain how students feel about the success of lectures, course content and even how they are assessed and examined. The results of these surveys are predictable enough. At best they produce banal complaints of the 'not enough handouts…too few seminars' variety and confuse quantity with quality. Understandably, undergraduates often complain of rigour and testing as problematic. What student spontaneously welcomes the pain and effort of being intellectually stretched? But the moans of students who might prefer study to be easy and to fit in with their social life should surely not be taken too seriously. But they are, and now the preferences of those fearful of being put to the test are accepted as good practice. So we have educational assessments which are promoted as more student-centred than the exam regime of the past — that is, they are easier and less challenging. Only a minority of students in the best universities rely on that three-hour ordeal to pass their degree. In fact, 'open-book' exams (in which you take the textbooks in with you instead of trying to write the answers on your shirt sleeve) are now routine, and exam questions are regularly issued in advance to help students prepare. Continuous assessment by course work and seminar performance is a common experience.

Pandering to this lowest common denominator approach, done in the name of listening to students, has dire consequences for what higher education really amounts to today. Take university teaching. The new Institute for Learning and Teaching (ILT), which was set up last year following Sir Ron Dearing's report in 1997, is based on the assertion that lecturers are not teaching properly. Sir Ron arrived at this conclusion on the question of lecturers' teaching abilities by using consultations with students. Dearing's justification for the ILT cited a Policy Studies Institute survey of 1200 students, where almost half of those who responded were less than satisfied. The National Union of Students' complaints about poor teaching techniques and too much emphasis on rewarding good research were quoted approvingly. After publication of the report, NUS President Douglas Trainer boasted that 'The student voice was heard, and we remain the most considered party within the report's findings' (*Times Higher Education Supplement*, 25 July 1997). The report itself claims that it 'puts students at the centre of the process of learning and teaching'.

But while taking on board the views of students sounds very empowering, what does it say about education when the people asked to rate the quality of HE are students who are after all the least-educated constituency in the university and the least likely to be able to judge what they should be getting from lecturers? How can academics function as mentors who inspire confidence and push students to the limit of their potential, when lecturers live in dread of end-of-term student assessments rather than the other way round. Witty lecturers do well, while others are written off as boring. But HE is supposed to be more than entertainment. Of course when you ask students about their lecturers there will be moans about bumbling, boring academics droning on and sending everybody to sleep. These stock images of other-worldly nutty professors, swotty academics and nerdy researchers were once associated with a philistine response to academia; now they are touted by trendy administrators as things of the academic-centred past.

Ironically the obsession with being student-centred has completely emptied out what a student can expect to receive from university. The aim to keep the student happy begets an unhealthy desire to do what pleases rather than what the curriculum or pursuit of higher knowledge requires. The consequences of the ILT, for example, means breaking the link between university teaching and research. This represents an assault on the very idea of higher education and shows how the language of empowerment is being used in reality to give the ever-growing number of students an inferior university experience.

The belief that research and teaching must be closely linked reflected a view of universities, held in the not-so-distant pre-access past, as special places of scholarship and knowledge, where academics were at the cutting edge of social progress, expanding ideas and researching new areas. Undergraduates were educated by interacting with this atmosphere and with the people who were pushing society's intellectual boundaries outwards. The education process lay less in the technical teaching of subjects and more in allowing the new recruits to academia access to the greatest minds in the field. This was not school, but an apprenticeship to becoming independent thinkers.

Of course, not all great teachers want to do groundbreaking research — nor should they have to. The relationship of research to good teaching is the understanding that what inspires young people is the stimulation and challenge of dealing with new and, yes, difficult ideas, the intellectual excitement that emerges from an atmosphere of originality and scholarship. If they are to be university teachers in any meaningful sense, lecturers need the opportunity to pursue an active and creative research relationship with their subject; and for students to be really satisfied, rather than pandered to, they need to be taught by people who are more interested in the topic in hand than in keeping their audience amused.

The irony is that the separation of research from teaching does not mean that no research occurs. Universities are obsessed with the Research Assessment Exercise. But those who are encouraged to research and are rewarded accordingly are often kept away from the chalk-face and students never benefit from the fruits of new ideas and devlopments. Instead they are offered a version of HE teaching which is entertaining and slick, full of flip charts and PowerPoint presentations—all style and no content. Or more often the tired academic who now spends all his/her time preparing, marking and teaching, with no time to think or research. Whichever option prevails, by removing the centrality of the link between teaching and research, students are sold short.

The dumb part of the new universities is that they are no longer places of intellectual stimulation and excitement for anyone concerned. In addition to what I have drawn out, the dead weight of utilitarian vocationalism and a subservience to relevance now dominate discussions about curriculum content. But then, we are told that for graduates to be socially included when they leave they must have employability skills. And so it goes on. What a shoddy deal we offer access to. What happened to inspiring a search for truth, a desire to experiment, a sense of wonder and curiosity, an unapologetic interest in the irrelevant and the arcane? All this has been lost in the pretence of being student-centred! Imagine what it must be like to be an undergraduate today; to get to university simply because a government wants you to be socially included, and then to be taught by people who tell you that you know best. This is patronizing, insulting to the intelligence and ultimately a mind-numbing experience. For the rest of us, to celebrate the uninitiated as wise, to give out degrees as badges of social inclusion rather than educational excellence, and then to claim this is all in the interests of students—now that is just dumb!

Andrew Williams

The Dumbing Down of the Young Consumer

Despite the repeated contemporary call for higher state spending on education, the early pioneers of mass education would be astonished at the lavish provision with which that dream has been fulfilled in the late twentieth century. Still more astonishing would they find the suggestion that such provision has not liberated the masses from ignorance. They would be baffled that so highly educated a populace could prefer bread and circuses to learning and culture, that the appetite for knowledge, understanding and competence which drove them and which they assumed to be universal could be so quickly satiated in so many.

Is such a situation inevitable? Must learning and culture ever be the pursuit of the few, an elite defined by common enthusiasm or conscience, imposed in dilute but compulsory doses on the many? Several thoughts suggest themselves, some rooted in the nature of our society, others in the nature of the young.

Faced with a choice of Shakespeare or *EastEnders*, the early pioneers of mass education would have had no difficulty asserting not just the aesthetic but the moral superiority of the one over the other, and the moral benefit of struggling with the initially inaccessible. No longer. In a consumer society, the act of choosing confers legitimacy: whatever I like is right, and the path to fulfilment must be a travelator. Take eating for example. Despite increased affluence, young people's diet and consequent health is poorer today than in the 1950s. Eat up my greens? I prefer a Big Mac thanks. The parallel between diet, nutrition and health of mind and body is close and instructive. If I don't find the taste congenial, why should I eat up my intellectual greens?

As for the young themselves, one could be philosophical about adolescent rebellion against education if the challenge were that of the rising generation against the last. However the problem today is not rebellion, but indifference. There is no nihilism as absolute as that of indifference, even when it is benign; of non-engagement, even when it is tolerant; and it is these that lie at the root of teenage dumbing down.

Even among those young people who value education, most view it in a purely instrumental light; to provide qualifications likely to open career doors. The narrow focus of league tables and examination performance has intensified this, suffocating many of the best elements of outstanding idiosyncratic teaching. I suspect, however, that alongside such instrumentalism is an anti- intellectualism; together they effectively annihilate (to borrow Skinner's definition of education) 'what remains when what is learned has been forgotten'.

One clue to this anti-intellectualism may lie in the extensive and anxious research into why boys, across the Western world, underachieve academically in their school years in comparison with girls. Many possible contributory factors have been advanced—including each commentator's personal hobbyhorse. Among them one in particular rings true in my experience: the susceptibility of the fragile adolescent male self- image to the views or perceived views of others. Whilst both genders suffer the pressures to conform in an ever-widening range of activities, styles and possessions, boys are particularly vulnerable to the 'uncool' connotations of academic attainment. Girls seem little affected by being taunted as a swot, a boffin; boys much more so.

At its extreme and most pernicious, I recall in a midlands' coal mining community the taunts of 'swot' and 'gay boy' being used interchangeably. What chance the inculcation of values embracing the intellectual or cultural? Understandably such bullying is most powerful when joined by girls, ironically themselves less susceptible to the negative connotations of academic pursuits. We routinely teach children about peer group pressure; perhaps we need to distinguish between 'cheer group' and 'sneer group'. While the Americans have practically institutionalized the process, the British have particular difficulty in cheering the achievement of their fellows. Sneering, on the other hand, is all-pervasive here, in both private and public arenas. Why we have no direct translation for *schadenfreude* remains a mystery: we excel at the process. So it is that among the young, of all classes it seems, the highbrow or intellectual pursuit has to be a closet affair, to avoid the lacerating sneer.

Changing such a culture and climate is not a hopeful prospect. As girls overtake boys at GCSE, A-level and shortly at degree level, the 'girly' associations of such achievements will intensify. Parents and even teachers connive in the assumptions that boys will be boys, relieved when an aptitude or at least an enthusiasm for, say, football manifests itself: thank God, the boy is normal! When the government is compelled to talk premier-league football clubs into running homework clubs it is evident just how much sugar it takes for the medicine to be palatable. Yet when a premier-league footballer reads a broadsheet newspaper and discusses art he is subjected to the most obscene taunts from the terraces about his sexuality. Which of us adults would take a stand in such a context. Our atavistic fear of being different, of defying the herd, is overwhelming. Spare a thought then for the adolescent, male or female, who nurtures a passion for Mahler rather than ManU, for Austen rather than Austin Powers.

At the end of the day, they say, what's in it for me? If the choice is indeed theirs, why bother, when the alternatives are so much more attractive? As the task of education falls to a generation of parents and teachers acculturated in such values, the echoes of those pioneering assumptions will grow ever fainter.

Joan Leach, Shaun Mosley and Ivo Mosley

Science: The Stuff of Dreams or Nightmares?

In the Greek tragedy 'Oedipus the King', a chorus of citizens tries to alert Oedipus to his obvious and impending doom. Oedipus, drunk on his own power and fortune, cannot see the truth of what they are telling him. The greater community are struck with more and more afflictions while they tolerate his freedom among them. Angry at their impertinence and blinded by his own arrogance, Oedipus takes no notice and proceeds to his predicted demise.

Science, like Oedipus, has enjoyed great good fortune. Its wrong deeds have been eclipsed or forgotten in the light of the material prosperity it has brought. Arrogant and sure of itself, it ignores the laws that nature has set out for us — laws it has grown great by disclosing.

The difference between the two scenarios is that the arrogance of Oedipus led to his own blindness and exile, and to a temporary plague upon Thebes. The arrogance of science — or to be more specific, the uses to which science is put — threatens the future of us all. The great tide of scientific progress is turning, leaving in its wake a world not of dreams but of nightmare. So how has this come about?

A passion for truth; the thrill of discovery; ambition for glorious recognition and achievement; these, we used to be told, are the motivations of the scientist. 'He who has once in life experienced the joy of scientific creation in the birth of a generalization will never forget it,' wrote Kropotkin. The 'scientific character' was discussed, at a time when such generalizations

were acceptable, by J.R. Baker[1]: 'Nothing but an intense interest in the subject as a whole—in things—could make a man
work so long with so many rebuffs and with so little hope of
profiting directly.' To contrast the scientific character with an
utterly non-scientific but otherwise admirable character,
Baker tells us this story:

> The great mountaineer, Whymper, was not a scien-
> tist. He devoted some pages of a perfectly serious
> book to the cretins and sufferers from goitre in the
> valleys of the Alps. He was horrified by these people
> in a way which would be impossible to a scientist,
> who would regard the diseases impersonally and
> look for a cause. Whymper allowed his horror to
> grow to hatred, and wished to think that the suffer-
> ers or their parents were themselves to blame. He
> wanted those suffering from goitre to be conscripted
> into monstrous armies, to be commanded by idiot
> cretins. He wanted illegitimate cretins to be subject
> to 'special disabilities', as though the frightful dis-
> ability of cretinism were not a sufficient punishment
> for innocent persons. That people should think in
> this way appalls the scientist.... Research has exhib-
> ited the folly of the mountaineer. Lack of iodine in
> the drinking water, not wickedness, is the cause of
> the diseases. One ounce of iodine in seven-and-a-
> half million gallons produces a drinking water
> which will ward off goitre, while feeding with thy-
> roid gland or its extract has a markedly beneficial
> effect on cretinism.

Contrasted with the superstitious attitude of Whymper, it is
easy to see how valuable the scientific attitude has been, leading to great advances in knowledge and to great benefits for
the human race. Yet this dispassion, which distinguishes the
scientist in many admirable ways, is only of value when it is
tied to a moral outlook; otherwise, it leads straight to experiments such as the Nazis conducted in their death camps and

---

[1] J.R. Baker, *The Scientific Life*, 1942.

the U.S. government allowed in the Tuskegee syphilis experiments.

Descartes laid the foundations for the exploitation of the animal world by arguing that humans had souls, but animals were machines. 'It is nature that acts in them according to the arrangement of their organs, just as we see how a clock, composed merely of wheels and springs, can reckon the hours.'[2] Armed with this belief, mistreating animals becomes morally the same as mistreating a clock—if a gain is to be made thereby, it is a perfectly rational thing to do.

Many scientists now propose that we humans are machines too. Does this justify mistreating humans—poisoning their environments, experimenting with their bodies, blowing them to pieces with 'smart' weapons—if some gain is to be made? If so, who is to reckon the gain? We are suddenly in a world of madness, a world of a type it has been the entire work of civilization to avoid. Some scientists look from this rationalist viewpoint in a different direction and express a kind of disappointed disgust of life and humanity itself. Stephen Hawking in a TV interview, sounding more like Baudelaire in a mood of disgust than an objective scientist, described humanity as 'a chemical scum on a remote and insignificant planet'.

It would be absurd to suggest that all, or even most, scientists share this negative world-view. It is certainly not the main reason why scientists from distant parts of a fragmented profession gather together to defend each other even when they—as specialists in other fields—have precious little idea of what is involved in the debate. A more fundamental reason is that scientists share a confidence, even a conviction, in the ability of the scientific method, properly applied, to reveal the dangers inherent in a process. Science is based upon measurement, statistical or mechanical. So far so good; but what if something cannot be measured? In the words of C.D. Darlington, himself a noted scientist, 'It is intolerable to many otherwise rational scientists to believe in anything they cannot

[2] Quoted in *The Boundaries of Humanity* ed. Sheehan & Sosna, UP Press 1991. 'On the whole, it does seem that he (Descartes) held the strong thesis usually ascribed to him' — Bernard Williams, *Encyclopaedia of Philosophy*, 1967.

measure.'[3] So we have the phenomenon of possibilities that cannot be measured being treated, for the purposes of the moment, as if they do not exist.

This principle of 'suck-it-and-see' applies in any situation where the experiment cannot be isolated because of its physical power or enormity. Scientists who developed the atomic bomb took bets, at the time of its first test explosion, on whether the Earth's atmosphere would become a vast fusion bomb. The bets were surely a bit light-hearted, for only one side could possibly have had time to collect.

The 'suck-it-and-see' principle is unavoidable in biology. When Ernest Rutherford said, 'All science is either physics or stamp-collecting,' he was referring to the fact that whereas a series of experiments can yield pretty definitive results in physics, they must always be to some extent inadequate in biology. They cannot fully predict the effects of the process in an open environment. Take for instance a new drug; no matter how many trials are done, its exposure to a wider variety of human subjects will always reveal new side effects because every human being is different. So the final release of a new drug is also an experiment, an experiment on a grand scale. The negative consequences of new pharmaceutical drugs will be in and around the unfortunate individuals who suffer; with biotechnology the negative consequences may embrace the whole human race.

When British government scientists approved the sale of meat products as feed for cattle, they could see no rational case against it. The instinctive revulsion of farmers and consumers was overridden by scientific 'rationalism'. But the unforseen occurred; a conduit for a new human disease was provided. Instincts were proved in retrospect right. In self-defence, and in retrospect, the scientific community branded the scientists involved 'bad scientists'.

When British scientists involved in anti-malaria experiments injected blood from chimpanzees into humans, they had no idea this could be a conduit for the development of a new strain of the AIDS virus. Indeed, at that time the AIDS

---

[3] Letter to *The Times*, 23 November 1976; quoted in *Biographical Memoirs of Fellows of the Royal Society*, **29** (1983).

virus still had no name, no diagnostic history, no scientific existence. Scientists still have no idea whether a new strain did in fact originate then; but it is acknowledged as an evident possibility. Other scientific practices have also been cited as possible sources for the AIDS epidemic. One in particular is the administration of polio vaccines made from the kidneys of infected monkeys, used in trials in Central Africa in the late 1950s. Tried first on crippled and mentally-retarded children, then on black Africans, then on Americans, it was responsible for transmitting a virus known as SV-40 to millions of humans; whether it also originated a strain of AIDS is fiercely debated. The possibility that it *could* have, however, is indubitable.

Researchers into these matters who try to get their findings accepted by the scientific community report a filtration system. 'Papers reaching optimistic conclusions are printed despite awesome errors; papers reaching pessimistic conclusions are rejected despite overwhelming evidence.'[4]

The examples above represent opportunities for new organisms to develop which could be of untold harm to the human race. Now, in a move that has no precedent, we are creating organisms with designer genomes. In the enthusiastic scramble to develop and profit from this technology, proper risk assessment is missing out on some factors, for sure: this has been proved by the speed with which introduced genes have spread 'horizontally' into other organisms. The science of this is not desperately obscure: to quote Darlington again, 'The dangers that arise from taking too seriously an axiomatic distinction between heredity, development and infection have long been evident. Common propagation by DNA was a prior property common to the three and is capable of overriding their differences.'[5]

It is only natural that the scientific community should want to protect itself from the possibility that it may be responsible for unleashing new plagues upon the human race. Such possibilities threaten profoundly its self-image as *the* great rational benefactor of humanity, and also its employment prospects:

---

[4]   Louis Pascal, quoted from the Internet.
[5]   *Nature,* **234,** 521 (1971).

should science shrink from the vast industrial enterprise it is today towards the economically modest search for pure knowledge from which it began, many scientists would be looking elsewhere for employment.

So although awareness of the dangers of scientific practice has increased both among scientists and among the public, there is a reluctance among the scientific community to accept moral responsibility for the downside of their activities, and thereafter to restrain the activities of its members. Indeed, some would say that moral considerations lie outside science altogether. But who *is* qualified to exercise control?

The knowledge of science is so vast, and so fragmented into different disciplines and sub-disciplines, that it is impossible for even a working scientist to be informed about more than one small area of knowledge and practice. So whoever does the policing has to do it on the advice of those who know, and — in the ever more commercial world of science — those in the know are also those with most to gain or lose.

This problem grows from the fact that the research is financed now not so much out of a desire for knowledge, as in expectation of the commercial rewards that exploiting such knowledge might bring. Programmes sponsored by corporations and governments are for the most part tied to possibilities of specific commercial gain. So experts in biotechnology, for instance, giving advice on whether a particular programme should go ahead, are being financed by the very processes they are being asked to monitor. Nadezhda Mandelstam's pithy and extreme expression of the problem should be on everyone's mind in these increasingly corporatist days: 'If you receive every morsel of your daily bread from the hands of the powers-that-be, then you are wise, if you want to be sure of getting a little extra, to give up thinking altogether.'[6]

The risks of genetic engineering may be small, and some of them are certainly unmeasurable, but factored up by the vastness of their potential consequences they are the stuff of nightmares. One new or mutated microbe, given the right conditions to flourish, is enough to originate an entire new disease for humankind. The risk is there; so what overrides it?

---

[6]   *Hope Abandoned*, 113.

Potential benefit to humanity, or potential profit to those who control the technology? This is a question many concerned scientists are asking, and the answers they come up with are not reassuring.

A group of concerned scientists and medical doctors has put the matter thus:

> The intentional or unintentional dissemination of genetically manipulated organisms into an ecosystem represents a risk. There have been a number of efforts to control these potential dangers by risk assessment strategies. However, by releasing these organisms, the main security barriers of laboratories and production plants are overcome. We are therefore directly and continually exposed to large amounts of genetically engineered organisms (plants, microorganisms, viruses) and are thus subject to an extremely high level of risk. The particular quality of risk inherent in genetic engineering resides in the fact that the source of the risk:
>
> • is alive,
>
> • reproduces,
>
> • cannot be retrieved in case of damage
>
> • and that horizontal transfer of genes can take place
>
> Should any damage occur, retrieval or disinfection is utterly impossible. This fact distinguishes potential damage caused by genetic engineering from risks caused by chemical or nuclear contamination which is limited to certain substances, certain times and certain locations. Genetic engineering turns nature into an open laboratory.[7]

The problem is further exacerbated by licences and monopolies being handed down like rain from governments anxious to take a share of the profits, especially in the ever-greedy

---

[7]   Dr Urs Guthauser, *EVU News*, Issue 2, 1997. Dr Guthauser is a member of 'Doctors for the Protection of the Environment', via Ubrio 2, 6616 Losone, Switzerland.

United States. Monopolies such as those granted by patents on genes are like faucets that turn on money. The justification given for these licenses is that the money finances research; but when the research produces more danger than benefit, that is scant justification.

The successful negotiation by the United States of new world trade agreements has opened up the world as a marketplace for new technologies in the exclusive control of Western corporations. Market enthusiasts may say that if a profit is being made, people must be benefiting. But this simple principle ignores several factors. First, speculative money follows speculative ventures, and huge fortunes have been chasing the biotechnology companies not for what they deliver but for what they promise. Secondly, producers are often forced, in order to survive, to adopt practices that give short-term benefit but spell long-term disaster; examples of this range from heavily chemicalized agriculture to built-in obsolescence. Third, one customer's benefit can be another's disaster — the most extreme example of this being the armaments industry, where the happy customer is able to physically eliminate the enemy.

Politicians and consumers are ignorant and greedy for the supposed benefits of science. Even when dubious practices are widely known, the public continues to buy the products concerned, for instance battery chickens. The farming community made no organized complaint about animal 'by-products' in certain cattle feeds until they were hit in their pockets. When scientists do get together to introduce a moral dimension, the political and press coverage is usually hostile — the most well known example of this happening being when the Pugwash group of scientists tried to control the spread of nuclear weapons. 'Who do they think they are?' was the response of public, press and government.

Recent practice has various combinations of politicians, scientists and some philosophically-minded 'great and good' types sitting in committee to monitor scientific activity. It is well known that when a committee is set up to investigate questions of scientific ethics, the elected politicians make sure this committee is packed with people who give the 'right' response. Alternative scientific opinion is brushed aside with the aid of government spin doctors.

In academic science conformism is encouraged by the career structure. Scientists advance by stages. First one is accepted as a PhD student; then one may rise through the ranks from the position of research assistant to professor; lastly one may be appointed to quangos or—even better— Royal Commissions. Steps one and two depend on demonstrating the requisite mental ability and being able to produce research judged to be valuable by one's peers, but progress is consistently easier if one learns not to rock the boat; otherwise one is labelled a 'maverick', a character-type normally sidelined. The few who make it to the very top are tolerated, even admired, but seldom asked to be on quangos. A notable exception was when Richard Feynman, the best-known physicist of his time, was asked to be on the committee investigating the 1986 Challenger Space Shuttle disaster; it seems the matter was so nationally traumatic that the truth simply had to be found. The effect of a truly independent-minded scientist on the committee was dramatic. Feynman himself has described[8] (in characteristically immodest fashion) how he single-handedly combatted the apparachiks on the investigation and found out the truth of what happened.

The third stage of the academic career—quangos and Royal Commissions—is extremely important to career scientists, since besides the considerable pay and expenses involved, it allows them to feel involved and valued in civilised interaction with their peers both from the wider science community and from other branches of society. It is quangos that decide scientific policy or ethics. To be accepted onto an important quango or a Royal Commission one must first have proved one is 'sensible' and 'reliable' on lesser quangos. Again, rocking the boat too far risks being labelled 'erratic' or 'living in cloud cuckoo land'. Under these circumstances, the government finds it all too easy to arrange a quango of 'independent' scientists and obtain a 'sensible' conclusion from its point of view.

---

[8] Feynman's *What Do You Care What Other People Think?* (1992) contains a fascinating account of this episode.

In commercial science, where more and more scientists find their employment and make careers, conformism is a *sine qua non*. In corporations, loyalty, and secrecy are paramount. Here the government has even less of a problem finding well-behaved committee-members.

Consider the many investigations (before the link was finally admitted) into the possible connection between feeding brains to cattle and 'Mad Cow Disease'. It was quite clear to investigators what the government wanted – a finding that any link was 'unproved'. In light of our previous considerations it would have been surprising if the usual 'quango' material had come up with any contrary result; not from any willful refusal to consider the facts, but more from the selection process as described above. A non-scientist may think this version lets the scientists off lightly – after all, why couldn't they just 'look at the facts'? But in reality, the link to 'Mad Cow Disease' was at first tenuous, becoming stronger over a number of years. The scientists involved would have concurred, at least privately, that there was *some* risk; the difficult decision was when to announce the drastic measures that had to be taken. What happened was that the government held on to an increasingly untenable position and then conceded everything in one fell swoop, so that according to their advice it was safe to eat beef on Monday but not on Tuesday.

If the government had really wanted an independent report, it would have appointed an outsider – even a 'maverick' – as chairperson, then included scientists of both viewpoints. Instead, what happened was that scientists of a contrary viewpoint, far from being included on the relevant committees, were vilified with the full weight of the government 'spin doctor' machinery. Worse, at least one scientist who came up with compelling contrary evidence was dismissed from his position, as well as receiving hate mail and death threats. The moral responsibility must lie with politicians when they let their desire for the 'correct' result override objectivity.

How can we progress? The politicians seem so wonderfully immune to morality, responsibility and truth it is a miracle any of us trusts them on anything. Take for example the safety of GM food. The government's emotional involvement has been for a long time clear — YES TO GM! Quite why they have been so keen is a mystery; the dubious propriety of a minister financially involved in GM technology has been noted by all except the government. Is the investigation being conducted in a rational manner? Are people with contrary viewpoints being included on the relevant committees? So far all we have heard is a sound of bleating such as one might hear from a flock of genetically engineered sheep; 'no discernible risk' etc. Soon, no doubt, the distaste of voters will make itself felt; then, sheep-like once more, government advisers will change their tune.[9]

So in the end, the opinions of non-experts (the voters) prevails — but sometimes it is too late to prevent some extremely nasty developments. Can this democratic wisdom be harnessed at an earlier stage?

Recent critiques of 'big science', and calls for a scaling down of science, have been greeted by wails: the public does not understand or appreciate the values of science. On the one hand, there is ample evidence to claim that 'big science' may not serve the interests of the majority of citizens; on the other, it does seem reasonable to claim that science itself is not well understood by the public. What can we make of these two partially contradictory and yet related claims?

The first claim, advocating a scaling-down of 'big science' or at the very least a tighter regulatory structure, leads us to consider the relationship between regulation in science and regulation of other forms of social and professional life. Scientists have long appealed to the 'peer-review' process as central to scientific self-regulation. Peer-review, so the story goes, weeds out fraud, irrelevance and even allows the scientific referees to determine what questions and methods are worthy of attention by scientific peers. Peer review, of course, is a regulatory process internal to science.

Suggestions of *external* regulation have been met with incredulity and resistance by the scientific community. The preferred argument of those who oppose it is that members of the

---

[9] As this book goes to press, so the process has begun; Tony Blair announces there is 'cause for legitimate public concern about GM foods' (28 February 2000).

public do not have the special technical knowledge it takes to understand science and so cannot possibly help to regulate it. So, critiques of science can usually be stymied by the simple claim 'you just don't understand.'

But do we need to understand the technicalities of science in order to participate in its governance? In one sense, this very question points out an asymmetry in the relation between science and society. Scientific autonomy and self-regulation have effectively meant that scientists have not been held accountable to democratic decision-making. Yet scientists find it perfectly acceptable to judge the public and find it wanting. This asymmetry reflects an assumption among scientists that the scientific method should hold sway in *every* human activity; it ignores the fact that subjective judgements become more and more important, the further one moves away from the most basic experiments of physics. But even if we ignore the dubious foundations on which questions of public knowledge or understanding sit, is 'public understanding of science' the answer to the governance of science question?

While most people would certainly argue in a general sense that more knowledge is better than less knowledge, there are two reasons to be careful about 'science literacy' movements. First, they foster a 'them' versus 'us' approach; scientists have knowledge, the public does not. This tends to encourage a sense in which scientists are seen as intellectually superior to non-scientists. Instead of encouraging the acquisition of knowledge, learning in this context becomes quite daunting when scientific elites are parcelling out knowledge to inferior minds. The second reason why knowing more science will not necessarily help us govern science better is that merely knowing more science does not help us participate in science. Given the fragmentation discussed above, even scientists would not have the intellectual resources to govern other parts of science. But if more knowledge is not the answer, what is?

One answer lies in democratic engagement in and with science. Democratic procedures which have enjoyed long histories are finally making their way into the governance of science. Two methods — citizens juries and 'consensus conferences' — have successfully mixed the adage that more knowledge is a Good Thing with the general principle that knowing science does not necessarily help one to govern science. In both, lay representatives chosen at random from the electoral rolls are presented with some technical background and then with a host of expert and lay views as to whether a certain area of scientific research is worth pursuing. After hearing this evidence, lay juries come to a verdict, and consensus conferences to a moderated view, as to whether the research seems reasonable and fair by criteria that they themselves develop. Scientists and political theorists have been surprised and impressed with the results. It seems that when citizens feel empowered to make decisions, instead of being positioned as ignorant receptacles of knowledge, then considered views on science are not impossible. These experiments in democratization should make us feel optimistic, but only if the consensus or the verdicts that have been reached have real clout in public policy. This will turn what could be a democratic ideal into a real democratization of science.

Another answer, not incompatible with the above, lies in the democratization of the way internal scientific opinion is itself represented. At the moment the public culture of science appears arrogant, self-seeking, obsessed with hierarchy (the title 'Nobel prize-winner' carries as much weight as ever did 'Duke' or 'Prince' at a royal court) and contemptuous of the unscientific mind. The arcane language of science is used publicly like the barking of dogs to intimidate and silence opposition. But does this represent the voice of the average working scientist? Certainly not — these spokespeople were not asked by other scientists to represent science; they were chosen by government and business to represent science. Would a body of scientists, elected from within the scientific community *by* the scientific community, be more responsible when it comes to regulating the activities of science? This is an experiment that has not been tried, but the system has proved successful in other professions. When members of a profession act not as individuals but as a body, selfish considerations give way to a desire that the profession should steer clear of disrepute. Such a body in science would have the advantage of being an international body, making international judgments. This point is extremely important, for the harmful effects of science are no respecters of borders.

Michael Polanyi has written that the false ideal of scientific detachment 'exercises a destructive influence in biology, psychology and sociology and falsifies our whole outlook far beyond the domain of science.'[10] Above all, this false ideal is used to avoid moral responsibility. Now, with no wise system of regulation in sight and with all the countries of the world competing to benefit and hope for the best, it is time for the scientific profession internationally to accept the principle of moral responsibility. Charges of irresponsibility lie heavy upon it; environmental degradation, weapons technology and new disease. Should *any* process be allowed to go ahead if a possible outcome is the destruction of most of the human race? This and other questions call out for proper answers, from the wider democratic community and from the science community itself.

---

[10] For a full exposition of this theme, see Michael Polanyi's *Personal Knowledge* (1958); the quote is from the Introduction.

John Ziman

Heeding Voices

To God the embattled nations sing and shout
'Gott strafe England', and 'God save the King';
God this, God that, and God the other thing.
'Good God!', said God, 'I've got my work cut out!'

Nowadays it's to Science that the People sing and shout. The voice of our Science is the voice of our God. Science, the provider of all good things, is also to save us from the follies of its own servants. By its aid we shall become more competitive, create wealth, avoid risks and conserve Nature. Let genetics give us abundant food and health, and the same genetics defend us from ecological and medical lunacies. Let information technology promote publicity and protect privacy. Science shall be our sword and our shield, for ourselves, against ourselves, evermore.

Having been brought up as monotheists, we address our King of Kings in the singular. Science United rules, OK? The astronomer shall stand up with the anthropologist, the physicist with the psychologist, the microbiologist with the macro-economist, all one great happy team, winning great goals of Truth together in the great Method game.

With respect, O People, not so. Look at the reruns. Star players those scientists may be, but when do they ever pass the ball to each other? They are playing in competition, and are not united by the same methods. Seismology is unpredictive. Animal behaviour is unquantifiable. Social scientists can't do experiments. Palaeontology is unobservable. Biological phenomena are not perfectly replicable. Evolutionary hypotheses are unfalsifiable. The big match looks more like an athletics meeting, with every science doing its own thing.

Don't be misled by the philosophers. Taking physics as their model, they have belittled the exploration of the world and spawned a million pseudo-mathematical misconceptions of life and society. The world is as it is, dead and alive, solitary and social, natural and constructed. We can experience it only in fragments, depict it only sketchily, grasp it only momentarily, glimpse it only myopically, in disconnected aspects, through a variety of clouded lenses. To each science its tiny porthole, from each its tunnelled perspective. Tell us, professors, what is a gene *actually*? A heritable trait? An evolutionary replicator? A developmental switch? A coded protein? A segment of DNA? A conglomerate of electrons, protons and neutrons? It is all those things and more: it is only one thing, yet it exists in a multiplicity of conceptual universes. We unify it metaphysically, through the enveloping veil of lived reality. The physicists' frenetic quest for a theory of everything is no way to a grander narrative or a fuller Monty. Their positivist ideology of reduction is the antithesis of synthesis. The scientific world picture is a ragbag of scrambled jigsaw puzzles, painted piecewise by numbers. Who will ever determine whether they connect?

Ah, but everybody knows that curiosity is a sharper instrument than rationality, and discovery trumps invention. Of course each science has a different notion of what counts as a discovery. The speculative shot that wins a prize in cosmology is judged a wide in chemistry and an own goal in economics. But curious folk have learnt to exercise their obsessions in concert: 'Just look at this! Have you ever seen anything like that before? I think this is how it works. Don't you agree?' Enlarge that conjoint operation, elaborate, co-ordinate, discipline, differentiate, professionalize and institutionalize it into a byzantine culture, with a community to practise it. Apply it to planets, polymers, pachyderms, percepts or plutocracies, and you have many sub-cultures. Watch the emergence of distinctive methodologies and paradigms. Call them all sciences, natural and human, housed together under the broad roof of the Academy.

So — science, the epitome of pantheism, has not mastered its own inborn polytheism. Whenever the people call upon it for aid, several voices reply, each from one of the many sacred clouds in which the gods of scientific truth are enthroned.

Their various warnings are often reliable, and ever to be heeded, but they are not securely grounded on a wide foundation of knowledge and understanding. What is more, there remain whole domains of mirth and misery over which no scientific deity presides. Indeed, the sciences are still only one of several divine families in the Pantheon of human belief systems. The empire of doctrine is not just a dyarchy of Science and/or Religion. The ancient palaces of Beauty, Justice and Love still stand high on Parnassus, alongside Truth and Faith; and in our pluralistic, multicultural ways of life, these great houses, too, are divided against themselves.

I hear a voice—'Don't tell me those poor deluded souls still believe in that sort of rubbish! Beauty, justice, love, faith and all those other social constructs?' Well I, too, used to think that a whiff of positive empiricism and absolute logic would be enough to dispel the mobs of junk thought and their gibbering prophets. What a pity! Back to the metaphysical drawing board, I suppose. But what has become of the holiest of all voices, the voice of the people themselves—common sense?

I'm glad you asked me that—which means I don't know. Opinions differ. Some scientists assert that common sense has been superseded by science. Others insist that science is but common sense writ large. Either way suits their book. Naturally, the truth must lie between these extremes. I suspect it's a lumpy mixture, rather than a custardy compound. Science and common sense are not quite separate, and not quite equal, but they each contain chunks of the other. Is an aspirin a folk remedy or a therapeutic agent? Is a personal computer a household appliance or an algorithmic instrument? Is hyperinflation a societal catastrophe or a monetarist miscalculation? Both, of course, in each case, which is no problem unless you are a card-carrying essentialist.

So even the mundane voice of folk knowledge — the whisperer of home truths, the source of life-world tittle-tattle, the Walkman guide to everyday things — is still but one of many media from which people learn how to live and for what to die. Despite their magnificent machines, scientists have created a thorny cultural bed to lie down on. How can they manage themselves without a supreme manager to call the final shots? In the name of Science, they said they had dethroned the old religions; so why can't they complete the revolution and acknowledge Science as their undisputed Lord? Why has their theoretical monotheism not brokered a theological tournament in which Science United always wins? Give it the co-ordination to prevail against every challenging doctrine and all must be its loyal fans.

But we, O People, are not just the guardians of truism. In the time of Enlightenment, it was we who sowed disobedience, and who now have to reap pluralism. Speaking discontents to earthly authorities, we released truths against heavenly powers. Science emerged out of great waves of political and religious discord. It has grown into a Leviathan, yet it is still a creature of the wild. It exerts its powers erratically, disconcerting those who try to ride it. Budgets and bureaux, designed to domesticate Science, enervate it with fat and complacency. Its strength is in its freedom from constraint; its mighty muscles would sag and its bones would crumble if it were caged and harnessed.

'But'—the Devil whispers—'Whoever said that humans should tame their gods?' Surely, sovereignty is for use and respect! Instead of trying to control Science, let the people be controlled by it. Let them worship it more devoutly, do its bidding more scrupulously, support it more wholeheartedly, proclaim its unity more widely, crusade more tirelessly against its enemies and exalt it with ever more imposing monuments, buttressed by massive computations and pinnacled with exotic algebra. Give Science absolute power, and it will provide absolute blessings.

But no! To do so would surrender humankind to a heartless monster whose very mind would soon be absolutely corrupted. Science can thrive only in the pluralistic climate that once germinated its seeds. It gains its nourishment from dissent and maintains its vigour through disputation. Unlike religion, it is poisoned by zealous rationalization and uncritical faith. Those who claim to be its entire servants are the worst enemies of Science and of humanity itself, and are often the unwitting lackeys of demonic corporate powers.

Science is an evolving organism. Free enterprise is its natural socio-economic environment. It survives in the doctrinal jungle by the fitness of its ideas. It is chronically sceptical and vulnerable to criticism. It adapts to self-induced change by continued variation and selection. It competes epistemically in the market place of credibility. Its niche in the ecology of knowledge has to be held by reasoned argument against a diversity of rival beliefs.

Science is not an alien theocracy that has enslaved humanity, but a living arm of democracy. Its practices are specialized components of the political and cultural apparatus of every free nation. Its norms are the same freedoms of speech and conscience, of assembly and justice, as of all the other institutions of an open society. The scientific voice is just one of the many voices that arise spontaneously in Liberty Hall. Science is no distant God. It is both the ward and warden, beneficiary and benefactor of the people themselves, supporting, protecting and correcting each the other, seeking least-worst modes of thought and action in a dangerous but many-splendoured world.

Jaron Lanier

Agents of Alienation

I find myself holding a passionate opinion that almost nobody in the AI community agrees with and I'm wondering: What's gotten into all of you? I find that in the wide, though shrinking, world away from computers most people find my position obvious, while infophiles find it impenetrable. I am trying to bridge a chasm of misunderstanding.

Here is the opinion: that the idea of 'intelligent agents' is both wrong and evil. I also believe that this is an issue of real consequence to the near-term future of culture and society. As the infobahn rears its gargantuan head, the agent question looms as a deciding factor in whether this new beast will be much better than TV, or much worse.

The idea of agents comes up in response to an obvious predicament of the new media revolution we find ourselves hurtling through. How do you make sense of a world of information available to you on demand? How do you find the grains of gold in the heaps of dirt that will be shipped to you on the infobahn every day? The 'official' answer is that autonomous 'artificial intelligence' programs called agents will get to know you by hanging out with you, and they'll figure it all out, presenting you with a custom morning newspaper, or whatever. This is the idea of Microsoft's 'Bob' program and the pitch presented in the AT&T 'You will' commercials, in Nicholas Negroponte's columns in *Wired* magazine (in which he has called intelligent agents the 'unequivocal' future of computing) and in the marketing of many products, like Apple's Newton.

While intelligent agents have been a dominant theme in anticipating the immediate future for some time, they can often not quite be found in the present. Offensively paternal 'Bob' and the Newton are rare examples of products that are actually shipped that claimed to have an agent capability. I will argue that the rarity of actual agents does not diminish their harm because they exist primarily in the minds of expectant beholders anyway, and in a way that damages those minds.

I should also make it clear that I am concerned with autonomous agents that people are meant to interact with in consequential ways; the term 'agent' is also sometimes used in fields like 'artificial life' to refer to experimental software elements in a closed system. These should be classified separately, though true believers in agents might not see the distinction.

So why am I enraged by the notion of agents? What galls me aren't just the practical problems, but I'll summarize those first, to get them out of the way:

- If info-consumers see the world through agent's eyes then advertising will transform into the art of controlling agents, through bribing, hacking, whatever. You can imagine an 'arms race' between armour-plated agents and hacker-laden ad agencies. Lovely.

- Since agents are little computer programs they'll have a lot more in common with each other than people do. Agents would become the new information bottleneck, narrowing the otherwise delightfully anarchic infobahn, which was supposed to replace the broadcast model with something more inclusive.

  An agent's model of what you are interested in will be a cartoon model, and you will see a cartoon version of the world through the agent's eyes. It is therefore a self-reinforcing model. This will recreate the lowest-common-denominator approach to content that plagues TV. 'You're interested in Balinese ritual, therefore you're interested in travel, therefore you're interested in the Infobahn Travel Game Show!'

- Agents will inevitably deliver an overdose of kitsch. Microsoft's 'Bob' is the agent of the moment and it proposes to the user a life of caricatured meaninglessness, sliding unintentionally into the grotesque, that is straight out of Diane Arbus.

Now true agent-believers can answer any specific criticism by postulating better agents. But the specific problems are not the ones that make my blood boil, anyway. *Agents make people redefine themselves into lesser beings.* THAT is the monster problem.

Am I making an inappropriately broad claim here? I don't think so. You see, the problem is that the only difference between an autonomous 'agent' program and a non-autonomous 'editor/filter' program *is in the psychology of the human user*. You change yourself in order to make the agent look smart. Specifically, you make yourself dumb.[1] Here is how people reduce themselves by acknowledging agents, step by step:

1. Person gives computer program extra deference because it is supposed to be 'smart' and 'autonomous'.[2]

2. Projected autonomy is a self-fulfilling prophecy, as anyone who has ever had a teddy bear knows. The person starts to think of the computer as being like a person.

3. As a consequence of unavoidable psychological algebra the person starts to think of himself as being like the computer.

4. Unlike a teddy bear, the computer is made of ideas. The person starts to limit herself to the categories and procedures represented in the computer, without realizing what has been lost. Music becomes MIDI, art becomes Postscript. I believe that this process is the precise origin of the nerdy quality that the outside world perceives in some computer culture.

5. This process is greatly exacerbated if the software is conceived of as an agent and is therefore attempting to represent the person with a software model. The person's act of projecting autonomy onto the computer becomes an

---

[1] Agent programs as a rule will also have worse user interfaces than non-agent programs.

[2] People have a tendency to yield authority to computers anyway, and it's a shame. In my experience and observations, computers, unlike other tools, seem to produce the best results when users have an antagonistic attitude towards them.

unconscious choice to limit behaviours to those that fit naturally into the grooves of the software model.

Even without agents a person's creative output is compromised by identification with a computer. With agents, however, the person himself is compromised.

For a recent example of the dumbing of human behaviour in the presence of a product that is designated 'smart', look no further than the Newton. Find someone who uses one, especially the agent features, and watch them closely. See how well they have adapted themselves to the project of making the product look smart? Don't they look silly?[3] Do you realize that if everyone was contorting themselves to take down simple notes, or emphasizing tasks that happen to fit into a database ('Call Mom!'), it would look *normal*?

If Ambrose Bierce were alive today I think he might add the following entry to *The Devil's Dictionary*:

> **Agent** *n*: A network/database query program whose user interface is so obscure that the user must think of it as a quirky, but powerful, person in order to accept it. *ALT. Definition*: A program that conceals a haphazard personality profile of a user from that user.

Now an agent supporter might say: Why does the personality profile have to be concealed? Wouldn't your objection be answered if users could edit what the agent does? Of course that would satisfy me! But where is the room for autonomy once you have such an editor? You have changed your psychology, empowering yourself at the expense of the agent. You have murdered the agent by exposing its murky guts to sunlight.

Agents are the work of lazy programmers. Writing a good user-interface for a complicated task, like finding and filtering a ton of information, is *much harder to do* than making an intelligent agent. From a user's point of view, an agent is something you give slack to by making your mind mushy, while a user-interface is a tool that you use, and you can tell whether you are using a good tool or not.

---

[3] If, on the other hand, you want to see a program that encourages people to be smart and autonomous, check out Eudora.

The extremely hard work of making user-interfaces to gen-uinely empower people is the true work of the information age; much harder, say, than making faster computer chips. The Macintosh was a prime example of this work. It didn't do any-thing other computers didn't, it just made those things clear to users, and that was a revolution. It should be remembered as an early step in a journey that goes much further.

So agents are double trouble. Evil, because they make peo-ple diminish themselves, and wrong, because they confuse the feedback that leads to good design.

But remember, although agent programs tend to share a set of deficiencies it is your psychology that really makes a pro-gram into an agent; a very similar program with identical capabilities would not be an agent if you take responsibility for understanding and editing what it does.

An agent is a way of using a program, in which you have ceded your autonomy. Agents only exist in your imagination. I am talking about YOU, not the computer.

II

Now, my objections to agents would surely be moot if agents were truthfully, in fact, autonomous and even perhaps con-scious. If agents were real it would be a lie to deny them. To address this possibility is to consider artificial intelligence. The problem with the AI school of technology development is that it doesn't say a thing about technology at all; rather, it redefines people. As Turing pointed out, the only objective measurement of humanity is the responses and judgments of humans.

If you don't know about the Turing Test, you should. It is the creation myth of artificial intelligence. It was invented by a brilliant mathematician, Alan Turing, considered a war hero for having broken a Nazi secret code...who happened to be gay and was imprisoned by the British government and sub-jected to quack treatments for homosexuality.[4] It was under these conditions, shortly before his suicide, that he created the mythical basis for smart machines. Einstein's thought experi-

---

[4] Turing was given large quantities of female hormones and developed breasts.

ments were in vogue, and Turing offered a thought experiment in their spirit. The Turing Test has now practically become an urban legend of the computing world. Here is the usual formulation: imagine two soundproof booths, one occupied by a man, the other by a woman, each typing at you, each trying to impersonate the other (a precursor to the current fun troubles with cyber-dating!). We then proceed to a booth with a man versus a booth with a machine. The claim of the Turing Test is that if you cannot tell the difference you have no scientific basis to claim a different status for people than for machines. When I first learned about the test at school I thought it was odd and superfluous to begin with the man/woman setup, and I only learned of its significance much later.[5] Turing was trying to escape the pain of his circumstances by fantasizing an abstract intelligence, free of the dreadful mysteries of the flesh.

The problem with the Turing Test is that it presents a conundrum of scientific method. We presume that improvement to machines takes place, so there is a starting state in our experiments where the human is considered 'smarter', whatever that means, than the computer. We are measuring a change in human ability to discriminate between human and machine behaviour. But the human is defined as the most flexible element in the measurement loop at the start, so how do we know we aren't measuring a state change in the human, rather than in the computer? Is there an experimental difference, in this setup, between computers getting 'smarter' and humans getting 'stupider'? I don't think so.

If I seem overly mean in attacking these ideas it is because I have been in a beleaguered minority for so long in the infophile community. Believers in the artificial intelligence world-view have a few standard insults for disbelievers. Here are two insults and my responses. First insult:

> Non-AI'ers must be 'dualists' claiming some sort of
> alternate track of reality for souls or something.

Experience is the only thing we share that we do not share objectively. I'm happy to assume that the study of the brain

---

[5] Turing's original paper doesn't start this way, but that is the way it is taught and I am most interested in its life as a legend.

can potentially proceed to the point where every tiny thought and feeling can be measured and even controlled, and still *experience itself* will remain unmeasured. Even though experience cannot be experimentally verified, and therefore can never be a part of science, we cannot ignore it in forming our philosophy, however tempted we might be by the simplicity of doing so, any more than a physicist could ignore gravity in order to have a unified field theory.[6]

Second insult:

> If you do not accept AI you are placing humans in a 'special' category, as onerous and silly as the placement of the earth at the centre of the solar system by the church in the face of Galileo.

What I am doing is avoiding judgment about what I cannot measure of myself, and keeping a general attitude of optimism about what I might be, that is all. In this case, unlike Galileo's, science will remain perpetually uncertain. We can, if we are unusually disciplined, accept this uncertainty in our platonic thoughts, but when it comes time to act we must choose a fantasy to act on. I am ultimately arguing the merits of the humanist fantasy versus the materialist fantasy.

III

There is a much higher stake here than a question of bad science and software design. It is a subtle question that might be described as spiritual, and it means all the world to me.

The agent question is important because it is part of a bigger question: do people keep an open mind about what they are, or might be capable of becoming? Or do people limit themselves according to some supposedly objective measure, perhaps provided by science or technology? A related question is also important: is information or experience primary?

The worst failing of Communism, in my opinion, is that it did not acknowledge the existence of human experience beyond the scope of its own ideas. The most stifling threat to freedom is to bind people within the limits of ideas, since we,

---

[6] I don't use the word 'consciousness' any more because it has been colonized by materialists and now means a specialized part of a computer that models another part and can exert executive control.

just like the rest of nature, are always a step ahead of our best interpretations. Thus under Communism we saw an attempt to destroy spirituality, sentimentality, identity and tradition.

In another context, discussing virtual reality, I came up with the slogan 'Information is Alienated Experience'. This phrase came to me partially in response to the imperialist tendency of theorists of politics, art and computer design to pretend that ideas or words can represent people.

The discipline of science is to only respect falsifiable theories. When you create a boundary for yourself or others by *believing* in a theory of what you or they are, you create a conundrum of scientific method in which you can never know what might have been, and therefore have no opportunity to test the theory.

Part of the beauty of the American idea of government is in its self-limiting charter. For instance, the phrase 'the pursuit of happiness' in an instant identifies an indefinable territory beyond the reach of law, or even language, that constitutes a critical part of 'freedom'. Let's limit the charter of computers and the infobahn in the same way.

This essay has been an attempt to find such limitations. It can be summarized by three limiting principles that I propose, to avoid a recurrence of agent-like confusions:

- treat computers as nothing more than fancy conduits to bring people together

- never treat information as being real on its own; its only meaning is in its use
  by people

- never believe that software models can represent people .

IV

Versions of this essay, excluding this final section, have been posted on the web and delivered in lecture form. There has been an extraordinary, sharply-divided response. The artificial intelligence question is the abortion question of the computer world. What was once a research topic has become a controversy where practical decisions must reflect a fundamental ontological definition about what a person is and is not, and there is no middle ground.

Feelings in the computer community run very deep on this subject. I have had literally hundreds of people come up to me after I have given a talk saying that it had completely changed the way they thought about computers and had answered a vague unease about some computer trends that they had never heard articulated before.

A fiery contingent (including Nicholas Negroponte) think the ideas in this essay are dangerously wrong. Nicholas has even expressed the opinion that it is 'irresponsible' for me to present my argument in public 'because it could mislead people'. Part of the reason for this might be that many in the computer world are attracted to the deathless world of abstraction, and nurture hopes of being able to live forever by backing themselves onto a computer tape.

Still other members of the community are, I believe, overcome with a reaction of denial, and convince themselves that I am saying nothing more than that agents aren't good enough yet. It is this final group that surprises and infuriates me. There is such a universal orthodoxy holding that artificial intelligence is a useful and valid idea that many in the computer community can read this essay and believe that I am only criticizing certain agents, or expressing a distaste for premature agents. They are somehow unable to grasp that someone could categorically attack ALL agents on the basis that they do not exist, and that it is potentially harmful to believe that they do. They have staked their immortality on the belief that the emperor is indeed wearing new clothes.

Ultimately there is nothing more important to us than our definition of what a person is. Isn't this the core question in a great many controversies? This definition drives our ethics, because it determines what is enough like us to deserve our empathy. Whether we are concerned with animal rights, whether we feel it is essential to intervene in Bosnia; our perceived circle of commonality determines our actions. Beyond ethics, our sense of what else is like us is the glue of our culture. The multiculturalism debate is another example of a struggle to define the centre and the extent of the circle of commonality.

I have long believed that the most important question about information technology is 'How does it affect our definition of what a person is?' The AI/agent question is the controversy

that exposes the answer. It is an answer that will have direct
consequences for the pattern of life in the future, for the quality of the technology which will be the defining vessel of our
culture, and for a spiritual sense of whether we are to be
bounded by ideas or not.

We cannot expect to have certain, universal agreement on
any question of personhood, but we all are forced to hold an
answer in our hearts and act upon our best guess. Our best
guess runs our world.

Walter J. Freeman

Happiness Doesn't Come in Bottles

Too little has been written about the biology of joy. Most of the articles in the medical literature about brains and emotions are devoted to explaining how we feel fear, anger, anxiety and despair. This is understandable, because we don't go to doctors when we are feeling optimistic, happy and joyful. Most of what we know about the chemistry of our emotions has been learned from the disorders and the treatments of people who are sad and depressed.

But we can't just accept this and say, 'Why bother?', because too many of us are seeking to find joy by taking chemicals. We need to ask, 'What happens inside our brains when we experience happiness? Is there a way to stimulate pleasure in our brains, and what really happens when we do that?'

Electrical Stimulation

We have known for 40 years what happens with rats, ever since a neurobiologist named James Olds learned how to put electrodes deep into their brains, connect the wires to an electric current generator, and give the animals a switch with which to stimulate their own brains. In some locations in the brain, if a rat accidentally presses the switch it jumps away and stays as far from the switch as it can get. We call those locations 'pain centres'. At other places, after discovering the effects of the electric current, rats press repeatedly for hours. They seem to be addicted to self-stimulation. We call these locations 'pleasure centres'. But does it make the rats happy?

We don't know, because we can't know what they are feeling. We can only know what they do.

Some neurosurgeons have placed electrodes into the brains of human subjects, who were suffering epilepsy. The surgeons were trying to locate the places in their brains in which a tumor or a scar might be triggering the epileptic fits, so that the damage could be surgically repaired. They stimulated the brains with electric current in order to try to control the epileptic seizures. For some locations, patients reported feeling profoundly depressed, as though they were about to die. One of them said, 'Doc, don't ever do that again!' In different places they reported feeling pleasure, sometimes sexual, but mostly rather bland. Some other patients, who were afflicted with chronic pain, reported that they got temporary relief from their suffering. They were given the opportunity to go home with a battery and a switch, so that they could treat their pain by stimulating themselves and adjusting their own dosage of electric current. But no one wanted to keep the wires, and no one got addicted. Some doctors feared that a black market might grow, with addicts going to third world countries to get fixed with wires and stimulators. That didn't happen, because whatever the pleasure is, it doesn't last, and it isn't happiness.

Chemical Stimulation

But a lot of people do get addicted to chemicals — alcohol, cocaine, amphetamine, heroin and nicotine. Why do they, and why aren't they happy? It is because brains have a variety of chemical systems that regulate their neural activities in waking and sleeping, and the addictive drugs artificially stimulate those systems, but the feelings are not those of joy.

For example, a chemical called 'dopamine' is broadly spread through the brain by specialized nerve cells. When a person achieves some kind of reward, such as by satisfying hunger and thirst, winning a game, or passing an examination, dopamine gives feelings of buoyant optimism, energy, power, and knowledge. It is often called a 'reward hormone'. Its chemical actions are produced also by closely related chemicals such as amphetamine and cocaine. It is not surprising that people who have no other avenues to success, living in poverty and hopelessness, will spend their food money on some transient chemical bliss. But that isn't happiness, and even people who are elated by academic or business success aren't liable to confuse that feeling with happiness.

Other chemicals called 'endorphins' act in the brain as natural pain relievers. Their action is imitated by heroin and morphine, also alcohol. Again, it is small wonder that people who suffer from emotional pain might find relief from their demons in forgetfulness. But that isn't happiness.

Yet another chemical called 'serotonin' is important in bringing mental relaxation as an important pre-condition for sleep. We don't really know yet what sleep is for, but we know we can't survive without it. The relief from agitation and anxiety that is mediated by serotonin leads also to recovery from some forms of depression. That is why the chemical fluoxitine (Prozac) has become so popular. It doesn't act like serotonin, but it prolongs the action of what little serotonin the brain is producing, if it is in short supply. But a return to tranquility from anxiety and depression is not the same as happiness.

So, is there a chemical for joy? Scientists are beginning to understand that there is no such chemical, and even to ask the question is to expose a deep ignorance about how brains — and people — actually work.

Lonely Brains

There is more to brain function than chemistry or electricity. Some pioneer neuroscientists have used the new theory of nonlinear dynamics to build mathematical models of brain function. They have come to some remarkable new insights, which at first may seem outrageous, but which are turning out to be much more in tune with human intuitions about brains and human nature than anyone had expected.

One conclusion is that brains don't take information from the environment and store it like a camera or a tape recorder, for later retrieval. There is no 'database' of memories in brains, such as we hold in libraries and computer chips. We have been misdirected by the makers of computers and the visionary Canadian neurosurgeon, Wilder Penfield, to search for hypothetical 'memory banks' in the temporal lobes. Human remembering is notoriously fallible, and what we remember is continually being changed by new learning, when the connections between nerve cells in brains are modified.

A stimulus excites the sensory receptors, so that they send a message to the brain. That input triggers a reaction in the brain, by which it constructs a pattern of neural activity. The sensory activity which triggered the construction is then washed away, leaving only the construct. That pattern does not 'represent' the stimulus. It constitutes the meaning of the stimulus for the person receiving it. The meaning is different for every person, because it depends on the past experience of the person. A stimulus is only successful in triggering the creation of the construct if the stimulus already has some relevance to the person; most particularly if it is being sought by the person through paying attention, or if the person has had some previous experience with it.

The implication of this dynamical model is that the meaning of a stimulus is different for everyone who receives it, because the sum of experience for each of us is unique. Since the sensory activity is washed away, and only the construction is saved, the only knowledge that each of us has is what we construct within our own brains. We cannot know the world by inserting objects or representations of objects into our brains.

Why not? Because the world is infinitely complex, and an individual brain can only know the little it can create within itself. It turns out this view is well known to philosophers. It is called existentialism. Many philosophers have been afraid that it is true, but they couldn't prove it or disprove it. Now neurodynamicists can show experimentally that it is true. Cognitive scientists have also proved that it is true, but in a negative way. Every robot or a computer they have made, using a fixed memory store of representations of objects, has failed miserably to handle problems in the real world.

Each successful stimulus also evokes a learning experience, so that the person is changed, and new experience accumulates. As existentialist philosophers from Kierkegaard to Heidegger and Sartre have concluded, each of us constructs our self by our own actions, and we know our self as it is revealed to us in our actions. The self is in dynamic readiness to act and bring into play its entire experience at each moment.

That is not the way a library works. It is far more flexible, rapid, and effective, though at the cost of reduced accuracy.

One reason that philosophers have been afraid is that existentialism seems to make it very difficult to account for shared knowledge. If everything each of us knows is made inside our brains, how can we know the same things? The answer is simple. We share almost the same things. Almost. That happens only if we go to the same school, or grow up in the same neighborhood and acquire the same language and the same culture.

Another reason for fear is that each brain is isolated from all others. No one can truly feel what another person is feeling, though we can empathize through shared experience. This separation has a good side, in that each of us has the inalienable right to privacy. The bad side is loneliness. And here, paradoxically, is where joy begins to enter.

Dancing is a Way to Happiness

Where we humans find joy is in surmounting this existential barrier by sharing our feelings and comforts. We cannot ever really cross it, but, a bit like neighbours chatting over a fence, we can be together. However, there is more to this communion than mere talking. There is trust, which underlies true friendships and partnerships. What is the chemistry of trust?

Answers are found when we look back on our mammalian ancestors. Raising a helpless infant to childhood requires intensive parental care, which comes with bonding between the parents and the infant. Now, how does a carefree child, when it has grown up, become a parent? This change in role requires a catastrophic change in beliefs, attitudes and values to make new parents. We humans would say that they fall in love, first with each other, and then with their offspring.

Scientists have learned that, when animals mate and give birth, specialized chemicals are released into their brains that enable their behaviour to change. Maternal and paternal patterns of nursing and caring appear. The most important is a chemical called 'oxytocin'. It doesn't cause joy. On the contrary, it may cause anxiety, because it melts down the patterns of connections among neurons that hold experience, so that new experience can form. We become aware of this meltdown most dramatically as a frightening loss of identity and self control, when we fall in love for the first time. Bonding comes not with the meltdown, but with the shared activity afterward, in which people learn about each other through cooperation. Knowing another person doesn't come with foreplay and orgasm. It comes in cooperative activities during and afterward. Trust emerges not just with sex, but also with vigorous shared activity in sports, combat and competition among work groups, through which people bond into teams by learning to trust each other.

Oxytocin is not a happiness chemical, but a brain tool for building trust. Perhaps a million years ago our ancestors learned how to use this mammalian mechanism to promote social bonding beyond sexual union, in order to form groups and tribes. They did it, and still do it, with dancing, rhythmic clapping and chanting, singing and making music together all day and night, often into exhaustion and collapse. When they awaken, they are reborn.

Nietsche realized this. Émile Durkheim and other anthropologists have shown how people engage in Dionysian revels and religious celebrations as the most effective way in which to create group identities. The joy they experience comes in dancing and singing with each other, thereby forming the bonds of trust. Trust comes when we are able to predict what other people will do, and we achieve that by repeated cooperative actions. Aristotle wrote: 'Happiness is activity of the soul in accordance with virtue.' We can see virtue as a set of shared goals for the good of ourselves and our children. Joy comes with activities that we share with people we have learned to trust, and that enable us to share meaning across the existential barriers separating each of us from all others.

So happiness is not made by a chemical. That would be like treating a violin sonata as nothing but rubbing horse hair on strings of cat gut in order to make a wooden box resonate. Violin makers have to know their materials to make one, and physicians have to know about the brain chemicals in order to treat patients, when the chemistry of brains has gone wrong, but they can't give us a pill to make us happy. We create our own joys, and we feel happiest in learning to trust each other.

Helen Oppenheimer

The Truth-Telling Animal

A good way to defend an affirmation is to explore what it implies. If indeed the glory of human beings has to do with communication, we need an ethic which gives *truth* its traditional place as a value alongside goodness and beauty. A proper human concern in a time when values are being blurred and diluted includes a concern about truth: that truth matters and is not to be 'dumbed down'.

When communication is given a central ethical place, untruthfulness must matter, even small untruthfulness. The right distinction is not between small and large but between honesty and dishonesty. There may be plenty of reasons for making statements which do not correspond to reality; but 'Why worry? – it's not important' is not one of them. The good reasons fall into two groups: where nobody is deceived and where, exceptionally, deceit is the least bad option among evils.

Some thinkers, not least Plato, have treated works of imagination as untrue and morally dubious: but Francis Bacon wrote more encouragingly, 'A mixture of a lie doth ever add pleasure.' Stories which grow in the telling are for enjoyment not disapproval. It would be strange for Christian moralists to renounce picturesque exaggeration, unless they seriously mean to refuse hope to the rich people who, like camels, cannot get through the needle's eye.

There is no need to make excuses for poetry and fiction. Far from hampering communication, the language of imagination is even a positive way of keeping in touch with the thoughts of other people. It illuminates reality from different points of view. We can say of an invented story, 'I never thought of that before: it's shown me something.' 'Telling stories' has a more excellent meaning than 'telling fibs', and is not to be put on the wrong side of a true/false line. Works of fiction, of course, may still convey false messages: Camus in *L'Etranger* built up to a conclusion that 'nothing matters'. We may enjoy the story and reject its message. What fiction does is give us the chance to see reality from different angles, to enter into other worlds. Works of imagination are forms of creation, indicating what it can mean to say that human makers are 'made in the image' of the divine Creator.

After approval of imaginative falsehood, it is time for disapproval of deception. If human beings are essentially language users, then treating people as human beings includes telling them truth not lies. There is no need to start an argument about which is more important, truth or love. They are not rivals: mutual love includes mutual transparency. Love and deceit combined are at best unstable and at worst incompatible. 'My *true* love hath my heart, and I have his.' Truth and love are so evidently connected that 'true-love' can naturally be written with a hyphen. The supposedly dry unemotional scholar has a *devotion* to truth. A friend is somebody I can trust. In a healthy community one can expect other people to be honest.

Does this mean an absolute prohibition of deception, regardless of the consequences? We understandably take fright at the priggishness, indeed the cruelty, of such an austere doctrine. The lawyers' concept of a presumption which is not absolute but rebuttable is what we need: a rebuttable presumption in favour of strict truthfulness.

A great big lie in a real emergency may be not just excusable but obligatory. Meticulous truth-tellers should ask themselves, 'Whose secret is this?' Self-righteous affirmation of damaging truth can be a positive wrong. It was right to say to the Gestapo, 'He's not here': and even, if one were clever enough, to spin a good story to put them on the wrong track.

In truly exceptional circumstances, the 'just lie' is like the just war. To save other people's lives it may be needful to be a conscientious objector to pacifism. Likewise to save other people's secrets one may be obliged to relinquish one's valued truthfulness: not just permitted but required to lie.

Suppose the secrets are one's own? Is self-defence a valid excuse for lying? Here the argument moves on from 'What *ought* I to do?' to 'What may I be allowed to do?' Self-sacrifice, humanly speaking, may be too much to ask. One may have a right, even if not a duty, to lie to people who have positively forfeited their human right to be told the truth. It is apparent in a cool hour that some kinds of threats and invasions break down the ordinary edifice of truthfulness. The principle that deceit is forbidden has to be rebuttable when we have to deal with people who exclude themselves from the network of trust which for most of us makes life worthwhile. The circumstances may not be dramatic. Most of us are more likely to be confronted by an inquisitive gossip or a badgering reporter than by the secret police.

The doctrine is still austere. It excludes a lot more than most people suppose. The presumption for truth-telling remains. A rebuttable presumption is not a matter of individual choice to opt in or out; nor is it an ideal aspiration unlikely to be fulfilled. Lying should be rare and reluctant. It is least harmful when, paradoxically, it is predictable. Victims of major or minor torments or invasions are hardly expected to speak the truth: if they lie, it is only natural. Communication is not impaired when it has already collapsed.

Truth is for trust. Saying what is not true may be justified only when, in the particular context, the general and normal human trust which makes communication possible is not impaired. Works of imagination are a happy example, free of deceit. The defence of other people, and even self-defence, are unhappy examples, where trust has been impaired already.

The 'kind' white lie is a hard case just because it necessarily belongs within the network of trust. If somebody asks me, 'Do you like this piece of work I have done?' and I give her the answer I think she wants, I am allowing her to live in a fog, cutting her off from the real world. Communication falters when, whatever answer I give, the questioner has to think 'But she would have said that anyway.' Real praise or real reassurance requires honest recognition that there are times when the wanted answer cannot be given. I need to find a way of offering the truth, or somehow declining to answer, with both honesty and gentleness.

Is equivocation a better answer than simply lying? To many honest people, equivocation is just a slippery way of 'dumbing down' truth. To treat it as an honourable expedient, while condemning every lie as intrinsically wrong, seems both shifty and harsh: certainly contrary to what most people think. In defence of equivocation, there is a distinction to be drawn. Equivocation *is* a kind of deception: if I deny this, I am deceiving myself. But equivocation gives people the choice of not being deceived. If they attend to what I have said and not said they can blow away the fog if they wish. The use of equivocation is not for allowing deceit but to protect the fragile right to abstain from revelation.

The rigidity of insisting that white lies are lies could be mitigated by finding ways of safeguarding the right not to speak. There is much to be said for useful social conventions like 'He is not at home', when 'to visitors' is understood: fences to sit on between deceit and brutality. Some of the burden of truthfulness could be lifted if people were taught not to confront one another with the choice of lying or hurting, not to ask for truth unless they want it, to respect each other's innocent silences.

Human beings have some responsibility for other people's truthfulness: for not inviting lies and for making truth-telling less hard for one another. Unreasonable demands for total frankness should be repudiated openly, before the difficulty has arisen. Human beings may honour one another by claiming the truth and nothing but the truth, but not always the whole truth.

Nicholas Mosley

Dumbing Down or Dumbing Up in Religion

lterations to the words of the traditional Anglican liturgy
seem to have been undertaken originally as an effort to
get meanings closer to those of other and earlier Church uses;
only secondarily to make old-fashioned language more
intelligible to modern worshippers in the hope that thus more
people might come to church. Church-going however has
declined during the twentieth century and the loss of the old
language has sometimes been blamed; but to many it seemed
that the changes had only been half-hearted, and the way forward was that language should be made still more homespun.
One result has been the 'Rite A' of the *Alternative Service Book*
of 1980; but the result of this seems to have been to make the
language more banal though hardly more palatable. Compare
for instance the words of the General Confession in the 1662
Communion Service with those in the 1980 'Rite A':

> Almighty God, Father of our Lord Jesus Christ,
> Maker of all things, Judge of all men: We acknowl-
> edge and bewail our manifold sins and wickedness,
> Which we from time to time most grievously have
> committed, By thought, word, and deed, Against
> thy Divine Majesty, Provoking most justly thy wrath
> and indignation against us. (1662)

> Almighty God, our heavenly Father, we have sinned
> against you and against our fellow men, in thought
> and word and deed, through negligence, through
> weakness, through our own deliberate fault. (1980)

What has been lost here is the incantatory mode of 1662, the style of which makes it evident that one is addressing someone or something numinous and portentous. The 1980 style is more like that of a suspect being obliged to make a statement to a policeman.

There are many such transformations. Perhaps the most irksome, because it confronts one at the very beginning of the Communion Service, is the reply to the Priest's greeting 'The Lord be with you'. In the old form the congregation replied 'And with thy spirit': by 1980 this had become the rather cheeky 'And also with you'.

All this seems to be in line with a trend amongst evangelical Anglicans to concentrate on the figure of Jesus as a homely friend rather than on the awesome mystery of God as Trinity; and recently with regard to church attendance at least this policy seems to be working. Evangelical or so-called 'happy-clappy' churches have packed congregations singing guitar-accompanied hymns of which the simple words are projected onto a screen, and hour-long sermons tell the good news of God being available to help with drug addiction. Traditional churches may have devout priests and heroic choirs, but except on festival days are often cavernously empty.

So—can it be said that some dumbing down has been beneficial?

It is interesting to compare this trend in religion with what has been happening at the same time in, say, philosophy. Philosophers have for long insisted that metaphysical matters cannot properly be approached or understood through rational language; they are best contemplated in silence (Wittgenstein) or in poetry and activity (Heidegger). Recently with the fashion for 'deconstruction' there has been the idea that no language has any meaning apart from what its users and critics make of it—so why should this or that form of religious language be any less valid than any other? In this light a state of grace would seem to be one in which authentic human language is that which is recognized as a form of game-playing. But this limiting view of language does not after all seem incompatible with a time-honoured Christian view—that the nature of God cannot be spoken about directly: one can say what God is not, one cannot say what He is.

Reading A.N. Wilson's compendious book *God's Funeral* one is struck by the grandiloquent verbiage with which eminent Victorians either perilously clung to their faith or explained how they could no longer cling to it. It seems they thought that by a clever use of words they might ward off despair and re-establish comfort. A reader wonders if they might have done better with a bit more activity and poetry—or silence.

In the Christian tradition there is a confusion about language. In the myth of the Tower of Babel humans once had a single language and were building a tower to heaven; then a jealous God inflicted on them a plethora of languages so that they found themselves in the confusion in which we find ourselves today. Medieval theologians wondered—what could have been the miraculously constructive pre-Babel language: Was it poetry? Was it more like an instinct? Why was God jealous! At the beginning of St John's Gospel there are the numinous words—'In the beginning was the Word and the Word was with God and the Word was God'; so what on earth did these words mean? Was the singular 'Word' different in kind from the multiple 'words' which form a language? Was it being suggested that the Word is what one hears when one listens to God, and the words of humans are naturally Babel?

It seems to me that the old poetry, the old incantations, of the Authorized Version of the Bible and the 1662 Prayer Book are the result of efforts to produce a language that might represent God's Word: that these efforts were made and indeed succeeded at a unique time—an age which embraced for instance the writings of Shakespeare—when poetry did seem to have something miraculous about it. This poetry is still there, and as potent as ever to those who wish to listen to it. There are few demands now for the dumbing down of Shakespeare.

For the rest—for the challenges and needs and experiments of daily life—might there not inevitably be some dumbing down? As to how far this goes, and what healthy reactions are stimulated against it, should not the outcome of all this, if one is religious, be left to God—or to what otherwise can be called natural selection. Whatever their mundane use of words, humans do have experiences of the numinous; and if they attend to these in whatever heartfelt way seems best to them, then this may lead to further revelation.

It is possible that a new culture of Listening rather than Talking might be growing, but this by its nature would have to be somewhat secret. Babels of words have led too many people and too many ideals astray; Babel should be left to the Media, which most people have a healthy contempt for anyway; and from the recognizable mass of rubbish we might learn some sifting—some attentiveness to complexity and possibilities rather than to prejudice and bombast. It has recently been suggested by geneticists (see Matt Ridley's *Genome*, quoting E.O. Wilson's *Consilience*) that if, as seems to be the case, morality and a sense of the transcendent are the codified expressions of our instincts, then a belief in a god can be said to be correct because it is natural. So—need much more be said about God? There would seem to be a case not for dumbing down but for dumbing up.

C.D. Darlington

The Impact of Man on Nature

Our ancestors first, using their earliest inventions, destroyed their nearest kindred species; in this way they gave their own surviving species a technological monopoly in the exploitation of nature. They then, secondly, used this monopoly to destroy a large part of their own richest food source, the great herbivorous mammals, in the continents which they successively colonised. They then, thirdly, destroyed in detail the vegetation and soil of great areas of land which their inventions of agriculture and pastoralism enabled them to occupy.

Man's short-term success in these operations with increasing speed transformed his own situation. It led to concentrations of his population which in turn favoured the growth of parasites and diseases attacking himself as well as his crops and stock. These were slow long-term effects which acted diversely on the separated races of mankind, so governing the distribution and partly the evolution of what had now become the most diverse and diversely complex of all animal species.

The lines on which these processes and habits of exploitation would develop had been laid down already before the Iron Age. Short-term natural selection had favoured man's urge to use his procreative and his inventive powers to the utmost, that is to their competitive limits. This urge had operated, and still operates, through instincts which are variously formalised by religion or encouraged by education in the various tribes and classes of human society — whence our difficulty now, when we recognise that our short-view success in control over our environment is being overtaken by a long-view failure. No other organism is known to have succeeded in making the kind of evolutionary right-about turn that is now necessary for the survival of man in the forms in which he at present exists.

The Scale of the Problem

The problem of man's impact on nature requires us to bring together two lines of enquiry which our forebears began for us long ago. On the one hand, thinking men in the ancient world observed, deplored and tried to limit the damage that less-thinking men had been doing to the world around them. Their tale was taken up a few generations ago by observant naturalists like Buffon and Humboldt who saw the devastation that was being spread over the habitable world and foresaw the calamity that was being prepared for us.

On the other hand, more speculative thinkers like Lord Monboddo, Erasmus Darwin and Charles Lyell were at the same time asking themselves just how long man had been at work on this planet; they had begun putting his operations on the time-scale which we have always needed if we were to take stock of our position. Now at last we have this time-scale safely in our hands. In the nick of time, perhaps, we can put together the observations and test the assumptions made by enquirers on these two lines of thought. How diverse are the ideas that have to be used will be seen from the range of historical and scientific inferences that I have to use in sketching my argument.

For we have to consider what happened, how it happened and why it happened. These questions can be answered only by looking at the whole problem. We have to begin at the beginning. We have to trace the course by which a hundred thousand human beings in Africa a million years ago swelled into three hundred million people spread over most of the earth at the beginning of the Christian era.

The expansion of numbers and of the area occupied is due, we suppose, to the increase in skill, knowledge and understanding, or collectively the intelligence, of the men and women concerned. And this in turn is due to the change in the size, shape and structure of their brains and of the hands, eyes, tongues and other organs connected with them. These changes in intelligence were not continuous or uniform. They arose from diversification of the human group, from competition and conflict between the species, races and tribes into which the group divided itself.

A striking feature of these conflicts was that they ended in a single inter-fertile group confined to Africa but sharply isolated from its nearest surviving relatives, the great apes. Man (or the common ancestors of man) had killed off his closest competitors. He had acquired a monopoly of the world's resources which his successive technical inventions in due course enabled him to exploit. This was man's first impact on nature.

Colonizing the Earth

How did he use this monopoly? First, he colonized the earth. He early occupied Europe and Asia. Much later, armed with projectiles, he moved into America and Australia. Last of all he spread over the oceans and their islands. In these various regions he had three great separate fields of exploitation: animal, vegetable and mineral. In all three fields he developed his intelligence. He came to know, presumably to name, and certainly to depict, the things he found useful. But whereas for a long time he merely collected the plants and the minerals, he hunted and killed the animals and sometimes destroyed them altogether, as he still does. The ones he pursued fell into two groups: those he killed for food, clothing and raw materials in general; and those he killed because they were predators and competed with him for the same victims.

If he had not been so quickly successful little harm might have been done. But competition between human tribes was the basis of their evolutionary advancement. And it must have been the short-term advantage of success in killing both food animals and predators that came to direct human evolution and made the success so overwhelming. It led to the extinction of many species of the great herbivorous mammals, first in Africa, then in America.

Of these extinctions one was notable beyond all others for its later effects on human history. The killing off of the horse in America by hunters meant that when agriculture followed hunting the horses were not there to domesticate; the process and the spread of civilization were delayed; the stratification of society was impeded; and the Amerindian peoples were themselves exposed to easy destruction when the European colonists arrived.

The immigrant Aboriginal in Australia fortunately lacked some of the superlative and diverse skills of the Amerindian races and although he brought his hunting dog, the dingo, with him he did not succeed in killing off the important marsupials that he found and fed upon.

When the Europeans came in their turn they brought with them their animals, wild and domesticated: asses, goats, pigs, buffaloes, camels, cats, foxes and rabbits. All of them, in part, like the dingo, ran wild. We may say in consequence that the wild fauna of Australia is richer today than it has ever been before. And the misfortune of the Europeans' arrival has fallen not so much on the animals as on the vegetation—and the Aboriginal.

The Invention of Agriculture

The climax of all man's earlier inventions came with the development of settled farming. It came some 10,000 years ago and independently in the Old World and the New. In both regions it happened between continents at the cross-roads of those human movements which followed the climatic upheaval at the end of the last ice age.

The Old World cradle or nursery of farming was the hilly border of the Fertile Crescent north of Arabia. For a long period, between 8,000 and 4,000 BC, the new farming peoples hardly expanded. These peoples seem to have been accumulating experience and genetic diversity. This is the period that I have called the Silent Millennia.

This was the period during which the character of civilization was established, the directions it was to take and the modes of man's great assault on the earth were laid down; society was stratified, spinning and weaving, pottery and the decorative and technical arts were developed. During this period the processes of agriculture were being more and more intelligently and industriously organized and the farming population must have multiplied some tenfold. How were all these things accomplished?

What happened is fairly clear. The origin of settled farming had been made possible by an inward movement of people. The stability of food production which resulted gave rise to a second inward movement. The settlements were a magnet for all the arts and skills of the uncertain unsettled world of the hunters and collectors. The neolithic centre sucked up what it wanted from the paleolithic world outside. And it was this attraction which generated, in the course of 4,000 years of dialogue, the wealth, strength and diversity at the centre.

The generation of wealth favoured not only the stratification of society but also the extension of the instinct or appetite for property which was inevitably extended from the ephemeral to the durable, from the marketable to the heritable; and with this change developed the law of property and the economic consequences of property in land and in goods, in men and in power. It was these changes which enabled the central people after four millennia of incubation, transformed in character by their success in their new activities, to spread out and colonize the whole of the habitable earth. But when they did this and made their great assault on the earth it was an assault on many fronts and we have to look at these different fronts in their different characters outside and inside agriculture.

Outside agriculture their most striking development was in the growth of mining. The demand for the best materials of all kinds and the ability of the settled peoples to pay for them meant that dispersed and sporadic collectors of flint and obsidian, lapis lazuli and amber, copper and gold were now able to establish self-supporting groups or guilds of specialist workers, miners and traders, craftsmen and artists, with trade routes all leading to the centre of agriculture; all leading to, and dependent on, what they were making the centre of civilization.

By our present standards these operations were on a small scale. But they were the beginning of one kind of despoliation of the earth.

Inside agriculture the purposes and the results were different. The control of soil and water by terracing, by drainage and by irrigation preserved the new settlements from the effects of drought and flood and the washing away of soil. The remains of these works we can still see marvellously preserved in Persia and Anatolia, Mexico and Peru. Their extension later across Europe and Asia from the banana plantations of the Canary Isles to the rice fields of the Philippines is still the basis at once of the cultivation of crops and the conservation of soil and water.

Meanwhile their crops show that these people developed all the arts of enriching the soil with animal and vegetable manure. Many of them had their unwritten Deuteronomies, mixtures of science and superstition, taught by forgotten sages to plant a fish with a grain of corn and feed the crop by enriching the soil. All this was the fruit of the work done and the skill and experience acquired during those early millennia. It is something we can put on the credit side of man's account with the earth.

Egypt, Mesopotamia and the Indus

These things were the business of primitive tillage with pick and hoe by the villagers on the southern hillsides of Persia and Anatolia. When these people were assisted by the plough and the ox, they were able to tackle the richer soils at the bottoms of the valleys and in the river deltas. Then the greater problems of the control of running water had to be solved. These problems were solved by the engineers, surveyors and astronomers of Sumeria and Egypt. Calendars were devised; floods were predicted; canals were built; property and labour were organized; and the state was controlled in relation to the needs of the land for the purposes of food production.

In due course the descendants of these experts spread out over the world. But especially spreading westward by sea into Europe they were concerned, we have reason to believe, with constructing the stone circles and avenues of Britain and Brittany as well as the canals of Lombardy and Holland. They were responsible indeed for European enterprise in engineering and science. These were men who in every country and generation have been skilled in protecting nature from other men's mistakes, men who, as Marvell puts it, unwisely scorning the Dutch:

> dived as desperately for each piece
> Of Earth, as if't had been of *Ambergreece.*

Their original works, however, were not all plain sailing. The governments they served took the longest view that we could expect of them, but they met with quite different results in different conditions. In Egypt they succeeded; in Mesopotamia they partly and significantly failed.

The reasons for this contrast seem to have been several but connected. In the first place the flood in Egypt came in September and spread its silt conveniently in the winter. But in Mesopotamia it came in spring and spread its silt in summer and it was — as the legend of the Flood informs us — less certain in the service it rendered. A second contrast made the first much more serious. The cities of Mesopotamia were exposed to attack; attack both from the desert and from the mountains. Time and again they were overwhelmed. And each time the delicate structure of society and the fragile organization for the maintenance and repair of canals were liable to be broken. For these various reasons the cities of Sumeria were in the end, after a millennium, totally ruined. Cultivation and civilization then moved together up the long valleys of the twin rivers leaving behind them (according to Jacobson and Adams) the silted waterways and salted lands which had slowly choked them.

The cities of the Indus had a similar beginning and met the same end, both being 500 years later. By the time the end came the whole region was irretrievably lost. The desert had claimed it and it lay buried under sand until Sir Mortimer Wheeler uncovered it 3,500 years later.

In Mesopotamia the period from 3000 to 50 BC repeats this story. But each successive disaster by war and misuse becomes a little milder. Step by step the centre of government moved northwards until it was to be found in Persia. And then it was no longer a small kingdom but a great state based on the iron and the horses of the mountains, a colonial and imperial government strong enough to protect its subject peoples in the valleys from the disturbance that had always threatened them and their works when they were, so to speak, free. Meanwhile Egypt lay protected not by its men but by its deserts. Its people could maintain their system of irrigation unchanged and undamaged for another couple of millennia. Unchanged also were the people themselves.

The lesson from this contrast is of universal application. Competition, conflict and war, as in Mesopotamia, advance the evolution and civilization of men. But they tend to destroy the environment in which the descendants of those men have to live. To be sure their descendants in the past did not have to live there. They could move on. That is what some of them always did, leaving their devastation behind them. The damage to the environment has always in a sense damaged the people. For the enterprising ones have taken over and colonized new territory, leaving the slow-witted ones established for ever in the impoverished possession of the homelands of their ancestors.

The Farmer and the Forest

So much we may say of the most skilful use that men have made of the land they have worked. This was what happened when they were applying all their abilities, energies and foresight to pass on the benefits of what they did to their children. But there were other things they did (and still do) whose consequences were less to be foreseen and also less to be desired.

They understood, or rather the best of them understood, the land that they worked and felt that they owned. But they did not understand the wilderness, the heath or the forest: those lands that Fraser Darling has fondly and aptly portrayed for us; those lands that belonged to no one or to everyone. Among those lands Deuteronomy, always exact and prudent, makes a wise distinction. It is a distinction which is still always observed by the Mediterranean farmer and must therefore have governed the spread of agriculture for many millennia. The lawgiver (in Ch. 20:20) tells the Israelites that the only trees they may cut down are those that 'do not yield food'. So it was that throughout the Mediterranean region, while forests and woods disappeared, the olive, the fig, the date and the vine, the almond, the walnut and the chestnut were preserved and propagated: save, of course, for the damage wrought by desert marauders and foreign armies.

But what happened to the general forest? Everywhere, the farmer felled trees for timber and fuel. The timber he used for building houses and ships. The fuel he burnt for heating and for baking both bread and pottery. And here the miner stepped in to demand far more for smelting and forging. In Sumeria and the Indus cities, having stripped their own woods, they went further afield. In Egypt they had to go very far afield to Nubia. All three fell prey to those newer nations who could keep their fuel and their smiths at home. Crete being well-forested and well-harboured was made for ships and for sailors. But, since Crete was an island, a few centuries of maritime supremacy and prosperity sufficed to destroy its forests and ruin its power for ever.

The greatest threat to the forests and woods of the ancient world, however, still lay in the future. It lay in the flocks and the herds of the pastoralist.

The Herdsman and the Forest

The herdsman seems to have taken his livestock, his spinning and weaving and his pottery from the settled farmer. But here and there as opportunity arose and inclination agreed, he cut adrift from this early partnership. Then he often went far afield and far ahead. In the great expansion which followed the Silent Millennia he took his flocks and herds westward, to the Atlantic, southwards through Arabia and Africa and eastwards into India and Central Asia.

In every direction the resources of the world and its opportunities for the herdsman seemed unlimited. But by the end of the Bronze Age the limits were being reached and his initiative was already taking a fresh direction. Already, grazing animals had extended their pasture at the expense of the woods and the forest. And the forest itself was retreating in a drying climate. Now he began to burn the scrub and the forest in order to enlarge and refresh his pasture. The forest seemed to him an enemy but it was an enemy that could be defeated without effort and even by accident. The felling and the burning, the sheep and the goat, later, on the African side, assisted by the camel, slowly depleted the forests and woodlands of the Mediterranean region.

To achieve this result, this terrifying result, the herdsman had to wage an endless war, and a finally successful war, on one remaining enemy, the wild predators. But every success he gained against lions, leopards and wolves was a success also for wild grazing animals. So that just as the cat domestically followed the mouse across Europe so we may say that later the rabbit pastorally followed the sheep; both of these pushing back the forest and preventing its natural regeneration.

In these ways it came about that the Mediterranean forests dwindled from 500 to 50 million acres, one-tenth of the area they had covered before the agricultural revolution struck them. In India and China we cannot so well estimate the extent of what has been lost. We merely know that the causes, the scale and the timing of the disaster have all been similar. What about its consequences?

The consequences of the destruction of forest were manifold and some of them irremediable. Forests, like the sea, represent a vast reservoir of water. And they can be tapped on roughly the same scale since they yield this store of moisture to the air and provide for rain. Hence we may say that, at the end of the ice age, subtropical forests constituted a vast buffer against the sudden parching effects on the vegetable and animal world of a warmer and drier climate. Conversely temperate forests helped to drain an over-watered land and their removal, notably in Britain, left uncultivable moors behind them. Yet another consequence of deforestation was the washing away of the soil which had accumulated under the trees largely during the last ice age and was not to be replaced by any conceivable human effort.

The last consequence of deforestation may be seen where an agricultural people is endeavouring to survive in a region that is now severely depleted of wood through its use for timber and fuel. In India perhaps 300 million tons of dried cow-dung, the proper means of restoring fertility to the soil, are burnt every year to furnish the fuel which was originally furnished by the forest. This practice is equivalent to the impatient or greedy habit of those in the urban world who live on hire-purchase. They are living on the future. They are taking a mortgage on posterity.

Mankind Divided

The farmer and the herdsman, carrying their crops and stock, their crafts and skills, spread over most of Europe, Asia and Africa during the fourth and third millennia BC. Interbreeding with the native peoples they undoubtedly went some way towards bringing mankind together. Yet when all this movement was over in the Iron Age mankind found itself once more frozen up in separate and remote racial compartments. Genetically and culturally the expansion had served to unite mankind, but when the expansion ended mankind once more fell in pieces. How could this be?

First, let us notice that one link was never broken, that between the ancient East and Europe: this connection was both by land and sea and never could be interrupted. The bronze craftsmen moved into Europe on a large scale carrying their arts with them and bringing the Bronze Age to its climax in that continent. But communication of the ancient centre with the Far East became intermittent. And as for the far south of Africa and India, bronze failed to make its way until iron and the iron workers had arrived. The conditions that stopped the expansion and severed the communication have now become clear.

Take first the connection with China. This was established with decisive effects several times in the third, second and first millennia BC. But at those times the Tarim Basin was still watered from the mountains around it. The cities discovered there by Sir Aurel Stein were buried, he supposed, only during the first millennium AD. There can be little doubt that the desert which buried them, as it has buried the Indus cities, was one which they themselves had helped to create. The grazing of the flocks and the felling of the trees had combined with a deteriorating climate to destroy them. In destroying them it had not severed but at least strangled the connection between Europe and China. And in doing so it had altered the course of history.

At the same time the same kind of change in the state of the Sahara was strangling the connections between tropical Africa and the Mediterranean. But other connections in Africa were being broken, as we can now see, not by drought but by quite other means.

The Heyday of Disease

One of the results of the successes of farmers and herdsmen was that their populations were now lying much thicker on the ground. Their ancestors had been protected from infectious disease by their rarity and by the isolation, at once geographical and biological, from all their neighbours which they had won for themselves. Now they became vulnerable.

Not only was man now vulnerable but so also were all the other animals he had assembled or attracted around him. These were not only cattle. Rats and mice, lice, fleas and mosquitoes and every pest and parasite, all of these in turn could prosper and multiply. New diseases could be, and were, transferred from animals and adapted themselves to the new conditions that man was now providing. All these changes proceeded with a speed in proportion to the density of the populations of the victims, human and animal; and in proportion also to the warmth and humidity of the climate. In other words they proceeded most rapidly in tropical Africa, India and South-East Asia, all of them regions which the new farmers and herdsmen were attempting to colonize.

In these countries different effects followed. In Africa the movement of cattle and cattle people colonizing the country was arrested. The spread of inventions and the development of civilization carried by these peoples (except modestly in the highlands of Abyssinia) was consequently frustrated. Bronze and the horse, the wheel and the plough all failed to break through the barrier of disease. Even the genetic remedies giving resistance to the disease of malaria, the haemoglobin defects arising in the Old World tropics, proved to be little less damaging to the men whom they protected than the disease itself.

In India the effects were again different, and indeed unique. The barrier to the spread of infectious disease was explicitly and plausibly the establishment and reinforcement by religious sanction of the system of castes which prevented contact between the clean and the unclean. Yet this system came to govern the evolution, or rather lack of evolution, of the whole society. By this indirect means it was able to impede the spread of civilization.

So far we have looked at one half of the story. Our interpretation of it, however, is not justified until we look at the other half. Every race of mankind, exposed to these new diseases, developed its own genetic devices for acquiring resistance to them. Some of these, like the haemoglobin defects, as we saw, handicapped the peoples that acquired them. Others inevitably failed when either the people or the disease crossed their established frontier. Suddenly on a great scale after the navigations of the fifteenth century this crossing of frontiers struck mankind like a hurricane. What happened then has been exactly recorded.

When America, Australia and Polynesia were discovered by Europeans they were inhabited by peripheral and isolated populations. Their peoples lacked both the diversity and the specific resistances to disease which had been developed by the central mass of mankind among whom the great diseases of civilization had already reached their epidemic climaxes. The results are well known: the destruction of the peripheral peoples. By man's own action the impact of man on nature had been reversed. Now we had the impact of nature on man or on some men and, because the impact in this case was sudden and recent, its cause could not be mistaken.

When Success is a Failure

We are lucky today in respect of what we know. We can survey the whole earth and, looking at the whole of geography, we can see a cross-section of history. The early stages of exploitation, wise or unwise, stages which have almost vanished from the advanced countries, are revealed to us by the backward parts and peoples of Africa, India and Indonesia. At the same time a devastation of a different kind but no less instructive is revealed to us in the most advanced industrial societies. Among them technical exploitation is approaching its terrifying limits and showing these societies to be in their different aspects at once the most enlightened and the most dangerous of all. Showing also, I believe, that the greatest enterprise in doing the damage can be connected, socially and genetically, with the greatest skill in understanding and perhaps repairing it. For the basis of understanding and repair is in one principle: that every invention of man has made his environment more favourable for his short-term multiplication. But it has made his environment less favourable for his long-term survival.

This is not the only unexpected or paradoxical conclusion that we are forced to admit. The driving force of human evolution has been selection for competitive success in invention and also for competitive multiplication of those who succeed. It is these two forces, largely instinctive forces, which have brought the full impact of man to bear on his environment. The effects of that impact are to threaten his means of sustaining life as an individual; and to favour the diseases that threaten his life in a community. He has been brought to the point where, tightly packed in numbers and partly fixed in character, in beliefs and in institutions, he has come near to being deprived of his initiative. He is no longer completely the master of his destiny that he once imagined himself to be.

Indeed we may be excused for putting to him an audacious suggestion. It is that he may have to reverse his initiative: to regard his virtues as vices, his successes as failures: to admit that all harm done to nature is harm done to man; and hence to scrap some part of his morals, natural or official, and of his religion, pious or political, to scrap them, strangely enough, both East and West. He may even have to allow that standards of right and wrong can never be uniformly applied to different peoples, to different classes or even to different age-groups in a world of rapidly changing structure.

This very diversity between and within societies offers us, however, our means of discovering a way out for mankind as a species. The groups and classes in which we exist are mutually dependent. In the long run we must recognize this enduring fact. And in some groups among some peoples there are always likely to be a few who can see far enough ahead to warn the rest. They will see that our values now have to be reassessed. Man depends on nature. The supply of what nature offers him is limited. He uses up nature in proportion to his numbers. But some men use up nature faster than others. Some employ nature more wisely than others, preferring the distant future to the immediate future. Some, for this reason, give more in return to nature and to mankind. What has happened in the past shows us that all these factors must influence our judgment in deciding how man will have to make his reckoning with nature in the future.

Demelza Spargo

The Cultivation of Society

Agriculture today is surely a living embodiment of the saying, 'fact is stranger than fiction'. Battery hens, neurotic pigs, mad cows, herbivores fed on the remains of other dead creatures or on human excreta. Sheep selling at less than the price of a cup of coffee, undeclared growth hormones, antibiotics in the food chain, distinct species conglomorated by manipulation of genomes, *etc. etc.* Yet, are we so very different, in all this, from the nineteenth century, when food adulteration was rife, cruelty to animals more acceptable, disease in livestock widespread and prices extremely vulnerable?

We are different in that we, in Western Europe, live longer and may enjoy better nutrition than ever before. But what about the British countryside? What about the suicides of farmers, who have walked out with their shotgun and turned it on themselves; the farmers found hanging from the rafters of their barns? The lives and futures of farmers are subject to the dictates not just of the Market, but also to a mountain of political regulations about what they may grow, how much, when and where. Subsidies are doled out and then withdrawn. Within a structure dominated by Brussels, they are forced to operate not as they think best but as they are instructed. Thus their liberty is curtailed, their time consumed furthermore by bureaucracy, one set of rules for producers, another for the global Market, which may go where it pleases. This is not the healthy functioning of democracy, it is being in hock to corporations and political whim. Furthermore, it gives agribusiness — which employs clerks to deal with paperwork, in order to stay up-to-date with policy and fashion, and to apply for grants—a mighty advantage over the individual farmer.

We are confronted with the breakdown of ancient patterns of rural settlement and commercial activity, and this makes us uneasy. Of course, agricultural life has experienced traumas before, and in fairly recent history: the massive depression of the 1870s, when European and American financial depressions coincided with a period of bad harvest; and the years between 1881 and 1911, when the agricultural workforce declined from just under two million to under one million—a figure which includes not only farmers and their workers but also skilled rural craftsmen, blacksmiths, saddlers and wheelwrights among them.

But our times are very different. What we are witnessing in Britain now is the agonizing termination of the life of the agricultural countryside. We are in an 'end game', a conflict between unequal forces in which the winner is taking all of worth, leaving the opposition in serfdom or extinction. One in which not only hierarchy, with its systems of responsibility and freedoms, but also its attendant vessels of communication—ritual and convention—have been discredited as irrelevant to a democratized partnership of equals. In the populist emphasis on equality, it is forgotten that individuals differ; that societies have existed in hierarchies precisely because of these differences.

Ancient hierarchies: church, monarchy and state have for all their shortcomings contributed to the circumstances in which, latterly, democracy has been born in Western Europe. The concentrations of industrialized labour arising from the Industrial Revolution gave rise to a democracy which has allowed the dismantling of the vestiges of traditional hierarchies in all areas of human endeavour. Ritual and convention are removed without a full understanding of the forces measured or controlled by those conventions. In theory, the collective voice of the majority, as represented by the democratically elected government, would dispense with the vagaries of philanthropic charity of the kind characterized by the high Victorian industrialists. Duties of care did exist, but the system was undoubtedly haphazard:

No lily-handed Baronet he,
A great broad-shouldered genial Englishman,
A lord of fat prize-oxen and of sheep,
A raiser of huge melons and of pine,
A patron of some thirty charities.

Tennyson, The Princess

The modern system of patronage has been to create the welfare state; the NHS, education by the state, state pensions — a system designed to mask the fact that its beneficiaries draw on charity; a system designed to be constant, not subject to withdrawal without redress, with no discrimination in its distribution. In short, democracy would care for all the members of its society.

Traditional hierarchies and religious beliefs in the countryside have now been almost entirely replaced by the new Holy Trinity of corporate agribusiness, the demands of supermarkets, and politically-imposed regulations. It is often forgotten that corporations are essentially hierarchies themselves — as are governments, however populist. The new hierarchies are apparently less objectionable, partly because with their ever-changing personnel they excite less envy. But are they better for our welfare in the long run?

Agriculture has, until now, stood for much more than its literal meaning of cultivating the land. It is the surplus food produced by agriculture that has enabled the creation of communities, cities and civilizations, of centres of cultural and technical exchange. The natural environment exerts an all-pervasive influence on human affairs, conditioning social, cultural and economic realities. By distancing ourselves from nature we may forget these realities for a time, but at our peril. The current enthusiasm for genetic manipulation chooses to ignore the fact that the species barrier is a barrier to disease. Just one new disease, given opportunity to rampage through humanity by open experiments with our genomes, could do unlimited damage. Both of the most recently alarming diseases — AIDS and BSE — crossed from other species to man, helped along by human malpractice. Instead of learning from this, we permit ever more perversions of accepted practise, which will make future occurrence more likely. When reason forgets, our instincts are still there to warn us; but the response of too many scientists to such instinctive recoil is defensive mockery.

The land and agriculture are a gift; a gift of nature, and of our ancestors. In its duty of care towards citizens, society looks to the corporations for the massive funds that are needed. But it ignores the fact that being alive can mean more than a full shopping trolley and a reliable TV. For many country- dwellers, living close to nature — the changing skies, the animals they husband, the seasons and the harvest — is as essential as breathing. The integrity of what country-dwellers do and the long-standing habits of country living are the stuff of life — destroy these, and you deny them life itself.

But what of the greater community, the 90% of our population who live in towns and cities? In an obvious way their welfare depends upon agriculture, for it depends on the wholesomeness of the food they eat. But there are ramifications; are society's morals, its attitudes to religion, to the primacy of human needs and to life itself damaged as we move away from an intimacy with nature? This is a large question, worth bearing in mind when we contemplate the future of the countryside as projected by government spokesmen and by farmers' representatives. In their version, the countryside will soon consist of a giant theme park, interspersed with huge agricultural factories producing food in vats, growing flesh without animals, flour without sunlight. No longer will man toil long hours, getting dirty and killing in order to eat. The countryside, which stands for drudgery and class exploitation, will be tamed once and for all.

For these purposes, traditional life in the countryside is painted in grim colours; but that was not always so. Traditionally, the imagery of art has celebrated the land, that which grows upon it and those who are nourished by it. In polytheistic ancient Greece, for example, we find images depicting Demeter, Goddess of Agriculture. This goddess was also the tutelary deity of legislation and social order, which first grew out of the appropriation, division and cultivation of the soil; she was acknowledged as such by society as a whole, as well as by those engaged in agriculture. Her gift, it was believed, was bestowed upon the earth by Triptolemus, who flew through the air in Demeter's chariot, scattering grain over Europe and Asia and Scythia. The cult of Demeter was highly successful, subsidized by the contents of three vast grain silos built at Eleusis to collect tithes. Demeter was still being worshipped at Eleusis as late as 1801.

The expanding Roman Empire, with its objective interest in the land and its cultivation, left a richly-detailed visual legacy of their practice. The medieval church in Europe was responsible for masterpieces of illumination showing the activities of the seasons, such as those shown in the Luttrell Psalter; while the cultural princes of the Renaissance, seeking a reflection of a new world order where man was the measure of his own existence, found it amongst the wonderful responses of artists such as Pieter Breughel.

In sixteenth century Europe, paintings reflecting the agricultural and horticultural empires of the Low Countries abounded. Still lives and market scenes were produced for the wealthy and cultivated merchants of those Empires. In Britain, the period 1780 to 1800 was one of the most innovative in the history of agriculture, and some of the finest works by English artists, painters and sculptors were produced: not only visual records of valuable livestock, but also of the appearance of the land, of model improved estates, and of activities both traditional and modern.

More recent developments originated in May 1840 when the Royal Agricultural Society received its charter. Its principal object was to perfect the 'System of English Agriculture by the union of practice with science'. Scientific developments and applications since then have been staggering. The quest for greater fertility and productivity was instrumental in the creation of the giants we see today — the agrochemical companies. Early applications of science were founded in man's belief that he was struggling to establish his superiority over nature. In our own times, there is a growing movement that would like to see science going in another direction, one more closely allied with our dependency on ecological balance.

The Government (as of December 1999) is largely oblivious to this movement. It endorses the countryside's future use as a so-called amenity, to be stewarded by ex-farmers; as a *tabula rasa*, a clean slate cleared of the past in preparation for the never-ending banquet of the global economy. The vision of the countryside as an extended and sanitized municipal park is surely just a sop to those trapped in polluted and over-crowded cities.

To this end our Government is setting up a series of 'rights' to be enjoyed by the population at large with regard to the countryside. The establishment of 'rights' without concomi-tant obligations or duties is troubling, and behind such populist high-handedness there is a troubling lack of under-standing of our ancient and historic relationship with the land.

British city-dwellers are especially unfamiliar with the countryside, since planning laws have for generations made it economically impossible for smallholdings to exist in Britain in the way they do in Europe, where many urban workers are able to keep their own smallholding. Most of the people of Britain have forgotten what a life in the countryside is like, and are ignorant of how the ties of community have depended on the land.

In the global market, the community has no relevance what-soever, other than being the site of the consumer. People who place a high value on the quality of life, on democracy and the free expression of the human spirit, are dumbfounded and confused by the impassive and anonymous nature of the global market economy and the assumptions it makes about our needs; for instance, that consumers place appearance above reality, and would rather consume damaging food colourants, preservatives, herbicide and pesticide residues, organophosphates and nitrates than face something less than a virtual reality apple.

With the most ambitious and inventive branch of modern science, genetic engineering, comes a widespread sense that agricultural practice has gone too far. We foot-soldiers in the army of a global economy are approaching the Rubicon, we see it ahead of us—its other name is Genetically Modified Food. Farmers and consumers alike experience an atavistic fear when confronted with the propositions of this system. Though mocked by many scientists, and by ideologues of the highly commercial scientific state, these feelings may be pow-erful enough not only to stop us from crossing the Rubicon but also to disperse the army of greed which has brought agricul-ture to its knees. We are beginning to demand something different.

The demand for change is showing itself in growth in the organic food market. It is clear that the market as a whole is aware of a growing desire for organic produce. It is equally clear that this cannot be produced for mass consumption overnight. One finds organic food ghettoes in supermarkets which, when one looks at the 'country of origin' labels, show that these foodstuffs come from all over the world. It misinterprets the demand, to offer for sale something supposedly superior in its 'purity' which has been transported huge distances in exactly the same manner as ordinary foodstuffs: by road, jet, road before reaching the supermarket. The correlation between food transport and pollution is part of the whole argument which is turning people towards locally-produced organic food. Where is the reasoning that brings organic Kiwi fruit on a journey of thousands of miles to a small English town, when it could be grown here? The concept of melding 'organic' to 'international sourcing', is a contradiction, rather as though Gandhi were to travel across continents bringing a message of peace in a heavily-armed tank, guns blazing.

The current response to the demand for organic produce is short-term. But the real demand for organic food is not one that can be met by a simple discontinuation of chemicals, *etc.* If it were ever to happen, any switch to wholesale organic cultivation and animal husbandry would be highly labour intensive and dependent on more localized markets. Such a change would require a transformation of society as a whole, involving long-term policies for education, and long-term immutable subsidies to enable the change to take place.

We in Britain live in a society of plenty, yet we are riven with misgivings. We see institutionalized dishonesty, political expediency and short-termism in successive governments' failure to adopt radical programmes to reassure us about the future of our planet. It is essential, in order to understand what may occur in the future, to recognize the interconnectedness of the agrarian and industrial revolutions. Under the Tudors, England ceased to be a self-contained agricultural community and began to develop her industrial resources, with assistance from foreign exiles such as Flemish weavers who helped to establish the supremacy of the woollen trade and the Dutch engineers who directed the first land- reclamation schemes in the Fens.

Up to the end of the eighteenth century the most important industrial raw material was wood — early machines were made of wood — and it was essential, in the form of charcoal, as the foundation of the metal industries which used it to smelt ore. It was in the Tudor period that coal began to replace wood as fuel.

In our times new energy sources, together with the internal combustion engine and that most astonishing development of modern times, the computer, have made the global market possible. But this, the apparent end product of the combined forces of the industrial and agricultural revolutions, has put us in a quandary. We have either to redefine our understanding of democracy as a way of organizing society for the mutual benefit of those involved in it, with social duties and obligations, or admit that we are no longer living in a true democracy.

We fear the ultimate domination of human freedom of choice by monopolies and multinationals. In our own time we have witnessed the effect of totalitarian societies and it is assumed we do not wish to be part of one ourselves. In Hungary, under Communism, the flowers that could grow in a garden were limited to those allowed by the Party. In the global economy, the major agrochemical companies wish to reduce the varieties of wheat, maize, rice and other food crops to a mere handful. Within a decade they want most of the world's staple crops to be grown from genetically modified seeds which they have engineered.

> Few traditional varieties will be available to farmers. These new strains will only be available from them, at their price. They will be resistant to the most powerful herbicides, which farmers will use to kill every other plant in the field.   (Soil Association)

The government acts in the name of the people, hand-in-glove with corporations, assuming that what people want is maximum prosperity. Yet from the people comes the voice of protest, the voice of conscience, calling the government to protect us all and in particular our children.

Worries about the cruelty involved in massed animal husbandry led to the Brambell Committee, formed in 1965, which produced a report on the welfare of farm animals. At roughly the same time Rachel Carson's *Silent Spring* chilled all those who read it and focused people's attention on the destruction of wildlife and flora. This resulted in the Countryside Act of 1968, which did much to attempt to foster principles of compromise between farmers and conservationists.

Yet many strange things occurred, and developed behind closed doors. Chicken started tasting of fish, and it was discovered they were being fed the refuse from fish processing plants. Chickens with enormous breasts punctured by suspicious-looking holes were found to contain a growth hormone which was giving humans enlarged breasts too. The gloss on fruit was found to consist of wax impregnated with chemicals. The list could fill a book.

In 1965, just as Britain was starting to 'swing', Anthony Sampson brought out the second edition of his classic work *Anatomy of Britain Today*. A fascinating and innovative guide to the workings and institutions of Britain, it contained no reference whatsoever to agriculture. It did however make the important link between the emergence of marketing as a profession in Britain and its use by the food industry in the promotion of 'new' products such as margarine. Was the omission of agriculture due to its irrelevance to the establishment or simply because it was taken for granted, on the assumption that changes would simply continue to achieve targets of perfectibility and productivity?

It was in the 1960s that the novelties of a new consumer society, based on the US model, arrived in Britain. In rural society the impact was a loss of jobs on the land, the development of villages and the growth of roads. Farming continued to become more intensive and mechanized, with correspondingly reduced options for the rural population in terms of employment and recreation. The heart of the countryside was slowly but surely being transformed. We could look to the prescience of John Stewart Collis who in the 1940s, after several years as a farm labourer, wrote of the combine harvester:

> It is a remarkable machine. A truly triumphant invention...It is a binder and thresher in one unit. The corn which has been cut and taken up by the binder is taken up but not bound; instead it passes through a threshing operation so that the grain

pours into a tank...thus it proceeds round the field, doing two jobs at once: that of cutting and threshing, and knocking out the necessity of three middle ones — carting, ricking and thatching. 'An absolute godsend to the small farmer', I reflected, to a man who runs a hundred acres by himself. But in relation to big farms I could not help feeling gloomy about its appearance. It is rather as if the future has arrived before we are ready for it.

It has just been reported that in liberated Ukraine, a girl combine operator, Vera Panchonko, has received a Badge of Honour for harvesting 260 acres in five days...Let us consider exactly what this means...Though the combine has evolved as naturally as the other machines, its effect is much greater upon the lives of the labourers. At one stroke it does away with harvesting, of gathering up the year's work, this taken away from the labourers. In their place, one big machine. We look across the land for human beings and we see — one engine. And in its wake a bare field; no rick meets the eye, and no work for thatchers and threshers.

Gazing across, we try and take in the total situation and we think it fair to ask — Is this fact a little thing or a big thing? In the old, far-away days, the whole village came out to take part in the haymaking and harvest. Bit by bit, as wages went up and machinery came in, the villagers had to stay at home...Does this constitute a problem? Hardly, in the eyes of the world, for it is not a utilitarian problem. It is a human concern...Gradually, each man will come to work more and more on his own. The real problem now turns out to be — leisure. We have reached the Leisure State...Owing to the failure of intellectual leadership, the breakdown of religion and the short cuts to culture, our minds are now for the most part demoralized.

If we wish to reverse the decline in the countryside and the decline of democracy, must we test our freedoms in order to know what they are? The price of freedom is eternal vigilance. Supermarkets are just one of the undeclared power bases in our midst. They have been granted a status in our society which has enabled their ideology to infiltrate the most intimate part of our lives — our domestic culture. They have permeated the infrastructure of our lives.

However, if their power is in a way political, then it is the consumer who represents their electorate. We keep them there, and we may yet reject them or demand that they change. They have grown great on the profits of food as an industry — processed food, ready-made meals, bulk purchasing. Their standards have been miserably low, 'value' constantly taking preference over quality.

Surely the challenge now, in our well-informed society is to recognize our duty to tackle the environmental concerns which worry us; to address the contamination of our food; to look for a real alternative to the decadent concept of a leisure society; to understand how we may incorporate technology without destroying our environment. We have colossal problems with the alienated young of inner cities, of urban conglomerations and the countryside. Surely these elements alone would suggest that the way forward is not by extension and reinforcement of the global market but a scaling down — increasing considerably agricultural and horticultural smallholdings to supply local markets, with an attendant elaboration of rural industries and commerce.

We have indeed, in our post-modern world, untuned the string of harmony between ourselves and Nature. We know not to whom we should defer in the matter of our present or our future. Traditionally we deferred to those above us, in the theory that they knew better — and we all know how fallible that system has been; the story of that is history itself . But now we defer to the market, which has no human sense or wisdom at all, however sensitive it is at meeting demand with supply.

The attitude that has debauched our agriculture reflects the political and cultural crisis at the heart of Western civilization. Politically, it reflects the conflict over democracy; whether we should elect representatives for their wisdom, honesty, devoutness and foresightedness or whether we elect them because they promise to give us what we want. Culturally, it reflects the replacement of God by Mammon — the market, money. These struggles are old and well-documented, but the arguments of the losing sides are no less real for having been lost.

'There must be order in human society, as in the universe', writes A.L. Rowse, introducing a passage by William Shakespeare[1]:

> How could communities,
> Degrees in schools, and brotherhoods in cities,
> Peaceful commerce from dividable shores...
> Prerogative of age, crowns, sceptres, laurels,
> But by degree stand in authentic place?

'When order is broken down in society', Rowse goes on, 'Shakespeare well understood that it is reduced to a power struggle':

> Then everything includes itself in power,
> Power into will, will into appetite;
> And appetite, an universal wolf...
> Must make perforce an universal prey,
> And last eat up itself.

Our historic relationship with the earth on which we live, our debts to agriculture, have been invisible for too long. For land is capable of much greater nourishment of the human race than mere diversion from decadence. It is a day-by-day reminder of the fact that we live within the constraints of an order outside ourselves.

---

[1] From *Troilus and Cressida*, 1 iii.

HOLDING UP A MIRROR
How Civilizations Decline
Anne Glyn-Jones

According to Glyn-Jones, the central dilemma of history is this: the dynamic that promotes economic prosperity leads inexorably to the destruction of the very security and artistic achievement on which civilizations rest their claim to greatness. This book argues that the growth of prosperity is driven largely by the conviction that the material world alone constitutes true 'reality'. Yet that self-same dynamic—developing a critique of all belief in the supernatural as at best superfluous, and at worst a damaging superstition—undermines the authority of moral standards and so leads to social and cultural disintegration.

Focussing on dramatic entertainment as the barometer of social change, the author shows in vivid detail how the thesis worked itself out in four different civilizations: those of Greece, Rome, medieval Christendom, and now in our own contemporary society.

Critical acclaim for *Holding Up A Mirror*

This is a visionary book. Painful yet true in its portrait of the present, it is clearly driven by the anxieties of a sensitive and conscientious observer. **Bryan Appleyard**, *The Sunday Times*

Those who share Anne Glyn-Jones's belief in objective values will congratulate her on a thoroughly researched and illuminating reinterpretation of what Sorokin saw as 'The Crisis of Our Age'. **Angela Ellis-Jones**, *TLS*

It is a strength of this rich and engrossing book that it provokes on almost every page a willingness to argue with the author. Her thesis is challenging, and her examples abundantly interesting. **Alan Massie**, *Daily Telegraph*

Her focus on the theatre . . . gives her book an interest and a solid core that lend credibility to the main thesis. **John Habgood**, *THES*

Glyn-Jones's intriguing book puts an entirely new gloss on the stereotyped picture of fanatical Islamic theocracy. **Frank McLynn**, *New Statesman*

She excels in vivid, informative presentation of detail drawn together into a lucid, robust and fair-minded narrative. **Helen Oppenheimer**

Imprint Academic, 652 pp., £14.95/$24.95, 0907845 606 (pbk.)
http://www.imprint.co.uk

The Rape of the Constitution?
Keith Sutherland (ed.); Foreword by Michael Beloff QC
Dedicated to Max Beloff

Lord Hailsham once remarked that if you removed a brick from the wall of the British Constitution, the building was likely to collapse; yet New Labour have embarked on a reckless path of constitutional change regardless of the long-term consequences. Has the steady increase in the power of the executive turned Walter Bagehot's 'disguised republic' into an elective dictatorship?

In *The Rape of the Constitution?* scholars, politicians and journalists from both the Left and the Right debate these issues. Contibutors include Tony Benn MP, Moshe Berent, Jeremy Black, Duncan Brack, Lord Carrington, Tam Dalyell MP, Mike Diboll, Jonathan Freedland, Peter Hitchens, Simon Hughes MP, Mick Hume, Lord Jenkins, Simon Jenkins, Nevil Johnson, J.R. Lucas, Peter Oborne, Anthony O'Hear, Gillian Peele, Michael Rush, Earl Russell, Lord Shore, Sir Michael Spicer MP, Keith Sutherland, Lord Tebbit, Andrew Tyrie MP, Lord Weatherill and Diana Woodhouse.

Advance praise (and brickbats) for the book

Incremental totalitarianism indeed! Such partisan exaggeration defames the memory of the dead. **Bernard Crick**

Throughout his life, Max Beloff brought spirit, intellect and independence to the study of the British Constitution. This book is squarely in his tradition. **Peter Hennessy**

Reform cannot be equated with rape without a considerable degree of teminological inexactitude. **Vernon Bogdanor**

I only wonder if you need that question mark in the title. **Margaret Thatcher**

A wonderfully eclectic group of people contributing to the debate we never had…This book could scarcely be more timely or more needed. **John Humphrys**

It is sad to watch the destruction of one's own country but will be sadder still if no one has the guts to fight back. **Frederick Forsyth**

Imprint Academic, 384 pp., £12.95/$19.95, 0907845 703 (pbk.)
http://www.imprint.co.uk